NEW LOW-COST SOURCES OF

Energy for the Home

Permissions

Sincere thanks go to each and every organization mentioned and displayed herein for its willingness to contribute and impart information to the general public on the vital national issue of energy. We have tried to mention each contributor fairly and equally but realize that we may, like others, have erred by inadvertant omission from time to time. But it was the teamwork which counted and the result is, we hope, to add even one drop of water to the depleted reservoir of energy resources.

If we have mistakenly used your name, services, — or misrepresented your organization or research in any way whatever, please let us know by letter and we will be only too pleased to correct in a subsequent printing.

NEW LOW-COST SOURCES OF
Energy for the Home

PETER CLEGG

GARDEN WAY  PUBLISHING

Charlotte, Vermont 05445

NEW LOW-COST SOURCES OF
Energy for the Home

Preface — 2

Introduction — 5

General References — 8

I ❂ SOLAR ENERGY

Principles: Solar collectors — 14

Storage of Solar Heat — 26

Heat Distribution — 29

Available Energy — 33

Costing — 34

House Design — 36

References and Further Reading — 46

Solar Energy Catalog — 50

II ❂ WIND POWER

Principles: Propellers and Turbines — 88

Generators — 92

Storage and Regulation — 93

Available Energy — 98

Costing — 103

House Design — 106

References and Further Reading — 108

Wind Power Catalog — 110

CONTENTS

III  WATER POWER

Principles: Traditional Waterwheels   **132**
              Modern Water Turbines   **138**
Available Energy   **141**
Costing   **149**
House Design   **150**
References and Further Reading   **151**
Water Power Catalog   **152**

IV WATER/WASTE SYSTEMS

Principles: Waste Systems   **164**
              Methane Digestion   **167**
Available Energy   **171**
Water Recycling   **172**
Costing   **173**
House Design   **177**
References and Further Reading   **180**
Water/Waste Systems Catalog   **182**

V WOOD HEATING

Principles: Fireplaces   **202**
              Stoves   **205**
              Furnaces   **208**
Available Energy   **210**
Costing   **214**
House Design   **216**
References and Further Reading   **220**
Wood Heating Catalog   **222**

CONTENTS

Preface

The Purpose of doing this book

Energy for the home is written for you, the average homeowner who wants to cut down on the high costs of living. A number of works have been written in the past few years on the subject of alternate energy sources, very few of which are for the homeowner. They can be divided into two groups: technical and popular works. The technical books are written primarily by architects, engineers and ecologists for their fellow scientists. They demand from the reader an extensive knowledge of physics, chemistry and mathematics. The "popular" books present a "how-to" approach to energy, without going into much detailed scientific explanation or background.

There are advantages and disadvantages to both approaches. Reading the first kind of book, the average homeowner is quite likely to throw up his hands after a few chapters, admitting that this stuff might be fine one day for his son or daughter now digesting the New Math but it's not for him. The reader of the popularized energy book is likely to be turned on by a particular "how-to" project, for example: building a waterwheel at the site of a small spring behind his house. He will go to the local hardware store, buy whatever materials seem appropriate to do the job and end up producing barely enough electricity to power the bulb of a small flashlight. If he's a good sport, he might say sportingly, one foot up on his adult erector set: "Something must have been missing from the plans." Or he might heave it back at the publisher.

At Garden Way, we felt the real need for a book which presented both technical explanation *and* practical information. We wanted to treat the subject of energy fairly. We realized that at times we would have to challenge the reader's full intellectual powers, because at times the principles of heating and light, for example, are very complex. We reduced complex formulas to simple terms, and stayed, where possible, within the *practical* applications of our subject.

In addition, we wanted a "book of ideas", in order to convey to you the tremendous recreative and money-saving possibilities of alternate energy sources. We wanted a book to open the mind, reading to stimulate independent thinking in a time when all we are ever asked to do is *plug in* and *pay up*. We know that after reading this book, you are not likely to run out and build that water wheel this year or install a solar panel on your roof this summer. But we feel that we will have at least helped you become pretty conversant with the subject of energy — enough so, as a matter of fact, so you understand the *basics* of creating, saving, and using your own energy in the home. Through an intelligent awareness of things, *you* might, for example,devise simple methods of using energy more effectively — caulking windows in a special way, re-insulating to cut fuel costs, planting trees climatically, etc. Then, too, you just might be one of the brave adventurous souls to go to wind power, solar heating or to methane for your home energy needs. Our book, then, will have inspired you with the courage and knowledge to do so. We felt that if our book could create *that* kind of awareness, it would be worth far more than its purchase price.

There is no question that producing new forms of energy is synonymous with the future. We hear it talked about every day in all the media, and it will continue to occupy man's mind in the future. But like all new ideas — the railroad, penicillin, telegraph, telephone, or computers, — further experimentation and testing have to be undertaken before really low-cost and practical alternate power sources for our homes and communities become completely feasible.

During the Truman administration, a number of scientists predicted that by the present decade, there would be 13,000,000 solar homes in the United States. There are perhaps a few hundred. Why? New solutions to any energy crisis for homes, like cures for the common cold, have moved slowly. Truly practical and useful inventions seem to really develop and thrive in hard times, when the need is greatest. People today are actually doing fewer things for themselves than they did years ago. Perhaps a valid question would be: Are we letting the world run us? Instead of the other way around. Prohibitive costs and depleted supplies have necessitated a return to the land and a need for knowledge about what to do with it. The present book will, we hope, serve this purpose.

Photograph by Robert Perron

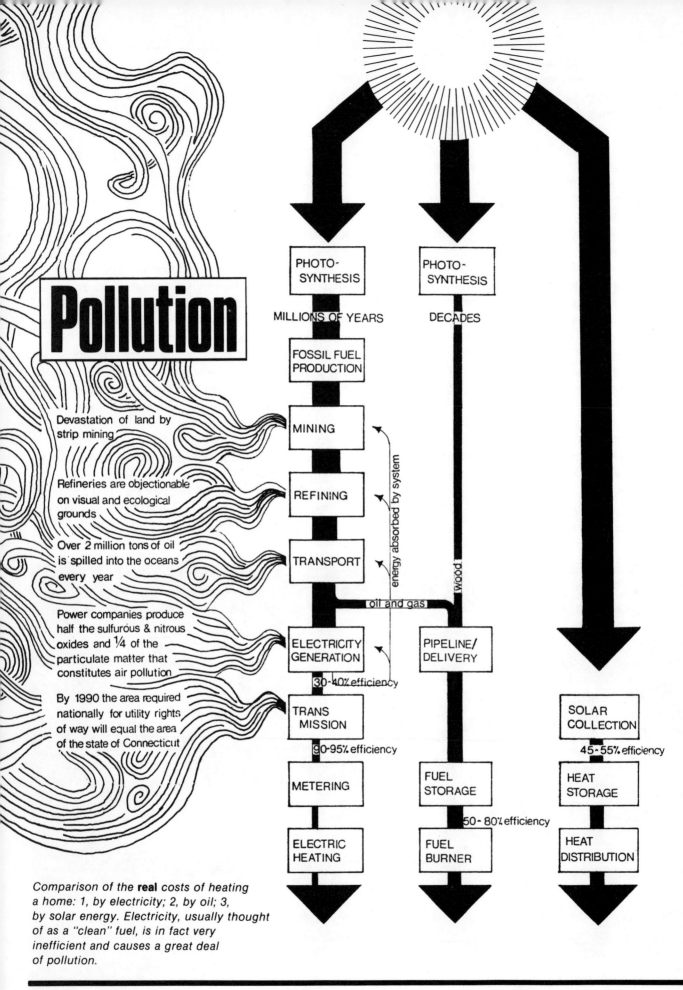

Pollution

Devastation of land by strip mining

Refineries are objectionable on visual and ecological grounds

Over 2 million tons of oil is spilled into the oceans every year

Power companies produce half the sulfurous & nitrous oxides and ¼ of the particulate matter that constitutes air pollution

By 1990 the area required nationally for utility rights of way will equal the area of the state of Connecticut

PHOTO-SYNTHESIS

MILLIONS OF YEARS

FOSSIL FUEL PRODUCTION

MINING

REFINING

TRANSPORT

energy absorbed by system

oil and gas

ELECTRICITY GENERATION

30-40% efficiency

TRANS MISSION

90-95% efficiency

METERING

ELECTRIC HEATING

PHOTO-SYNTHESIS

DECADES

wood

PIPELINE/ DELIVERY

FUEL STORAGE

50-80% efficiency

FUEL BURNER

SOLAR COLLECTION

45-55% efficiency

HEAT STORAGE

HEAT DISTRIBUTION

*Comparison of the **real** costs of heating a home: 1, by electricity; 2, by oil; 3, by solar energy. Electricity, usually thought of as a "clean" fuel, is in fact very inefficient and causes a great deal of pollution.*

Introduction

Energy for the home is a source of information on natural energy and available technology which could allow you to live independent of public utilities. It is primarily concerned with using the "free" and renewable energy sources of sun and wind, with productive and non-polluting methods of water and waste treatment, methane generation, and heating with wood. There is also a chapter on water power.

The book is intended (1) for all those who are interested in building houses which are not totally dependent on the vast, expansive, sprawling and generally inefficient network of sewers, power lines, and water mains that stretch across most of the country. (2) It should also be of use to architects, whose knowledge should be strong enough for them to assess the possibilities and advantages of using alternative energy systems in house design. (3) The book is, moreover, intended for people interested in both designing and building their own homes.

The ideas are presented so as to be understandable to most readers, and the technology at a level so as to assist most self-builders. Sun, wind, water and wood are all sources of energy that we can see, feel, and understand. There are no tricks or mysteries about the operation of your own, on-site, power-systems, — no "clean" energy which miraculously appears from nowhere. You need not be dependent on fuel mined on the other side of the world, nor on water from a reservoir that has flooded someone else's farmland.

Most of us tend to accept our utility industries with a shrug. Electricity *appears* clean and efficient. Since it is easy to use, we put up with the costs, and since it usually doesn't pollute our *own* back yards we conveniently ignore the hidden costs which indirectly involve us in pollution and ecological disruption. But if we look at the process of producing electricity, from the mining of the fuel to the construction of the transmission lines, we get a more accurate picture of the overall cost and efficiency of the network. Just compare the processes of heating a house by electricity, by direct fossil fuel combustion, and by solar energy.

The whole "energy question" is in the hands of the world's political leaders and the largest and richest multinational corporations. McLuhan's "global village" is fast becoming a reality. The individual is fast becoming enslaved to so-called *public* service facilities. Are our independence and sense of self-awareness rapidly giving way to a world machine somewhat beyond our control and mandates?

Getting back to the "natural" things and self-sufficiency on a national and personal level can restore people's independence and confidence,— opposite is an energy flow system for an "autonomous" house, which could be self-sufficient in terms of its energy and water supply. The house is represented as a self-contained environment which supports both human and plant life and balances the energy flows between them. Following are the principles:

• Heat is captured by absorbing energy from the sun, and retaining and using this heat as long as possible before it is inevitably lost to the environment or radiated to the sky.

• Wind generated electricity is used to run appliances.

• A small water powered generator might be installed to produce power.

• Water consumption can be minimized by recycling.

• Rainwater collection or well water could replace the mains water supply.

• Waste products are recycled on-site to provide fuel-gas and fertilizer.

• Wood stoves could be used to provide a back-up source of heat.

• A diesel generator or input of mains electricity could be used as a back-up system.

In areas where centralized servicing is available, a totally autonomous system would not be necessary, nor would it always be desirable.

In the United States, extravagant energy consumption has led to a standard of living we are loath to relinquish. But it *is* possible to use free and natural sources of energy and still get the kind of "automatic" service we have come to expect from electrical outlets (when there isn't a power failure or an unpaid power bill), from faucets, and radiators. The technology we habitually associate with "alternative" (and therefore inconvenient) lifestyles has and continues to be upgraded to satisfy the expectations of the well-serviced average American household — and can provide a significant saving in energy consumption and cost. Doing-it-yourself can be justified in many areas on a pure *cost-saving* basis, and it is this alone, perhaps unfortunately, that will increase its popularity. But the other, less measurable, advantages should not be ignored. The systems outlined in this book can provide energy *without pollution,* independence *without inconvenience* — and a closer relationship between man and his environment.

ENERGY SOURCE

COLLECTION

APPLICATION

AND PROCESSING

STORAGE

UTILIZATION

WASTE COLLECTION

TREATMENT

RECYCLING

– – – – – HEAT
——————— ELECTRICITY
▰▰▰▰▰▰▰ MOTIVE POWER
•••••••• FOOD
◦◦◦◦◦◦◦◦◦◦ ORGANIC WASTE
— · — · — · WATER
·················· RESPIRATION
▨▨▨▨▨▨▨▨ METHANE GAS

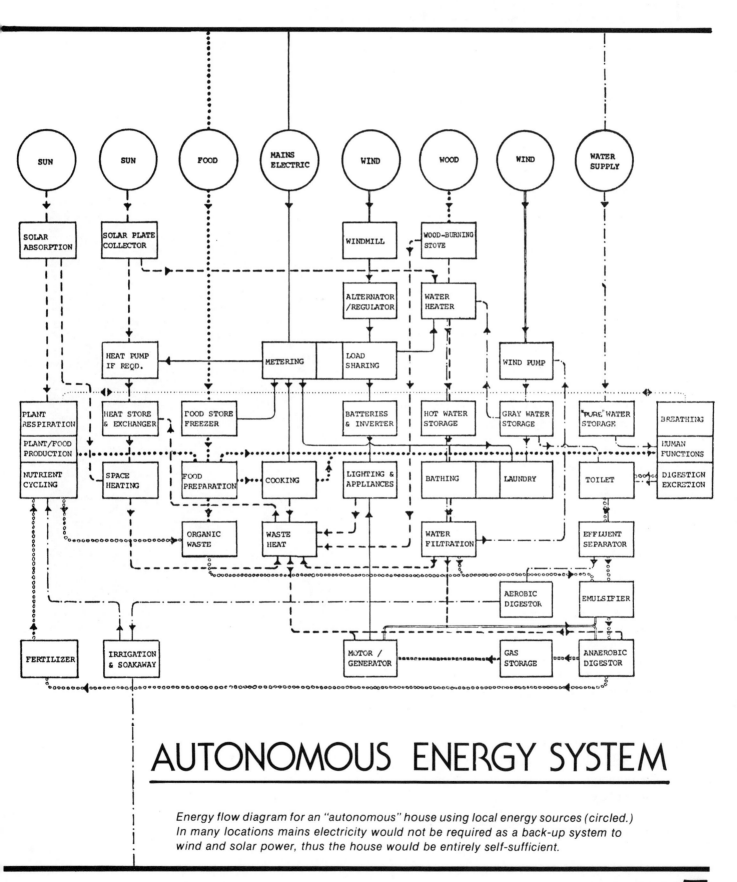

AUTONOMOUS ENERGY SYSTEM

*Energy flow diagram for an "autonomous" house using local energy sources (circled.)
In many locations mains electricity would not be required as a back-up system to
wind and solar power, thus the house would be entirely self-sufficient.*

General References

1   *Architecture and Energy.* Richard Stein.
    Forum. July-August 1973.

2   *Blueprint for Survival.* Goldsmith, *The
    Ecologist.* London, February 1971.

3   *The Climate of Connecticut.* J. Brumbach.
    State Geological and Natural History Survey
    of Connecticut. 1965, (general reading).

4   *The Ecol Operation.* A. Ortega et al. Minimum
    Cost Housing Group. School of Architecture,
    McGill University of Montreal, 1972.

5   *Eco-Unity.* Rye Loope and Peter Clegg. Award-
    winning entry for the ASC/AIA competition
    on Energy Conservation in Buildings. January
    1974. (university pub.).

6   *A Handbook of Homemade Power.* Collected
    articles from *Mother Earth News.* 1974.

7   *Patient Earth.* Harte and Socolow. Princeton,
    1966. (See chapters on energy and water).

8   *Patterns of Energy Consumption in the USA,*
    Office of Science and Technology.
    Washington D.C., January 1972.

9   *Service Systems and Cost Options.* James
    Thring. *Built Environment.* London, June
    1972.

10 *Towards a New Environmental Ethic.* (Leaflet
    published by the E.P.A.) Washington D.C.,
    1971.

11 *Producing Your Own Power.* Editor, Carol
    Hupping Stoner. Rodale Press Inc. Book
    Division, Emmaus, Pennsylvania 18049.

12 *The Limits to Growth.* Meadows, Randers,
    and Behrens, Massachusetts Institute of
    Technology, 1972. Published as a Signet
    Paperback.

13 *Energy for Survival.* Wilson Clark. Anchor
    Books, 1974.

Journals

Alternative Sources of Energy Newsletter, Editor, Don Marier, Route 1, Box 36B, Minong, Wisconsin 54859.

Architectural Design. 26 Bloomsbury Way, London WC1A 2SS. England.

Compost Science: Journal of Waste Recycling. Rodale Press, 33B. Minor Street, Emmaus, Pennsylvania 18049.

The Journal of the New Alchemy Institute. P.O. Box 432, Woods Hole, Massachusetts 02543.

Mother Earth News. P.O. Box 38, Madison, Ohio 44057.

Solar Energy. Journal of the International Solar Energy Society. P.O. Box 52, Parkville, Victoria 3042. Australia.

The Solar Energy Digest. P.O. Box 17776, San Diego, California 92117.

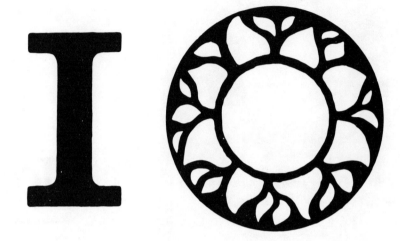

SOLAR
ENERGY

Energy From the Sun

Nearly 60% of all the energy used in the average house goes into heating it. Another 20% is consumed by domestic water heating, cooking, air conditioning, and other processes which require heat.

Most of this heat is eventually lost to the atmosphere or radiated to outer space, as the earth continues the process of balancing its heat gains and heat losses. A well designed house will lengthen the time the heat is **in use.** In large cities, however, heat is released so fast that it contributes to such familiar and devastating phenomena as smog and air pollution and adversely affects the natural climate over a very large area.

By comparing the available heat potential of known fossil fuel reserves (coal, peat, oil, and natural gas) of the world with the amount of heat the earth receives from the sun every day, we find that the total fuel reserves amount to about 3 weeks sunshine. Despite this fact, however, we are still consuming these fuel reserves at such an astonishing rate that we are even beginning to slightly affect the heat balance of the earth. The problem is a very real one in terms of both the future environment and the skyrocketing costs of traditional fuels used by the average homeowner.

If instead of relying on non-renewable resources, we could start to use natural resources —such as solar power — to service our homes and buildings, the problem of waste heat pollution would be eliminated. Moreover, we would also benefit by conserving our short supply of the fossil fuels. At present, we utilize solar energy indirectly through hydro-electric power generation. But this source only provides about 4% of the total United States electricity supply.

Research in solar energy has been ongoing for many years, but only recently, with the rise in the price of coal, oil and natural gas has it become economically worthwhile.

The whole field of solar energy is now expanding so rapidly that this book can only hope to offer a selective view. We have omitted a number of methods which are currently being researched for long-range development, such as photo-voltaic cells, and chosen to concentrate on using solar energy for heating houses in average or temperate climates such as New England.

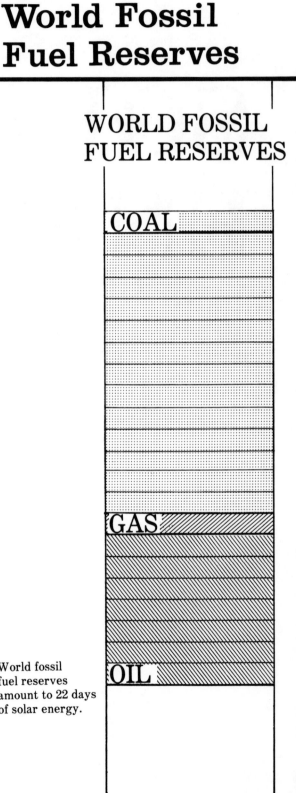

World Fossil Fuel Reserves

WORLD FOSSIL FUEL RESERVES

COAL

GAS

OIL

World fossil fuel reserves amount to 22 days of solar energy.

Twenty-two Days of Solar Energy

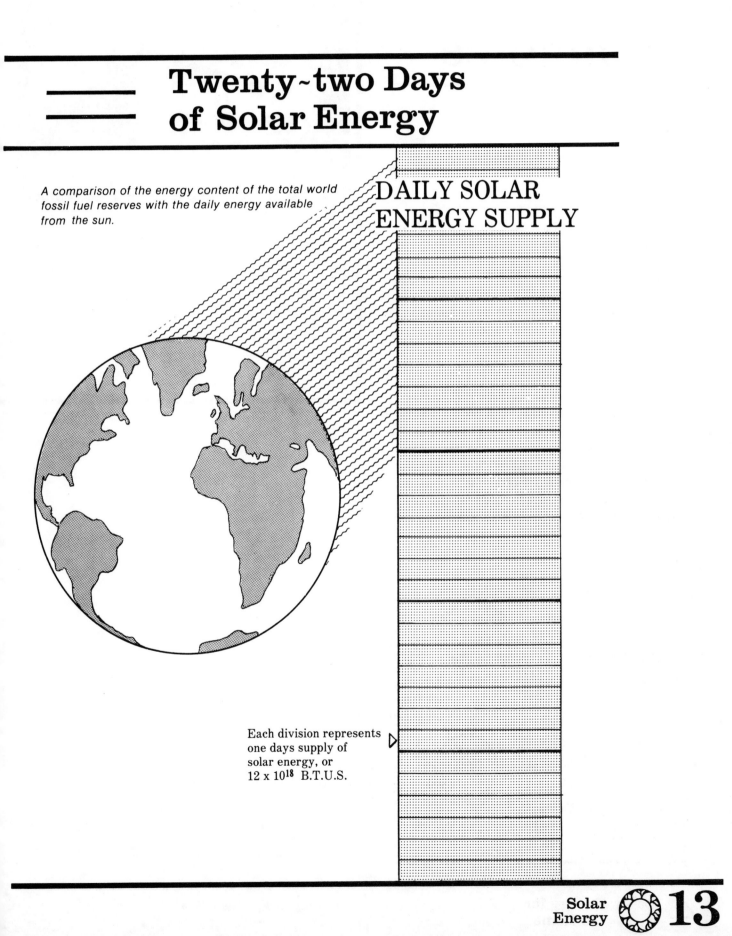

A comparison of the energy content of the total world fossil fuel reserves with the daily energy available from the sun.

DAILY SOLAR ENERGY SUPPLY

Each division represents one days supply of solar energy, or 12×10^{18} B.T.U.S.

Principles

Solar Collection: the background

Any surface exposed to the sun will rise in temperature as it absorbs radiant solar heat. When the surface becomes hotter than its surroundings, it will begin to lose heat in three ways: (1) by conduction — through any object with which it is in contact, (2) by convection — through contact with, for example, air or water, and (3) by re-radiation to the sky or to other surrounding cooler objects. By minimizing the heat losses and diverting the heat to a storage facility or to a radiator, a "solar collector" has, in effect, been created.

Various conditions must be met, however, before a useful amount of heat can be collected. The collector must be facing toward the sun and tilted normal to the sun's rays . . . the best angle to collect the maximum radiation. The conduction of heat from the surface to another medium where it can be easily stored must be both rapid and efficient and the heat lost from the absorber surface must be kept to a minimum.

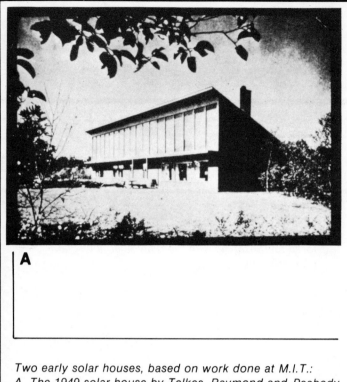

A

Two early solar houses, based on work done at M.I.T.:
A. The 1949 solar house by Telkes, Raymond and Peabody.
B. M.I.T. Solar House IV, 1957. Anderson, Dietz and Hottel.

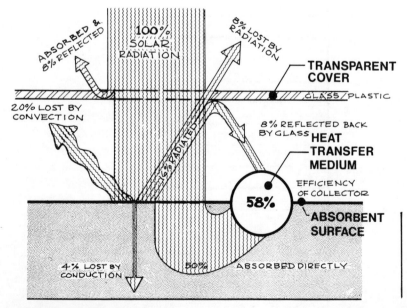

Section through a typical liquid-type solar collector, showing what happens to the incoming solar radiation (all percentages are approximate values for a single glass covered collector with a selective surface).

B

The Solar Collector

A transparent cover of glass or plastic permits the sun rays to enter. But it will not allow the longer wave *thermal* radiation produced by the heated surface to escape. This simple covering increases the heat absorption of the collection surface tremendously, since it prevents heat losses by contact with the cooler outside air. The *transparent cover,* the *absorbent surface,* and the *heat transfer medium* are the three main elements of any solar collector. With these principles in mind, it is possible to devise a range of different collector designs of varying cost and complexity.

Sections through various types of solar collectors using water (left) or air (right) as the heat-transfer medium.

LIQUID-TYPE SOLAR COLLECTORS

AIR-TYPE SOLAR COLLECTORS.

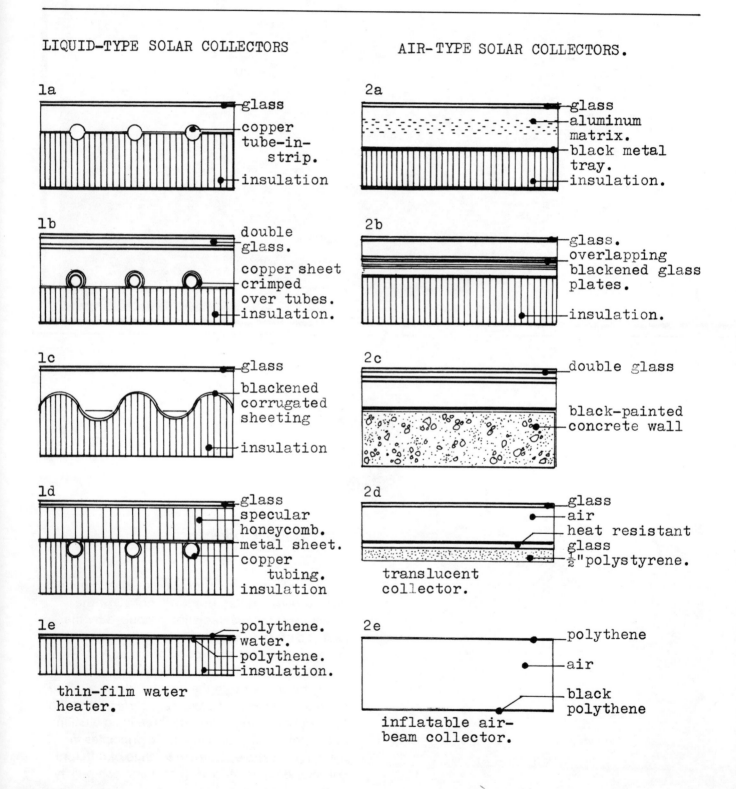

1a
- glass
- copper tube-in-strip.
- insulation

2a
- glass
- aluminum matrix.
- black metal tray.
- insulation.

1b
- double glass.
- copper sheet crimped over tubes.
- insulation.

2b
- glass.
- overlapping blackened glass plates.
- insulation.

1c
- glass
- blackened corrugated sheeting
- insulation

2c
- double glass
- black-painted concrete wall

1d
- glass
- specular honeycomb.
- metal sheet.
- copper tubing.
- insulation

2d
- glass
- air
- heat resistant glass
- $\frac{1}{2}$"polystyrene.

translucent collector.

1e
- polythene.
- water.
- polythene.
- insulation.

thin-film water heater.

2e
- polythene
- air
- black polythene

inflatable air-beam collector.

Sunworks collector
(see Solar Catalog).

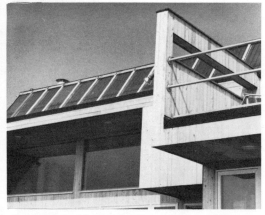

Solar heated house in Connecticut, 1974.
Architect: Donald Watson, A.I.A.
Engineer: Everett Barber Jr.

Focusing Collectors

The prior examples are all flat plate collectors Since these collectors absorb both direct sun and diffuse solar radiation, they will collect heat even on a cloudy day. The other type of collector is a focusing collector which concentrates the sun's energy, by means of a mirror or lens, onto the absorbent surface. It operates in direct sunlight only, and must be mounted in such a way as to follow the sun as the earth moves. Focusing collectors can achieve very high temperatures — over 400 degrees Fahrenheit, and can be used to power steam generators, solar cookers and other devices which require high temperature. They are, however, still very expensive and presently not suitable for domestic heating.

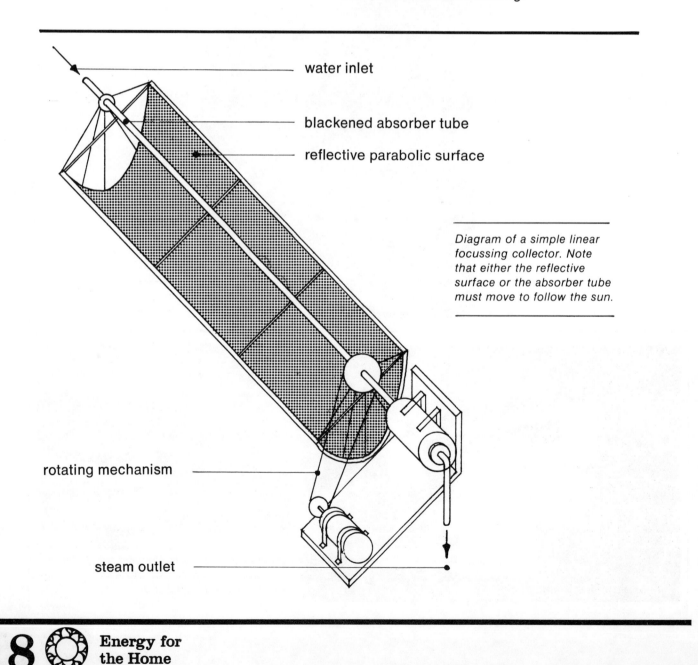

water inlet

blackened absorber tube

reflective parabolic surface

Diagram of a simple linear focussing collector. Note that either the reflective surface or the absorber tube must move to follow the sun.

rotating mechanism

steam outlet

Absorbent Surfaces

The way in which the surface of any collector absorbs solar energy, is a major determinant of its efficiency. Matte black paint, for example, has a high quality of absorption but quickly gives off heat. In order to overcome this problem, various selective surfaces have been developed to readily absorb but very slowly re-radiate heat.

Most selective surfaces consist of a very thin, but highly absorbent coating, generally a black metal oxide applied to a polished metal sheet. There are at present a number of such coatings. Most, however, are rather expensive, and require complex application processes. For the interested layman experimenting with his own designs, matte black spray paint ("Krylon" and "Nextel") are available commercially and will give good results.

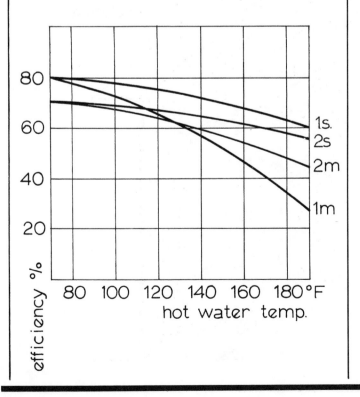

Efficiency of various flat-plate collectors plotted against the difference between the temperature of the outside air and the temperature of the fluid at the collector outlet. Note that the hotter the temperature of the fluid, the less efficient the collector.
1m: Collector with matte black absorber and one glass cover. 2m: Collector with matte black absorber and two glass covers.
1s: Collector with selective absorber and one glass cover.
2s: Collector with selective absorber and two glass covers.

See Reference 12

The Transparent Cover

The transparent cover on a collector serves as a protection against dirt and precipitation, and as a barrier to heat loss by convection and thermal radiation. Both glass and transparent plastic film have been used as covering materials. Plastic has a much shorter lifetime, and gradually becomes less effective as it loses its transparency, but is significantly cheaper than glass. Plastic films have been developed which last much longer than the normal polyethylene. Mylar and Tedlar are as clear as glass, and will stay clear for three to five years. However, plastic films are made from hydrocarbons which are likely to become more expensive and less available in the near future. Though plastic films are at the moment useful for low-cost, do-it-yourself collectors; glass, because of its durability, is more suitable for mass-produced units with a long lifetime.

A standard 3/16 inch glass cover will transmit approximately 85 percent of the solar radiation but will easily compensate for this by reducing the heat loss from the collector. More expensive glass is available with a transmission value of up to 95 percent for solar wave lengths. For a collector without a selective surface, the efficiency can be increased by adding a second glass cover. If a selective surface is used, however, the second layer of glass is not particularly helpful, since heat loss by radiation has already been minimized by the selective surface itself.

The heat loss from the collector also depends on the size of the air gap between the outer cover and the absorbent surface. A gap of about ⅜ to ½ an inch is the optimum one for minimizing the heat loss — a larger air gap allows greater heat loss by convection.

One of the major ways in which heat is lost from the collector is by convection. A layer of reflective honeycomb material in the air gap prevents the formation of convection currents which would cool the absorbent surface, but does not reduce the impact of radiation on the surface. If the honeycomb is cut at an angle, it can be used to reflect light onto the absorbent surface, thus allowing the collector to be installed vertically.*
For complete elimination of heat loss by convection, a vacuum could replace the air gap. The vacuum has to be built into the collector which adds considerably to the cost of constructing the unit.

*For a complete discussion of Honeycomb Devices in collectors see K. T. G. Hollands. "Honeycomb Devices in Flat-plate Solar Collectors" in **Solar Energy.** Volume 9, Number 3 July-Sept. 1965.

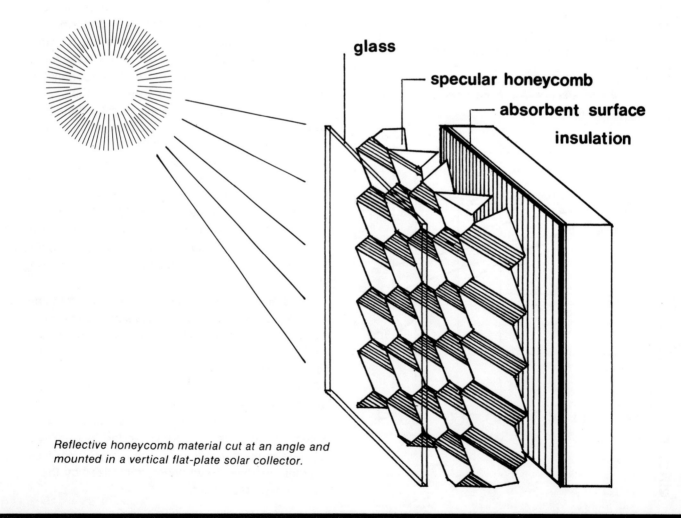

glass

specular honeycomb

absorbent surface

insulation

Reflective honeycomb material cut at an angle and mounted in a vertical flat-plate solar collector.

How Heat is Transferred from Collector to House

Water and air are the two most common heat transfer media used in flat plate solar collectors. Water has a low ratio of volume/heat carrying capacity, but it can cause problems if leaks occur in the pipework which is under strain due to temperature changes. Air collectors are generally bulkier, requiring larger ducts and heat exchange areas and more insulation than water systems, but they are cheaper and easier to construct.

Most collectors using water as the transfer medium consist of a series of metal tubes either welded to or built into the sheet metal absorber. Thin-wall tubing with a diameter of ⅜" to ½", placed 3" to 6" apart on the absorber sheet seems to be the most efficient and practical way of transfering the heat. The water, which generally contains glycol to prevent freezing and raise the boiling point, flows through the tubes and absorbs heat from the collector.

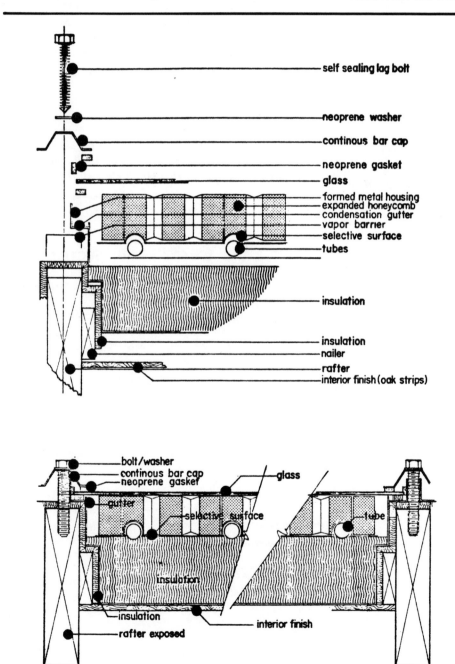

self sealing lag bolt
neoprene washer
continous bar cap
neoprene gasket
glass
formed metal housing
expanded honeycomb
condensation gutter
vapor barrier
selective surface
tubes
insulation
insulation
nailer
rafter
interior finish (oak strips)

bolt/washer
continous bar cap
neoprene gasket
glass
gutter
selective surface
tube
insulation
insulation
interior finish
rafter exposed

Section through a typical solar collector showing assembly of various components. This drawing based on a Sunworks collector designed to fit between the roof joists of a house (see Solar Catalog).

Other collectors using a liquid transfer medium consist simply of a black corrugated absorber sheet with a transparent cover. The water trickles slowly down the grooves in the sheet, absorbing the heat as it goes. This system has been developed and patented by Harry Thomason.

Solar Air Heaters

Solar air heaters vary from a simple black-painted duct, with one side made of glass and oriented towards the sun, to more elaborate designs which include layers of absorber material within the duct. Collectors containing several layers of slit-and-expanded aluminum-foil have been shown to have very high collection efficiencies. The aluminum can be replaced by several overlapping layers of glass, — each one partially blackened. Both of these devices have the effect of maximizing the area of the absorber in contact with the air flowing through the collector. In other air heaters, the heat loss by convection is minimized by incorporating a "dead" air space between the absorber sheet and the transparent cover. In this case the heated air flows behind the absorber sheet.

In hot air collectors, natural circulation will cause the air to rise along the length of the airspace, assuming the collector is on a slope or placed vertically. In direct sunlight, very high air velocities will build up. The faster the airflow, the lower the outlet temperature. In order to increase the temperature of the air in the collector, its velocity must be reduced by slowing down the natural flow, and causing a kind of turbulence which brings interior air to the surface where it is warmed.

The overall efficiencies of air and water collectors are very similar. They both average around 50 percent for a temperature difference of around 80 degrees to 120 degrees Fahrenheit between the outside air and the fluid in the collector. The choice between the two depends mainly on the relative cost and the ease with which they can be adapted to suit a particular building.

*Solar air heater with a dead air space for extra insulation between the absorber and the transparent cover. The air which is heated flows **behind** the absorber sheet.*

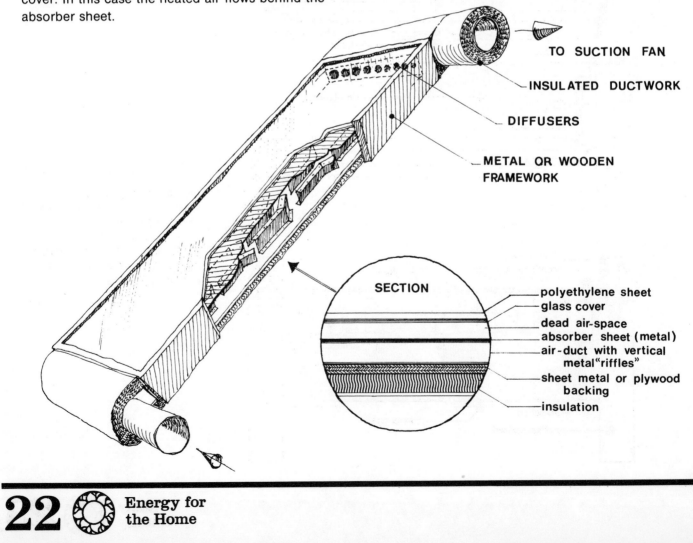

TO SUCTION FAN

INSULATED DUCTWORK

DIFFUSERS

METAL OR WOODEN FRAMEWORK

SECTION

polyethylene sheet
glass cover
dead air-space
absorber sheet (metal)
air-duct with vertical metal "riffles"
sheet metal or plywood backing
insulation

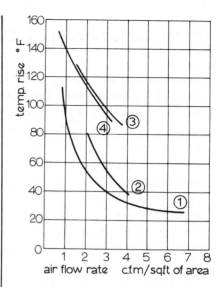

Air temperature vs. flow rate for a gauze-type solar air heater. Note that the faster the rate of flow, the lower the temperature. Models tested:
1: Empty black metal tray 1" deep.
2: 7 layers of gauze in a 1" deep tray.
3: 7 layers of gauze in a ¾" deep tray.
4: 17 layers of gauze in a 1" deep tray.
See Reference 8

slit-and–expanded aluminum foil matrix several layers thick painted black. layed skew in metal tray to encourage maximum heat transfer

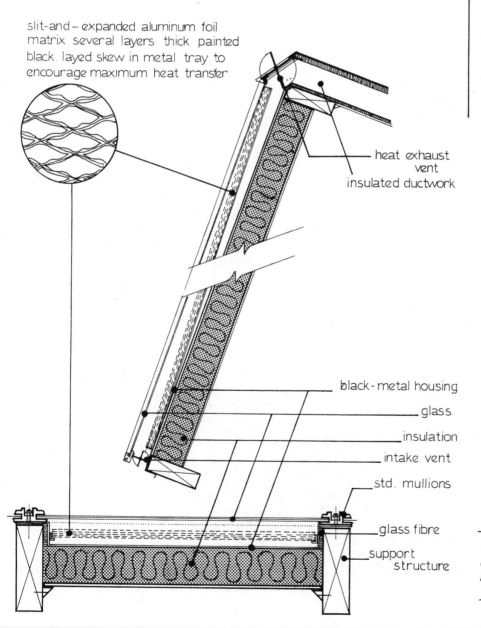

heat exhaust vent
insulated ductwork

black-metal housing
glass
insulation
intake vent
std. mullions
glass fibre
support structure

Gauze-type solar air heater based on models tested by Choui, El Wakil and Duffie (see Reference 6.)

Solar Collectors for Hot Water

Solar water heaters are commonplace in many parts of the world, particularly Japan and Israel. Many different types are available. The simplest of these is a large plastic pillow filled with water which can be installed on the roof of the house to collect whatever solar energy is available. More efficient collectors are sold which use 4 or 6 inch diameter pipes of glass, plastic or steel to hold the water. The absorbed heat then travels by convection to a storage tank above the collector Both these collectors heat the domestic water directly, but since the water is exposed to the danger of freezing, these methods are suitable only in warmer climates. To avoid the possibility of freezing, an indirect heating system could be used where an anti-freeze solution is circulated between the collector and a heat exchanger in the storage tank

Since these water-heating systems provide only low-grade heat (100-140 degrees Fahrenheit), back-up heating will be required from time to time in order to maintain a constant temperature of about 150 degrees Fahrenheit in the domestic water tank. A thermostatically-controlled electric resistance coil or a gas burner would suffice.

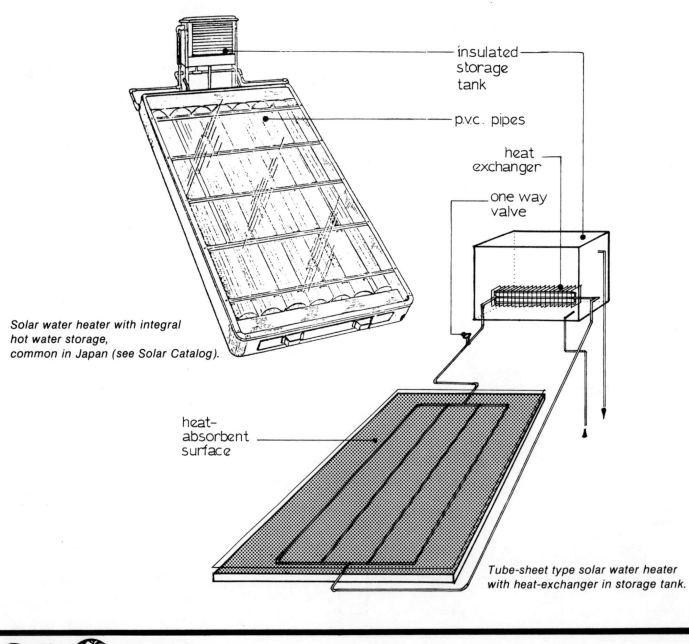

Solar water heater with integral hot water storage, common in Japan (see Solar Catalog).

insulated storage tank

p.v.c. pipes

heat exchanger

one way valve

heat-absorbent surface

Tube-sheet type solar water heater with heat-exchanger in storage tank.

Energy for the Home

simple solar heating system

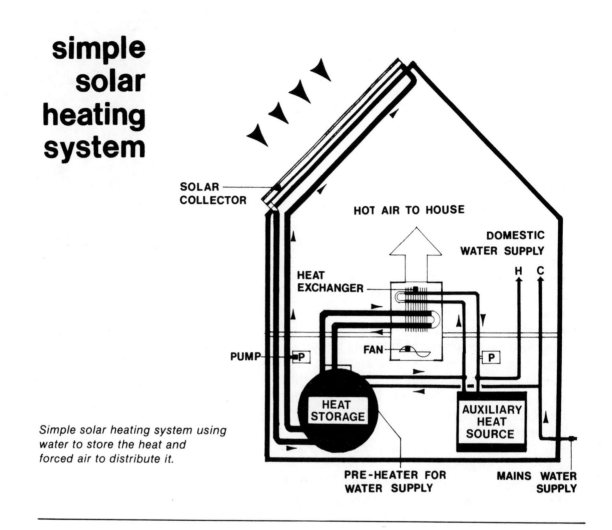

SOLAR COLLECTOR

HOT AIR TO HOUSE

DOMESTIC WATER SUPPLY

HEAT EXCHANGER

H C

PUMP — P

FAN

P

HEAT STORAGE

AUXILIARY HEAT SOURCE

PRE-HEATER FOR WATER SUPPLY

MAINS WATER SUPPLY

Simple solar heating system using water to store the heat and forced air to distribute it.

Solar Collectors for Space Heating

A simple solar heating system is shown above The collector supplies heat to the heat storage area, from where it can be drawn off whenever desired. A collector without storage facilities is less efficient than an ordinary window at providing heat for immediate use. The storage area must be large enough to accommodate three or four days heat supply in order to provide for successive days without sunshine. Ideally, this quantity of heat should be able to supply both the space heating and hot water requirements of the house.

The collection and storage of heat is a dynamic process, and daily as well as seasonal variations in the supply and demand of heat must be taken into account. A collector needs time to warm up in the morning, for the heat is usable only when it will no longer lower the temperature of the fluid in the storage tank. Hence a thermostat is needed to start the circulating pump working when sufficient heat is available.

The sizing of both the storage and the back-up systems depends upon how much heat can be collected under the worst design and weather conditions. The auxiliary system needs to be capable of handling the total heat load in cases of prolonged adverse conditions or failure in the solar heating system, but it must also be capable of running efficiently at less than its maximum output. A large electric water heater would meet these demands fairly well.

Storage of Solar Heat

Solar energy may be stored in one of two ways: either by raising the temperature of substances such as rocks or water (heat-capacity storage), or by using the heat to change the state of a material, such as forming a solution out of salt crystals, (chemical heat storage).

Any medium for storing heat should be able to retain heat well in relation to its weight, volume and cost. The material which best satisfies these demands is water. Water has the advantage of allowing heat to spread through it fairly rapidly by convection, and is easy to use in heat exchangers which require a large exchange surface area within a small volume.

Rock beds and cinder blocks have a very high heat capacity and are particularly convenient for storing heat from solar air collectors. Spherical stones provide maximum surface area and minimum resistance to the air moving through them. Generally the resistance to the flow of air increases as the size of the pebbles decreases — two inches in diameter is a reasonable size for household heat storage. Other materials could be used for direct heat capacity storage. Industrial wastes such as coke, or raw materials such as bauxite or iron-ore would be suitable, but they are not as easily available as pebbles.

Heat storage can be part of the structure of the building. If the south facing wall of a building is made of a material with a high heat capacity, painted black to absorb the heat, and covered with two layers of glass to retain it, the wall itself will act as a solar collector. According to tests done on an experimental building, approximately half the solar radiation is absorbed directly into the wall, slowly conducted through the wall and radiated to the inside; some is absorbed by the air between the wall and the glass, and is convected into the house through vents in the top of the wall.

The original C.N.R.S. Trombé-Michel Solar Wall, Odeillo, France (see References 2 and 13).

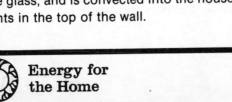

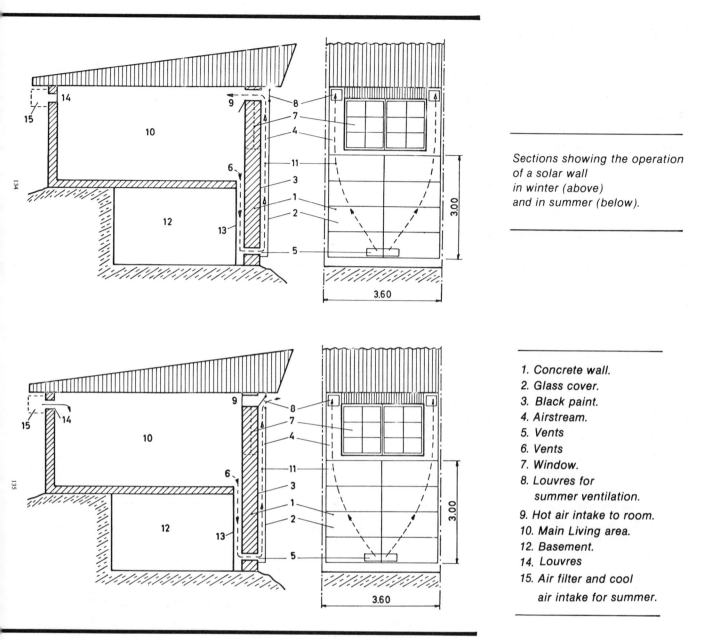

Sections showing the operation
of a solar wall
in winter (above)
and in summer (below).

1. Concrete wall.
2. Glass cover.
3. Black paint.
4. Airstream.
5. Vents
6. Vents
7. Window.
8. Louvres for
   summer ventilation.
9. Hot air intake to room.
10. Main Living area.
12. Basement.
14. Louvres
15. Air filter and cool
    air intake for summer.

Model of a three person house to
be built by the C.N.R.S. Laboratory.
From "Space Heating with Solar Energy
at the C.N.R.S. Laboratory, Odeillo,
France", J. D. Walton. Reference 2.

Chemical Heat Storage

When a chemical compound changes state from solid to liquid or from liquid to gas, it always takes in heat. The formation of water from ice, or of a salt solution from hydrated crystals are examples of this process; the actual change of state requires an extra input of heat. When the salt crystallizes out of solution, or the water changes back to ice, it releases this "latent" heat. This cyclical process can thus be used for heat storage.

The advantage of chemical heat storage is the great reduction in both the weight and volume of the storage material required. This is evident from our data in which the two types of heat storage are compared. The main problem with chemical heat storage, however, is that under certain conditions the solution when cooled fails to form crystals and enters a "supercooled" liquid phase where it still retains its latent heat. This can be overcome by the equal distribution of a "nucleating agent" (molecules of a different material around which the crystals can form) throughout the solution. One of the most successful combinations for heat storage is Glauber's Salts. Borax can be used as a nucleating agent. This mixture has a lifetime of about 3000 cycles, and the materials themselves are very inexpensive. Where volume and weight must be kept to a minimum, chemical heat storage is the best answer. However it is not fully tested or yet commercially available.

The performance and characteristics of various thermal storage materials, including the cost per million BTUs of heat stored. From "A Study of Energy Storage Media", James Eibling in Reference 2

	Temp. Range, F	Melting Temp., F	Heat Capacity	Latent Heat Capacity	Material Cost, $/lb	Per Million Btu		
						Vol., ft³	Weight, lb	Cost, $
Water-ice	32	32	0.49	144	Nil	111	7,000	Nil
Water	90-130	32	1.0	-	Nil	400	25,000	Nil
Steel (scrap iron)	" "	-	0.12	-	0.003	430	210,000	630
Basalt (lava rock)	" "	-	0.20	-	0.002	680	125,000	250
Limestone	" "	-	0.22	-	0.002	730	114,000	228
Salt Hydrates								
$NaSO_4 \cdot 10H_2O$	" "	90	0.4	108	0.012	90	8,000	96
$Na_2S_2O_3 \cdot 5H_2O$	" "	120	"	90	0.05	90	9,400	470
$Na_2HPO_4 \cdot 12H_2O$	" "	97	"	120	0.034	78	7,350	250
Water	110-300	-	1.0	-	Nil	85	5,300	Nil
Fire brick	110-800	-	0.22	-	0.01	33	6,600	66
Fused Salts $NaNO_3$	" "	510	0.38	80	0.024	21	2,920	70
Lithium	" "	370	1.0 $\pm$	286	10.00	31	1,020	10,200
Carbon	" "	6,750	0.2	-	0.20	52	7,200	1,440
Lithium hydride	1,260	1,260	1.0 $\pm$	1,200	10.00	23	833	8,330
Sodium Chloride	1,480	1,480	0.21	223	.02	33	4,500	90
Silicon	2,605	2,605	-	607	-	11	1,647	-

Energy for the Home

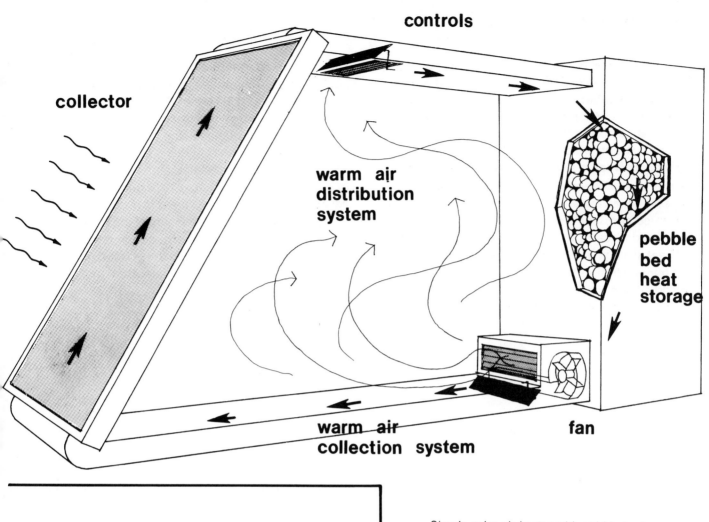

controls

collector

warm air distribution system

pebble bed heat storage

warm air collection system

fan

Simple solar air heater with pebble-bed storage and forced air distribution.

The Heat Distribution System

Once the solar energy has been captured and stored, it is necessary to provide a heat distribution system which can be controlled as easily as any conventional house-heating system. During the winter months, a collector operating at approximately 50 percent efficiency will provide hot water at a maximum temperature of about 130-150 degrees Fahrenheit (low grade heat). This temperature is not high enough for a conventional hot water heating system with convectors or radiators. But it could be used in a radiant floor or ceiling heating system, or as the heat source for a hot air system, all of which require only low grade heat.

A forced air system would necessitate a heat exchanger where the heat from the collectors could be spread out over a large surface area across which the air is blown. A standard fin-tube exchanger could be used. The drawbacks of this system are the bulkiness of the ductwork and the cost of not only the heat exchanger but also the circulating fan. These are offset however, by the total efficiency of the system and the ease with which the temperature of individual rooms can be controlled. In a system using pebble beds or concrete blocks as the storage medium, a hot air distribution system is easy to install since the air is merely drawn through the warmed rocks.

Heat Pumps

Using a heat pump to provide a supply of high grade heat (160-180 degrees Fahrenheit), a normal hot water distribution system becomes practicable. Essentially, a heat pump adds energy from an electrical compressor. It consists of a closed loop of a refrigerant, which evaporates and condenses continuously (as in a refrigerator). Low-grade solar heat is applied to one side of the heat pump and causes the refrigerant to evaporate. An electrically driven compressor then raises the pressure of the vapor and forces it to condense again, thus giving off heat at a higher temperature than was put in. As the temperature difference between the heat absorbed and the heat given off increases, the heat pump uses the electrical energy less efficiently.

When the temperature difference is less than 30-40 degrees Fahrenheit, a good heat pump can provide around 2½ BTU's of high grade heat for every BTU of energy the compressor uses. Commercial heat pumps using outside air as a source of heat are sold in this country by General Electric and other companies, and might be adapted to a solar heating system. A heat pump has the advantage that the cycle can be reversed and used for cooling in summer. The inside of the house then becomes the evaporator, and the condenser, outside the house, is cooled by convection or is buried in the ground which in summer is cooler than the air above it.

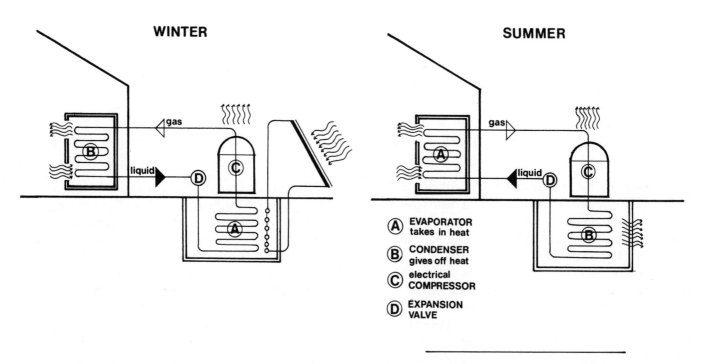

WINTER   **SUMMER**

Ⓐ EVAPORATOR takes in heat

Ⓑ CONDENSER gives off heat

Ⓒ electrical COMPRESSOR

Ⓓ EXPANSION VALVE

Simplified diagram of a heat pump.

Solar Cooling

Solar cooling is one of the most promising future applications of solar energy. Once again, the subject is so broad that only a short summary of the principles involved is possible. The system which has received most attention is absorption cooling which operates like the heat pump. In absorption cooling the refrigeration cycle involves two changes of state.

Looking at a simplified diagram of the system, high grade solar heat is applied to a solution (1) of ammonia (or other highly volatile substance) and a salt water (or other less volatile substance). The heat causes the ammonia to vaporize and pass into a second chamber where it cools and condenses (2). Pure ammonia liquid then absorbs heat from the space to be conditioned (3) which causes it to vaporize again. The ammonia vapor is then reabsorbed by the original solution and the cycle begins again. Commercially available gas refrigeration units work on a similar system; heat is applied to one end to provide cooling power at the other.

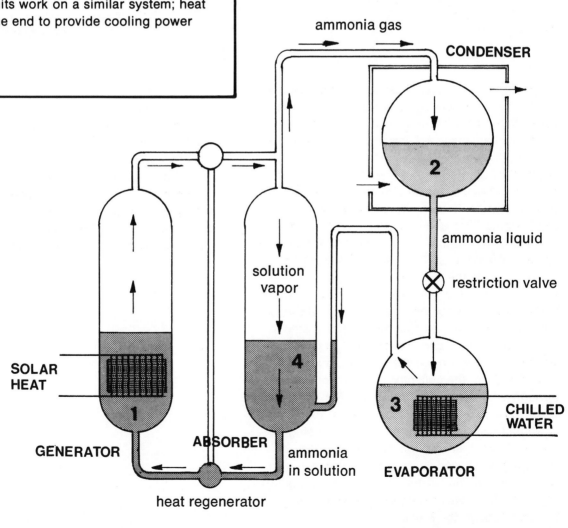

Simplified diagram of the operation of an absorption cooling system.

ammonia gas

CONDENSER

2

ammonia liquid

⊗ restriction valve

solution vapor

4

ammonia in solution

SOLAR HEAT

1

GENERATOR

ABSORBER

heat regenerator

3

CHILLED WATER

EVAPORATOR

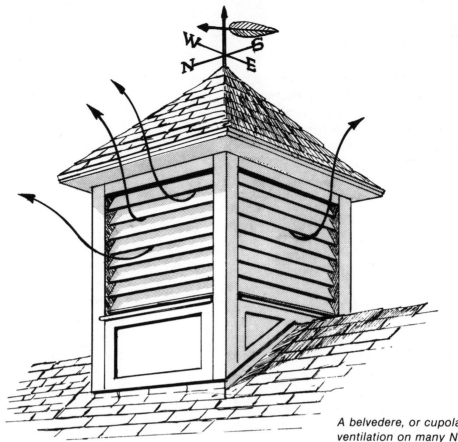

A belvedere, or cupola, used for ventilation on many New England barns.

In climates where air conditioning is needed, there is generally enough solar energy to run an absorption chiller. Well-constructed flat plate collectors can easily achieve temperatures of around 300 degrees Fahrenheit in hot climates, during the summer, which is well above the 180 degrees Fahrenheit needed to operate this kind of cooling system. In more temperate zones air-conditioning is an extravagance; and it is more reasonable to design the building to "cool itself" by natural ventilation. The use of overhanging eaves, for instance, will reduce heat gain in summer while allowing the winter sun to penetrate the house. A *belvedere* (cupola) on top of the roof can be used to exhaust the air from inside the house. (A chimney can also be used to bring cool air into the house in summer.) It would also be possible to run the collector return manifold through a fin-coil array of tubing in the belvedere which would serve the dual purpose of exhausting unwanted heat to the outside air and causing an upward flow of air through the house. With appropriately placed vents, a comfortable environment could be maintained by drawing cooler air from the shaded side of the building all the way through the house.

The possibility of developing technologies to use solar energy is virtually limitless, but we must reexamine our basic requirements to avoid developing systems which use the energy wastefully or extravagantly. At the moment the pressing need is for the investigation, installation and testing of the more straightforward applications of solar energy, such as processes which require low grade heat. These systems can be installed using very simple technology and readily available materials.

Available Energy

The conventional unit of measurement of solar radiation is the "langley", which is equal to one calorie per square centimeter, or about 4 BTUs per square foot. The radiant energy reaching the earth's surface is a combination of direct radiation from the sun and radiation from clouds in the upper atmosphere, diffuse radiation. On a clear day, as much as 10 percent of the radiation reaching the earth comes from the upper atmosphere, and in New England, for instance, about 40 percent of the annual solar radiation is atmospheric.

The average direct and diffuse radiation falling on a horizontal surface near the ground varies, in Connecticut, from about 135 langleys per day in December, to about 520 langleys per day in June. Average monthly figures are shown for solar radiation in various places in the Northeast. There is a great reduction in intensity over urban areas, where smog and air pollution cuts down the solar radiation by over 10 percent in winter and by 3-4 percent in summer.

Throughout the winter in this part of the country, there is more than enough solar radiation to accommodate a conventional house and all its heating requirements. Because of collection inefficiencies, however, and the difficulties in adapting the large area of the collector to the house, it is not easy to provide all the heat required.

New Haven, Connecticut has an average of 12 cloudy days (with 80-100 percent cloud cover) and 10 clear days (with 0-30 percent cloud cover) in the months of December through February. No specific data is yet available on the length of cloudy spells, but long periods without sunshine are apt to occur in winter and early spring, and a solar heating system should be capable of storing enough heat for at least four cloudy days.

Average daily solar radiation for various locations in the Northeastern U.S. For complete data on locations throughout the U.S. see Reference 18	Boston, Mass.	Blue Hill, Mass.	New York, NY.	Sayville, NY.	Newport, R.I.
January	135	148	144	160	151
February	197	213	211	249	229
March	290	301	316	335	329
April	365	383	381	415	395
May	473	474	464	494	494
June	498	519	532	565	539
July	497	504	518	543	518
August	420	434	429	462	452
September	339	352	361	385	381
October	240	252	262	289	275
November	143	159	160	186	175
December	122	132	126	142	141

Costing

The market prices for solar collectors at the moment range between 20¢ and $20 a square foot. It is very difficult for the homeowner to decide **where** he should spend his money, let alone **why** this price range is so great. If you are buying a collector system to provide you with space heating you should look in depth at the collectors designed to do this, which in general are the more expensive ones.

You should consider first, the durability of the collector. If it is going to pay for itself in ten years in the savings you make in fuel costs, the collector must be able to last ten years. This means that the absorber plate, the selective surface, and the whole fabric of the collector must be designed to withstand rapid and large variations in temperature and weather.

Calculations

In order to determine how much collector area you need, you will need to know the efficiency of the collector. Most reliable manufacturers will provide figures either for annual average efficiency (at the moment for the best systems this is between 40 and 70 percent depending on the temperature difference between the absorber and outside air) or for daylong efficiency (the collector's response to a given set of climatic conditions over one day). Study the manufacturer's data carefully! You will need twice as much collector area if the collector averages 30 percent efficiency, than you will if the collector averages 60 percent efficiency. This largely accounts for the wide price range in present equipment.

To calculate the energy available from the sun, you need to consult tables of solar radiation at various latitudes. These can be found in the Ashrae 1974 *Handbook of Fundamentals,* an excellent and very useful source book if you are interested in installing a system. From the *Tables,* you can read off the average amount of solar radiation (in BTUs per square foot) falling on a surface at any angle, and at any time of day for each month of the year. You then need to know the monthly average cloud cover for your area which will give you the percentage of sunshine actually received. Once you have this meterological data, and all other necessary figures, you can plug them into the following simple equation:

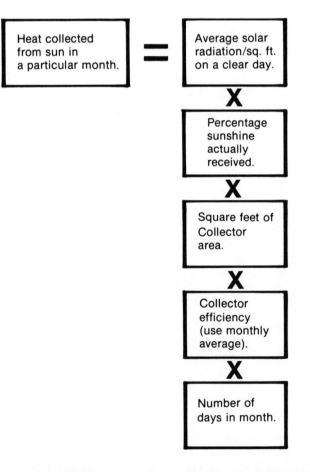

You can then compare this figure with the heat loss of your house, to see how much of your heating can be done by solar energy. The heat loss of the house can be computed either by looking at your heating bills (in an existing situation) or by calculating the design heat loss (for a new house). An architect or engineer can do this for you very easily or you can figure it out yourself from Reference 18.•

Storage Volume

In using water as a heat storage medium, it is usual to allow about one gallon of water for each square foot of heated floor space. A typical family house installation might use a 1500 gallon storage tank (about 10' x 4' x 5') in the basement. In a climate such as New England, a storage volume of that size would provide for about three or four days without sunshine.

The system can be made to store heat longer by increasing the collector area, the efficiency of the collector, and the storage volume. Some suggestions have been made to incorporate a huge cellar-sized storage tank which used heat collected in summer to heat the building in winter. The major problem with this idea would be insulating the stored heat effectively.

Domestic Hot Water Heaters

As a "rule of thumb" for calculating the area of collector required for a domestic hot water installation in a temperate climate, allow about one square foot of collector area (with an average annual efficiency of around 50 percent) for every gallon of hot water required per day. The daily hot water requirement for an average family is about 10 gallons per person (exclusive of appliances such as dishwashers and washing machines). Therefore, a typical hot water installation might use about 40 square feet of collector area. This would provide about 70-75 percent of the annual hot water requirement, with a simple gas or electric water heater providing the remaining 25 percent of the energy.

• For a well-insulated house in a temperate climate, the design heat loss may vary from 20-40 BTUs per hour for every square foot of floor area.

For winter heating in temperate or cold climates it is inadvisable to try and design an installation to provide for all your heat requirements. To do so would require a very large collection and storage area and a very efficient collector. But to provide 75 percent of your heating budget, you would probably need one square foot of collector for every two square foot of floor space (assuming a fairly high annual collection efficiency of around 50 percent). The rest of the heat you need could be provided by a woodburning stove or any kind of conventional heating system acting as a back up to the solar energy system.

It is important to realize that energy conservation should have priority over energy collection. There is no point in collecting solar energy and then wasting it in a poorly designed house. Minimizing the infiltration of cold air, using extra insulation, double glazing and shutters or insulating drapery over the windows at night will help reduce the heat load of the building. The size and number of windows facing north, or toward the prevailing winds must be kept to a minimum, whereas windows facing south can act as solar collectors themselves and help to heat the house during sunny days.

House Design

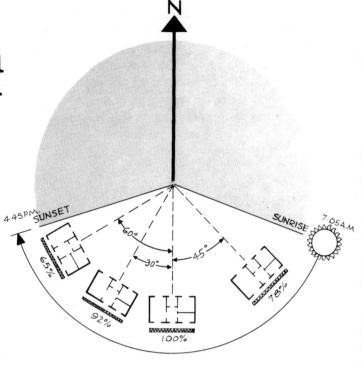

The use of solar energy will affect the design and hence the form, orientation and construction of a building, as well as the landscaping around it. Nevertheless, you can use these limitations to your own advantage and produce a well designed, energy-conserving house. By failing to understand the principles of solar energy systems, you could conceivably construct a building that functioned badly and was, in the bargain, an eyesore.

The percentage reduction in collection efficiency of vertically mounted collectors oriented away from due south (latitude 35° to 40° N). See reference 5.

Exposure

Solar collectors will work most efficiently when perpendicular to the sun. To maximize the efficiency of a collector for winter heating it must face the equator and should be tilted so that it is perpendicular to the mean maximum altitude of the winter sun. This angle is approximately equal to the angle of latitude at the site plus 15 degrees (in Connecticut this means an angle of 56 degrees to the horizontal).* As the angle of the collector varies from this (particularly towards the horizontal), the efficiency of the collector decreases.

If the collector is incorporated into the building, a large proportion of the south side of the house must contain collectors. This in turn means cutting down on the window area facing south, and can reduce the amount of natural lighting in the building. A number of configurations are shown which the form of the building could take in order to accommodate a collector area equal to 45 percent of the floor area.

*For optimum collection all year round (i.e. if the solar energy is to be used for cooling as well as heating), the angle of the collectors should be closer to the horizontal (latitude plus about 3 degrees).

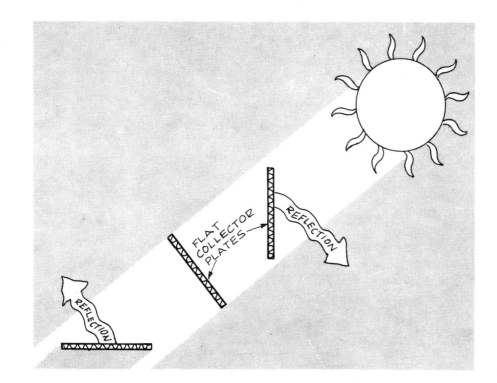

The loss in collection efficiency as the collector is tilted away from the optimum angle of inclination (which depends on the latitude of the site).

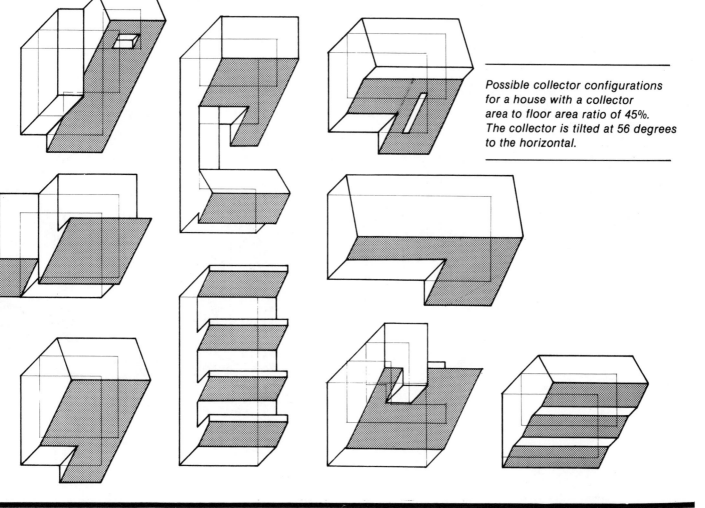

Possible collector configurations for a house with a collector area to floor area ratio of 45%. The collector is tilted at 56 degrees to the horizontal.

The Site of The House

To insure maximum exposure to the winter sun, shading from trees and other buildings must also be considered. Evergreen trees provide year-round shading, whereas deciduous trees provide much less shade in the winter period — though they still cut down on solar radiation. Shadows cast on the collector by other buildings or by protruding parts of the same building must also be avoided.

A collector which is completely exposed to the sun is, unfortunately, likely to be exposed to the cooling effect of winds. A 15 mph wind across the surface of a collector will cause a heat loss of 6 BTUs/Ft.^{2}/hr. (reducing the collector efficiency by about 5%). Planting trees and shrubs to the east and west of the collector could help to shelter it from the wind, without shading it from useful incident sunlight.

Solar collectors applied to a simple pole built house. For further information see **Pole-Building Construction** *by Doug Merrilees and Evelyn Loveday. Available from Gardenway Publishing Co., Charlotte, Vermont 05445.*

Courtesy of Irwin Abrams,
Burlington, Vermont.

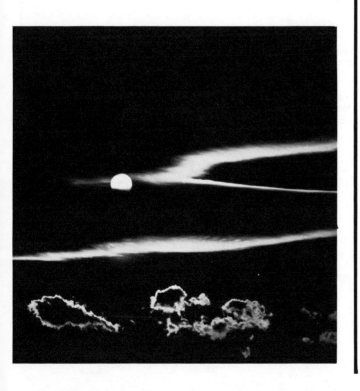

Constructing a Solar House

Harnessing solar energy for use in buildings contributes indirectly to the conservation of non-renewable energy resources. It is just as important to approach energy conservation by designing the building so that it retains heat in winter and excludes excessive heat in summer.

To make the best use of collected solar energy, the building must be well insulated. Low thermal insulation and large areas of glass facing north or exposed to the prevailing winds waste the available solar energy. Conversely, to reduce the heat loss of the building, reduces the required collector area.

A complete solar heating system with collectors, storage and distribution can add about $8,000 to the cost of a medium-sized house, but will pay for itself in about 8-10 years, (Reference 10) *
A system for providing a hot water supply only, will pay for itself in less than 5 years. Less efficient collectors can be incorporated more easily into the structure of the house at a lower initial cost. The designs on pages 44-49 show the range of collection systems available, from the mass-produced flat plate collectors with a relatively high efficiency, to a simple modification of the skin of the building to increase solar absorbtion.

In the 1950's the term "solar house" was used to refer to buildings which had large picture windows facing south, but this was a very misleading definition. The essential principle of a solar house is that it absorbs and stores the sun's energy for use as required. Large glass windows will rapidly lose as much heat at night or on a cloudy day, as they gain during hours of sunshine.

The approach towards environmental control in a building must be to create a skin which can admit, repel, absorb and retain heat as required. This means that the skin must be flexible, and easily adapted to changing external conditions. For environmental controls, we may be moving towards more sophisticated versions of windows, shutters, vents, and curtains instead of towards more eleaborate thermostats for more extravagant fossil-fuel heating systems.

*Approximate figures based on the calculations, research and experience of Everett Barber, Sunworks Inc.

SOLAR WATER HEATER

"*Eco-Unity is a project for a self-sufficient housing community of 32 units, utilizing solar energy and wind power and ecologically sound methods of waste treatment. The houses extend in terraces from the central community building. Heat from the collectors on the terrace is stored in the community building and is returned to each house via a service runway running under the terrace. Considerable benefits are to be gained from sharing plant and maintenance costs when using decentralized servicing systems.*

Eco-Unity. Ryc Loope and Peter Clegg. Award-winning entry for the ASC/AIA competition on Energy Conservation in Buildings. January 1974. (university pub.).

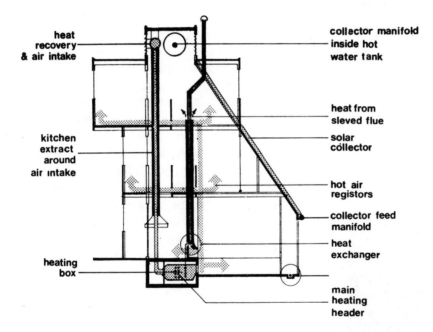

heat recovery & air intake

collector manifold inside hot water tank

kitchen extract around air intake

heat from sleved flue

solar collector

hot air registors

collector feed manifold

heat exchanger

heating box

main heating header

A simple cabin design using solar air-heaters and pebble-bed storage integrated into the structure and skin of the building. The air collectors can be used for ventilation during summer. One electric fan powers the entire system.

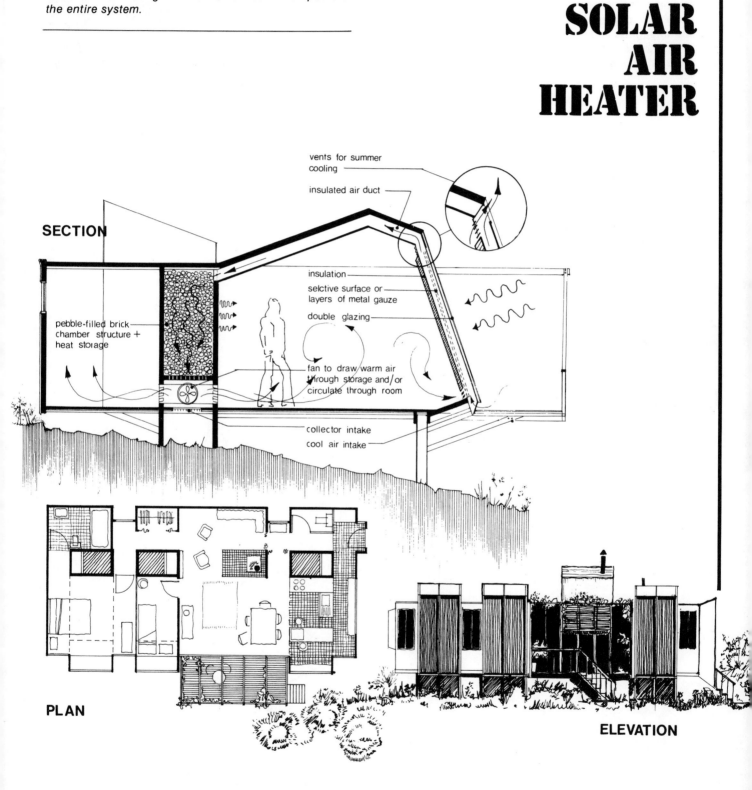

SECTION

vents for summer cooling

insulated air duct

insulation

selctive surface or layers of metal gauze

double glazing

pebble-filled brick chamber structure + heat storage

fan to draw warm air through storage and/or circulate through room

collector intake

cool air intake

PLAN

ELEVATION

Bringing the collector inside the house overcomes the problem of excluding natural light from the building. The collector efficiency is reduced by the extra layer of glass and the convection losses between the outer glass and the collector. An angled honeycomb could increase the radiation incident on the collector. Insulating blinds are necessary for use at nighttime.

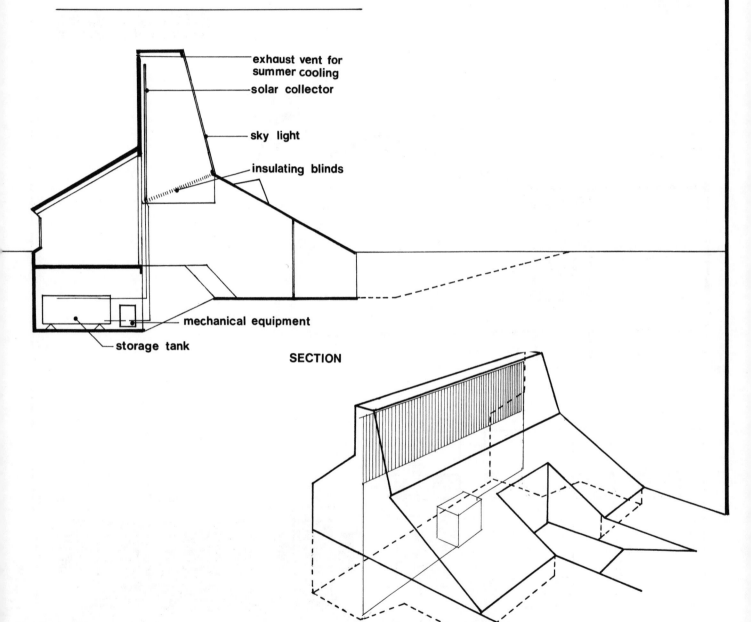

exhaust vent for summer cooling

solar collector

sky light

insulating blinds

mechanical equipment

storage tank

SECTION

SKETCH

In this design, based on the Trombe-Michel solar wall, the collector is completely integrated into the south-facing wall of the house. The concrete block wall provides both heat storage and cladding and could also be structural. Roller blinds operated from each window sill insulate the heat absorbing wall beneath it during the night. A precast modular system could provide a variety of collector configurations to suit different room layouts. The design is particularly well-suited to high-rise buildings, especially in northerly areas, but it is not very efficient, and would only provide a small portion of the heating requirements.

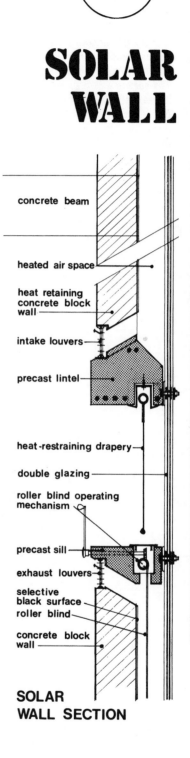

④
SOLAR
WALL

concrete beam

heated air space

heat retaining
concrete block
wall

intake louvers

precast lintel

heat-restraining drapery

double glazing

roller blind operating
mechanism

precast sill

exhaust louvers

selective
black surface
roller blind

concrete block
wall

**SOLAR
WALL SECTION**

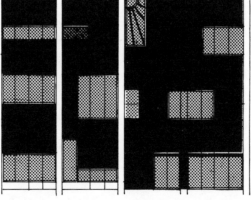

Elevation showing different arrangements of window and solar wall, using a 2 foot square modular system. Heat intakes are located above the wall panels, but near the floor in every room. The sketch above shows a "one-of-a-kind" house using a similar system.

This design shows how a simple lean-to glasshouse can become a winter sun trap and a barrier against heat loss from the heated portion of the houses. It also serves as an extension to the living area of the house when the climate is favorable, and as a greenhouse for plants. The block wall, laid so that airspaces in each block form ducts, and painted a dark color serves as a heat sink.

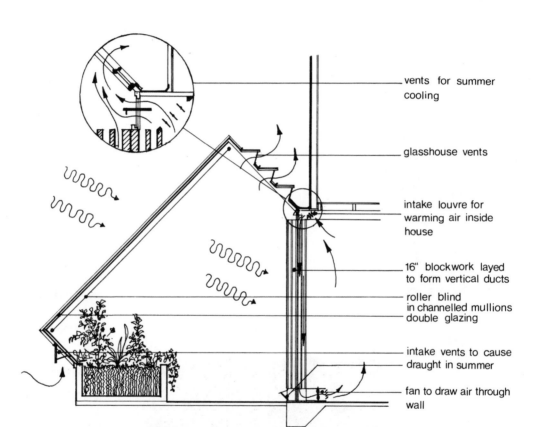

vents for summer cooling

glasshouse vents

intake louvre for warming air inside house

16" blockwork layed to form vertical ducts

roller blind in channelled mullions double glazing

intake vents to cause draught in summer

fan to draw air through wall

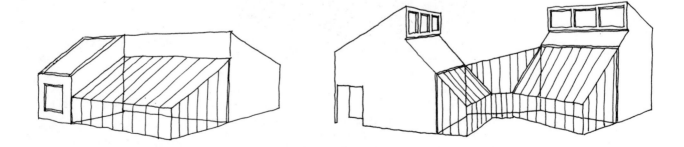

self~sufficient house plan

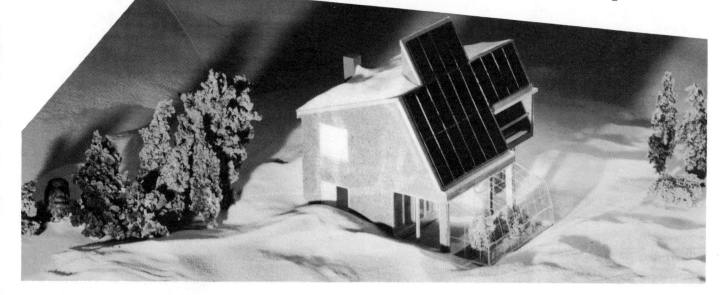

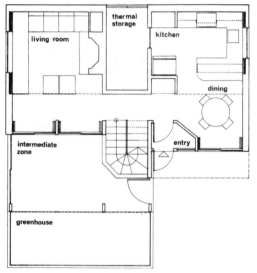

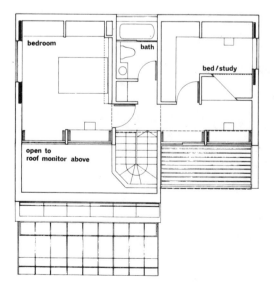

SELF-SUFFICIENT HOUSE PLAN for adaptation to various northern climates.

Features:

Greenhouse zone for multiple use. Self-heating with underfloor rock storage heated by return air that rises to top of space and can maintain above freezing temperatures year round.

Internal minimal living zone can be insulated from greenhouse in coldest weather.

Fireplace to augment heat of living zone and water storage tank.

Insulating shutters on all windows.

Solar collectors, either air-cooled or liquid-cooled can be used.

Masonry walls and floors optional in interior to serve as low temperature heat sink with insulation on exterior.

Roof "monitor" (skylight-cupola) for natural ventilation and illumination of greenhouse zone.

These features may be combined to accomodate different plans and climates.

DONALD WATSON, AIA ARCHITECT
Guilford, Connecticut.

References

1 **Direct Use of the Sun's Energy.** F. Daniels. Yale University Press 1964. Ballantine paperback, 1974.

2 **Proceedings of the Solar Heating and Cooling of Buildings Workshop.** Washington D.C. March 1973, sponsored by N.S.F./RANNU of of Maryland.

3 "Solar Energy in Housing." C. Moorcroft. **Architectural Design.** October 1973.

4 "Solar Heating and Cooling: Untapped Energy Put to Use." G. Loef and D. Ward. **Civil Engineering.** September 1973.

5 **U.N. Conference on New Sources of Energy.** Rome, 1961. Volumes 1-6. New York, 1963.

6 "A Slit-and-Expanded Aluminum-Foil Matrix Solar Collector." Chiou, El Wakil, and Duffie. **Solar Energy.** Volume 9, Number 2, 1965.

7 Honeycomb Devices in Flat Plate Solar Collectors". K. G. G. Hollands. **Solar Energy.** Volume 9, Number 3, 1965.

8 Notes on a Solar Collector with a Unique Airpermeable Media." M. J. Shoemaker. **Solar Energy.** Volume 5, 1961.

9 Performance of Black-Painted Solar Air Heaters of Conventional Design." A. Whillier. **Solar Energy.** Volume 3, Number 1, 1964.

10 **Solar Energy vs Fossil Fuels: Nomograph for Economic Comparison.** E. M. Barber. Yale School of Architecture. 1973.

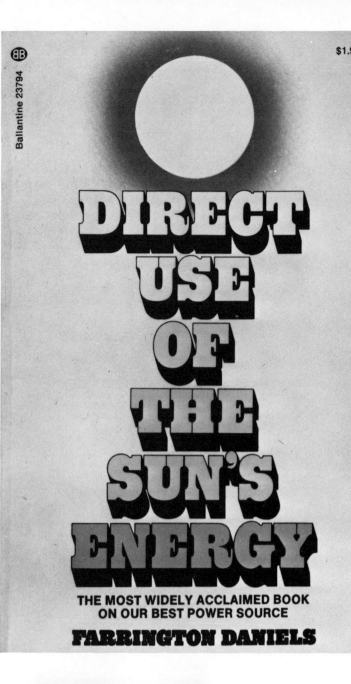

11 "The Thermal Performance of Solar Water Heaters." A. Whillier and G. Saluja. **Solar Energy.** January 1968.

12 "Solar Energy Collector Design." H. Tabor. Conference paper at the **Conference on the Utilization of Solar Energy.** Tucson, Arizona, 1955.

13 "Utilization de L'Energie Solaire." J. Michel. in **L'Architecture d'Aujourd-hui.** May-June 1973.

14 "Space Heating with Solar Energy." R. W. Hamilton, Ed. Massachusetts Institute of Technology (Cambridge, Massachusetts 02139), 1954.

15 "Adapting Design to Climate." (Reprint from *Connecticut Architect.*) Everett Barber, Jr., Sunworks Inc., 669 Post Road, Guilford, Connecticut, 06437.

16 "Criteria for the Preliminary Design of Solar Heated Buildings." Everett Barber Jr. and Donald Watson. 1974. Available from Sunworks Inc., 669 Post Road, Guilford, Connecticut 06437.

17 **Solar House Plans.** Dr. Harry E. Thomason. Edmund Scientific Company, Barrington, New Jersey. 1973.

18 **Ashrae Handbook of Fundamentals,** 1974. Published by the American Society of Heating Refrigerating and Air-Conditioning Engineers.

The planet is now the object of design: the consequences of building design are global through the consumption of energy and resources that it requires and the place it takes in an existing ecosystem. If the car and the water-flush toilet rank as the most inefficient tools now used for human ecology, our buildings may not be far behind, particularly those that consume large amounts of energy in order to compensate for the designer's disregard of climate.

Architects once studied the rules of proportion for the styles and orders of the Classic temple. The earth is now that temple: the rules are those of building and living within the limits of the world's balance of material resources and energy.

Energy Conservation in Architecture
Part 1: Adapting Design to Climate

by Donald Watson, AIA

Further Readings

"Intermittent Vapor Absorption Cycle Employing Ammonia-Water and Ammonia-Lithium Nitrate." J. C. V. Chinnappa. **Solar Energy.** Volume 6, Number 4 (October-December 1962), pages 143-150.

"Solar Space Cooling." R. Chung, G.O.G. Lof, and J. A. Duffie. **Chemical Engineering Progress.** Volume 55, Number 4 (April 1959), pages 74-78.

"The Varied and Early Solar Energy Applications of Northern New Mexico." Jeffrey Cook. **A.I.A. Journal.** August 1974.

"Solar Air-Conditioning System." E. A. Farber. **Solar Energy Journal.** Number 291, 1966.

"Power From the Sun: Its Future." Peter E. Glaser. **Science.** Volume 162, Number 3856, November 22, 1968, pages 857-861.

Proceedings of the World Symposium on Applied Solar Energy. G.O.G. Lof. Stanford Research Institute, Menlo Park, California 1956.

"Solar Absorption Refrigeration." N. R. Sheridan and J. A. Duffie. **Australian Refrigeration, Air Conditioning, and Heating.** Volume 18, Number 8 (1964), page 14.

"Low Temperature Engineering Applications of Solar Energy." Ashrae, 345 East 47th Street, New York 10017.

"The Complete Steve Baer Solar Energy Reprints." Steve Baer. Sun Publishing Company, P.O. Box 4383, Albuquerque, New Mexico 87106.

"Economics of Solar Collectors, Heat Pumps and Wind Generators," Gerry Smith. [Available from:] University of Cambridge, Department of Architecture, Technical research division. Scroope Terrace, Cambridge, England. $1.00.

"Solar-House heating and air-conditioning systems: Comparisons and Limitations," Thomason and Thomason. Available from Edmund Scientific Co., 555 Edscorp Bldg., Barrington, N.J., 08007.

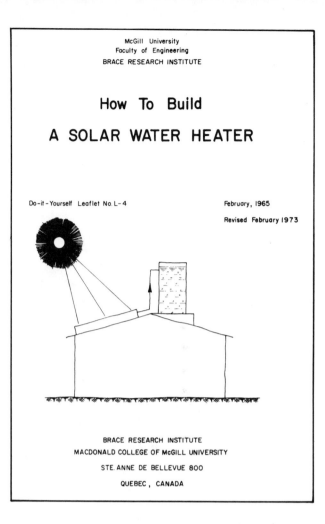

McGill University
Faculty of Engineering
BRACE RESEARCH INSTITUTE

How To Build
A SOLAR WATER HEATER

Do-it-Yourself Leaflet No. L-4   February, 1965
                                        Revised February 1973

BRACE RESEARCH INSTITUTE
MACDONALD COLLEGE OF McGILL UNIVERSITY
STE. ANNE DE BELLEVUE 800
QUEBEC, CANADA

How to Build a Solar Water Heater. D. A. Sinson and T. Hoad, rev. ed. Quebec: Brace Research Institute, 1973.

Solar and Aeolian Energy. Proceedings of International Conference on Solar and Aeolian Energy. September 1961. Plenum Press, 1964,

"Alternative Energy Sources," D. Watson and E. Barber in **Connecticut Architect** magazine. May-June 1974.

"Solar Heated buildings — a brief survey," W. A. Shurcliff, August 1974. Available from Solar Energy Digest. A.P.O. Box 17776, San Diego, CA 92117. $7.00.

Solar Energy Applications. Available from Arthur D. Little, Inc., 20 Acorn Park, Cambridge, Massachusetts 02140.

"Use of Solar Energy for Cooling Purposes." H. Tabor. Paper E 35 GR18(S), UN Conference on New Sources of Energy, Rome, 1961.

"The Effect of Materials and Construction Details on the Thermal Performance of Solar Water Heaters," **Solar Energy,** Vol. 9, No. 1, Jan., 1965.

"The Performance of Flat-Plate Solar Heat Collectors," H. C. Hottel and B. B. Woertz. **Transactions of the American Society of Mechanical Engineers,** Feb. 1942.

Solar Energy Research, ed. by F. Daniels and J. A. Duffie, University of Wisconsin Press, Madison, Wisconsin. 1955.

SOLAR ENERGY CATALOG

Dear Reader,

The information appearing on the following pages was forwarded to us from the manufacturer or organization whose name appears in the book. We wrote to each organization requesting information about the work it was doing in the particular field of energy in question, explaining that they were welcome to send to us whatever copy they thought would represent them well.

Our goal was and is to make this helpful information available to you, the reader. Should you become interested in obtaining a product or further information from one of the companies displayed herein, we request that you **not** write to Garden Way Publishing Company but directly to that particular company whose product or research interests you.

Performance Data

	HEATING			AIR CONDITIONING
	Swimming Pools	Domestic Water	Building	
Usual Fluid Temperature Range (°F)	70-90	100-140	120-200	160-230
Maximum Design Temperature of Fluid Above Ambient (°F)	25-30	Summer 60-80 Winter 80-110	Fall/Spring 80-120 Winter 100-150	90-140
Number of Tubes Per 2' Wide Panel	2-3	Summer 3-4 Winter 3-4	Fall/Spring 3-4 Winter 3-5	3-5
Usual Number of Transparent Covers	0	Summer 1-2 Winter 1-2	Fall/Spring 2-3 Winter 2-3	2-3

Note: Insulation for each of the above applications will vary according to geographical location and type of insulation used.

The table summarizes design ➡ and component variables for Revere Solar Energy Collectors for the applications mentioned above. This table will assist in the selection of the best collector configuration for a given application.

Collector Appearance

Figures 1 and 2 show the Revere Copper Laminated Panel System and its adaptation as a solar collector. The Revere Solar Energy Collector may be installed as a modular unit for existing structures, or it may serve a dual function as both roof and collector in new buildings.

To convert an installation of the Revere laminated panel system to a solar collector, rectangular copper tubes are secured to standard 2 feet by 8 feet panels with copper clips. A special high conductivity adhesive is applied between tube and panel to insure a good heat transfer characteristic. Tube spacings may vary from 4 inches to 10 inches on center, depending upon efficiency requirements.

A specially constructed copper batten supports one or two layers of glass or other transparent material.

Revere has also developed simple adapter fittings to facilitate the connection of the rectangular tubes to conventional round copper water tubes.

An installation made in this manner can function as a combination roof and solar collector in new buildings.

Preassembled modular units in 3 feet by 7 feet sizes are also available for use on existing structures.

REVERE COMBINATION LAMINATED PANEL ROOF & SOLAR COLLECTOR

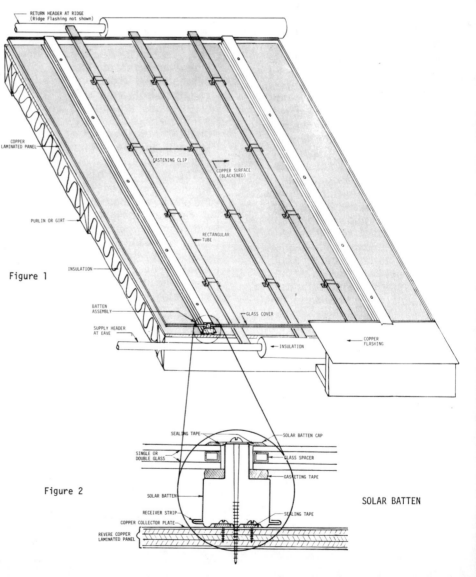

Figure 1

Figure 2

SOLAR BATTEN

Example

A total system capacity of 250,000 BTU/hr. is required from a 2000 sq. ft. solar energy collector system with an average panel water temperature of 120°F, a solar input of 250 BTU/hr./sq. ft. and an ambient temperature of 80°F. The panel configuration that meets these capacity requirements can be determined as follows:

$$\text{Required output} = \frac{250,000}{2000} = 125 \text{ BTU/hr./sq. ft.}$$

$$\text{Required panel efficiency} = \frac{\text{output}}{\text{input}} = \frac{125}{250} = 50\%$$

Average panel water temperature minus ambient temperature = 120°−80° = 40°

At the above conditions, a standard two-foot wide panel with three tubes and a single layer of glass has an efficiency of 52% and an approximate output of 130 BTU/hr./sq. ft.

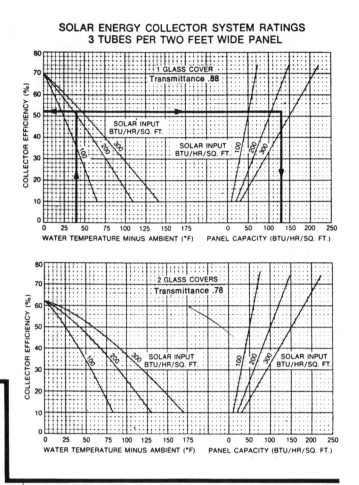

SOLAR ENERGY COLLECTOR SYSTEM RATINGS
3 TUBES PER TWO FEET WIDE PANEL

REVERE COPPER AND BRASS INC.
P.O. BOX 191, ROME N.Y. 13440

Revere gets the prize for the most concise and informative product literature on solar collectors. The panel they advertise is an adaptation of a laminated copper and plywood roofing system (see opposite). The first major installation will be made on the palatial "Decade 80" solar house (below) in Tucson, Arizona sponsored by the Copper Development Association.

Collector Piping Design & Use of Antifreeze

Ethylene glycol, the most commonly used antifreeze, is slightly more dense and has a lower specific heat than water. As a result, an ethylene glycol/water solution holds less heat than a corresponding amount of water. The following equations will aid in the computation of heat content and friction pressure drop for different ethylene glycol/water mixtures.

BTU/HR = GPM × (Ent. fluid temp.− Lvg. fluid temp.) × 500 × C
Friction pressure drop = pres. drop for water × frict. correction factor.

ETHYLENE GLYCOL CORRECTION FACTORS

% Glycol	Temp. (°F)	C	Friction Correction Factor (For Equal Flow Rates)
0	100	.995	1.00
	200	.975	1.00
25	100	.956	1.05
	200	.944	.96
50	100	.830	1.10
	200	.820	.92

Note: Do not use an antifreeze solution with greater than 60% ethylene glycol since this may result in damage to the system.

Tube sizing and pressure drop calculations for the remainder of the system are calculated in the same manner as in conventional heating systems.

The rectangular collector tubes have an internal area and pressure drop rate approximately the same as ¾" (Nom.) Type K copper water tube.

Materials for Solar Energy Collectors

Revere's Research Center has generations of experience with many materials. After thorough analyses of a wide variety of metals and non-metallic materials, we came to the conclusion that *copper has the best combination of properties for solar energy collectors* for these reasons:

■ **Copper transfers heat best.**
Copper's heat transfer values are two to eight times better than any other material considered for collector plates.

■ **Copper resists corrosion.**
No other metal has a better record of long-term corrosion resistance than copper.

■ **Copper is easy to install.**
The use of solder fittings, familiar to the trades, insures fast, simple, inexpensive installation. With the Revere system there are no expensive or complicated joining procedures.

■ **Copper stays strong.**
High temperatures such as 210°F water do not cause any significant loss of strength.

■ **Copper requires no inhibitors.**
Other materials need inhibitors, which require periodic replenishment, to prevent corrosion. Copper does not need such inhibitors.

In the Revere system the collector plate surface, tubes, clips, fittings and battens are all 100% copper and are compatible with copper or other distribution piping materials.

sunworks

Specialists in solar energy engineering and equipment

669 Boston Post Road   Guilford, Connecticut 06437
(203) 453-6191

Sunworks collectors have been installed in several homes in Connecticut both for space-heating and domestic hot water heating. The first installations have shown results which indicate a higher collection efficiency than was expected. The Sunworks collector comes in two different modules:- "flush mounted", for installation between the joists of a roof, and "surface mounted", for installation separate from the structure of the building. Selectively coated absorber tube-sheets are available in various sizes for do-it-yourself enthusiasts. Sunworks is also developing a high-efficiency solar air-heater which should be available in March 1975. Sunworks collectors carry a five-year guarantee.

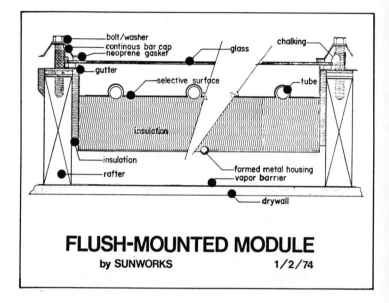

FLUSH-MOUNTED MODULE
by SUNWORKS   1/2/74

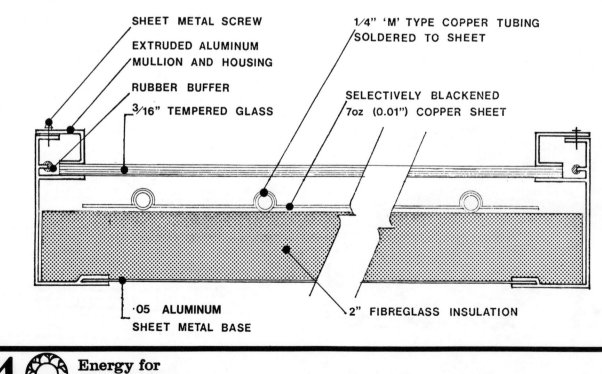

SHEET METAL SCREW

EXTRUDED ALUMINUM MULLION AND HOUSING

RUBBER BUFFER

3/16" TEMPERED GLASS

1/4" 'M' TYPE COPPER TUBING SOLDERED TO SHEET

SELECTIVELY BLACKENED 7oz (0.01") COPPER SHEET

·05 ALUMINUM SHEET METAL BASE

2" FIBREGLASS INSULATION

The first installation of Sunworks
collectors. A house on the
Connecticut shoreline. Architect:
Donald Watson AIA; engineer:
Everett M. Barber Jr.

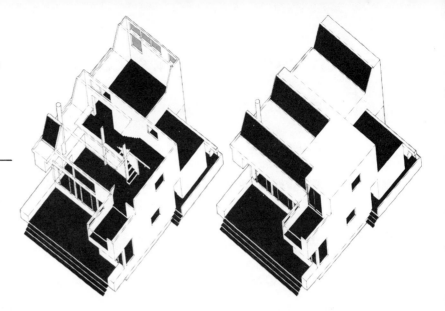

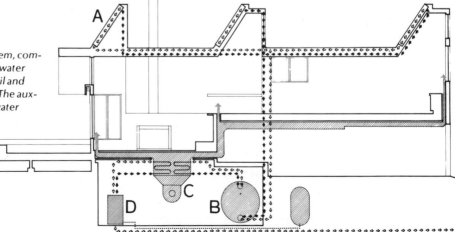

A cross-section of the solar house
which diagrams the solar heating system, composed of collectors (A), a 2000-gallon water
thermal storage tank (B), and a fan-coil and
forced hot-air distribution ducts (C). The auxiliary system is an oil-fired domestic water
heater (D).

why choose sunworks collectors?

● **1** FIVE YEAR PRODUCT GUARANTEE

● **2** FIELD TESTED AND PROVEN

● **3** HIGH EFFICIENCY PER UNIT AREA OF ABSORBER
SELECTIVE SURFACE, ABSORBTIVITY 0.9, EMMISSIVITY 0.1

● **4** CHOICE OF MODULES, COMPONENTS AND SIZES

● **5** WEATHERPROOF AND DURABLE ALUMINUM CASING

● **6** COPPER TUBING USED THROUGHOUT
PRESSURE TESTED TO 250 PSI.

Barber residence in Guildford Conn. Architects Charles Moore and Associates, Essex, Conn. Completion date March 1975. Besides a complete Solar-heating system, this house incorporates several fascinating energy-conserving features. ▶

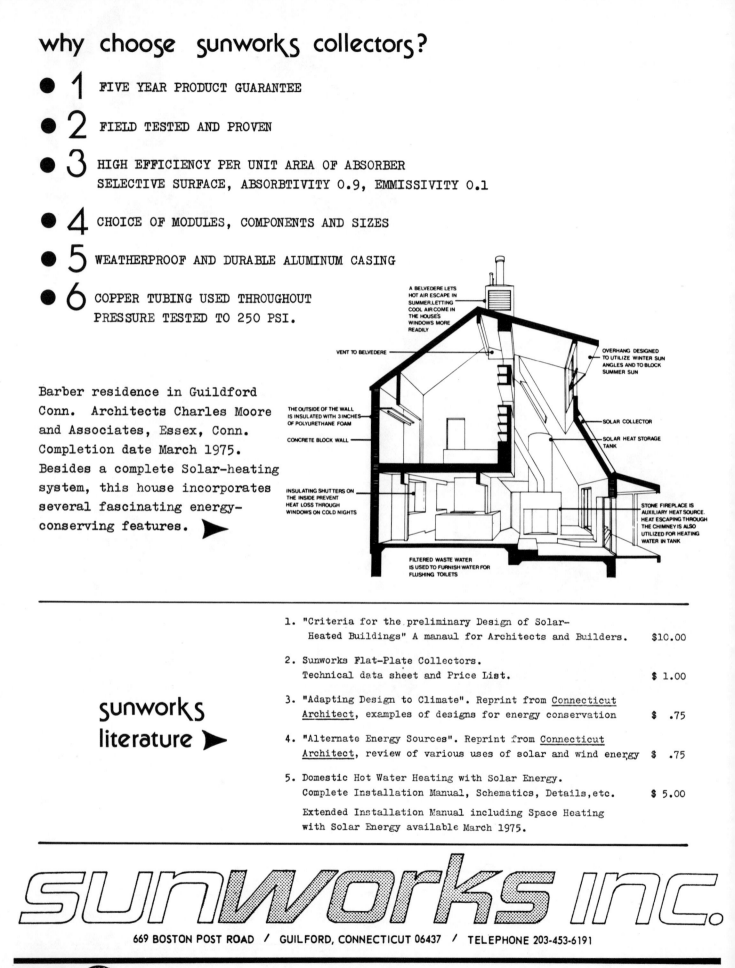

A BELVEDERE LETS HOT AIR ESCAPE IN SUMMER, LETTING COOL AIR COME IN THE HOUSES WINDOWS MORE READILY

VENT TO BELVEDERE

OVERHANG DESIGNED TO UTILIZE WINTER SUN ANGLES AND TO BLOCK SUMMER SUN

THE OUTSIDE OF THE WALL IS INSULATED WITH 3 INCHES OF POLYURETHANE FOAM

CONCRETE BLOCK WALL

SOLAR COLLECTOR

SOLAR HEAT STORAGE TANK

INSULATING SHUTTERS ON THE INSIDE PREVENT HEAT LOSS THROUGH WINDOWS ON COLD NIGHTS

STONE FIREPLACE IS AUXILIARY HEAT SOURCE. HEAT ESCAPING THROUGH THE CHIMNEY IS ALSO UTILIZED FOR HEATING WATER IN TANK

FILTERED WASTE WATER IS USED TO FURNISH WATER FOR FLUSHING TOILETS

---

sunworks literature ▶

1. "Criteria for the preliminary Design of Solar-Heated Buildings" A manaul for Architects and Builders. $10.00

2. Sunworks Flat-Plate Collectors.
Technical data sheet and Price List. $ 1.00

3. "Adapting Design to Climate". Reprint from <u>Connecticut Architect</u>, examples of designs for energy conservation $ .75

4. "Alternate Energy Sources". Reprint from <u>Connecticut Architect</u>, review of various uses of solar and wind energy $ .75

5. Domestic Hot Water Heating with Solar Energy.
Complete Installation Manual, Schematics, Details,etc. $ 5.00

Extended Installation Manual including Space Heating with Solar Energy available March 1975.

---

sunworks inc.

669 BOSTON POST ROAD / GUILFORD, CONNECTICUT 06437 / TELEPHONE 203-453-6191

56 ⊙ Energy for the Home

ABSORBER TUBE - SHEETS

ALUMINUM
COPPER
STEEL

Preformed absorber sheets can be purchased from three manufacturers. Tranter makes a carbon steel and a stainless steel "plate-coil" unit. Olin Brass manufactures a "rollbond" sheet of copper and aluminum.

Sunworks sells a selectively blackened copper tube-sheet. Different metals have very different properties. In deciding which absorber metal to use, the following should be considered:

1 The Lifetime of the Unit and Its Resistance to Corrosion from the Heat Transfer Fluid. Copper has the longest lifetime (copper solar heaters have been working for over fifty years in Florida). Steel has a considerably shorter lifetime, and aluminum has serious corrosion problems with water based heat transfer fluids. Check for guarentees of durability.

2 Use of Selective Surfaces. These can be applied to almost any surface with expensive techniques like electro-plating or vapor deposition, but on a copper base the selective surface appears to be the least expensive and the most durable.

3 The Conductivity of the Material. The greater the conductivity, the less material is required. Copper has a conductivity of about 220 Btu/sq.ft.hr.°F/ft, Aluminum about 119 and steel about 26.

4 The Cost of the Unit. The Aluminum unit is by far the cheapest, and the copper unit is generally the most expensive. But the price of metals fluctuates rapidly, affecting the price of the metal absorber sheets. Make sure you get up to date prices.

ROLL-BOND® PRODUCTS

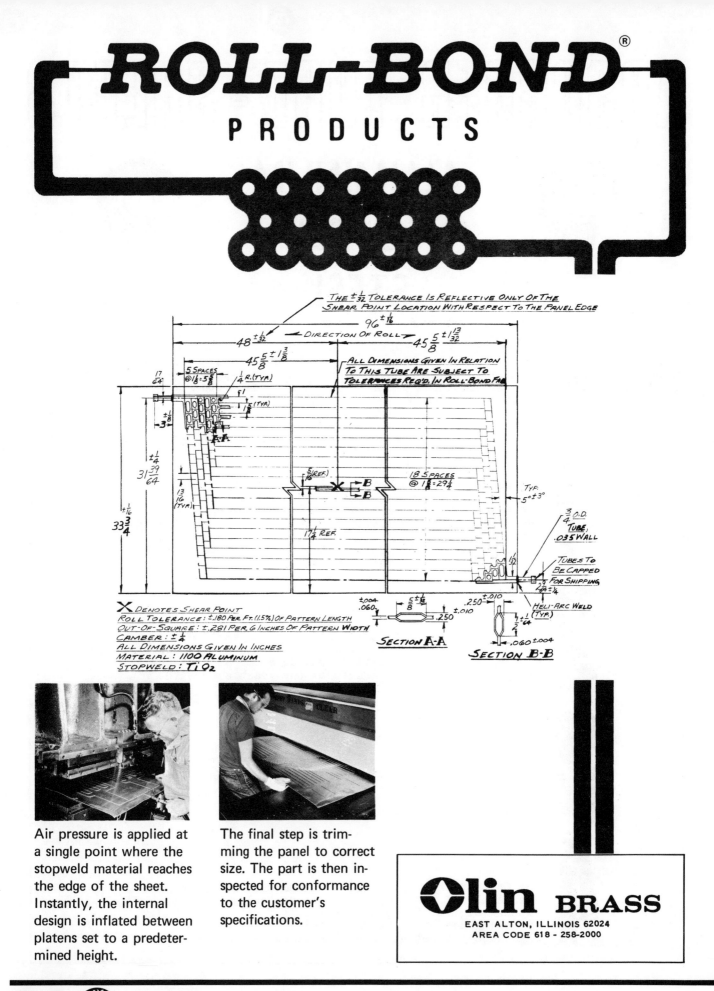

X Denotes Shear Point
Roll Tolerance: ±.180 Per Ft. (1.5%) Of Pattern Length
Out-Of-Square: ±.281 Per 6 Inches Of Pattern Width
Camber: ±¼
All Dimensions Given In Inches
Material: 1100 Aluminum
Stopweld: TiO₂

Air pressure is applied at a single point where the stopweld material reaches the edge of the sheet. Instantly, the internal design is inflated between platens set to a predetermined height.

The final step is trimming the panel to correct size. The part is then inspected for conformance to the customer's specifications.

COST ASSUMPTIONS: Metal (1100 Aluminum)
@ $.57/lb., Scrap @ $3.50/lb
Waffle Headers—Tube Height .180"

FABRICATION AVAILABLE: Forming
Hole and notch piercing
Welding (includes attachment of connector tubes)
Finishing (alodine prefinish, baked paint)

QUOTATIONS AVAILABLE UPON REQUEST

Size: 22" x 96"
Gauge: .040" (.020" wall)
Material: Alloy 122 Copper
Weight: 27.287 pounds
Sq. Ft.:   14.667 sq. ft.

Quantity	Unit Price
100 pieces	$53.40 each
250 "	49.40 "
500 "	47.50 "
1,000 "	46.65 "
2,500 "	46.25 "

Additional Costs

Weld 2 copper connectors
to panel edges.....................$4.85 each

Sampling Program

A small quantity of parts will be stocked
and available at:
$60.00 each (w/connectors)
+ $25.00 packing charge per shipment

OLIN BRASS
ROLL-BOND PRODUCTS
SOLAR ENERGY COLLECTOR PANEL SUPPLIERS

Alten Associates, Inc*
Suite 200 D
3080 Olcott St
Santa Clara CA 95051
--Frank Verprauskus, VP

Phoenix Of Colorado Springs, Inc
PO Box 7246
Colorado Srpings CO 80933

The Theodore Bross Line
Construction Co
42 E Dudley Town Rd
Bloomfield CT 06002
--Theodore D Bross, Pres

Solar Heating Systems*
13584 49th St N
Clearwater FL 33516
--C.H. Breckenridge, Pres.

W R Robbins & Son*
1401 NW 20th St
Miami FL 33142
--WR Robbins, Jr, Owner

Energy Design Associates, Inc *
3003 NE 19th Dr
Gainesville FL 32601
--Richard C Rodgers, Pres.

Sun Systems, Inc
PO Box 155
Eureka IL 61530
--YB Safdari, Pres.

SunSav, Inc*
250 Canal St
Lawrence MA 01840 --Peter Ottmar, PA

Solar King, Inc *
277 Gould St
Reno NV 89502
--Brian D Pardo, Pres.

Grumman Aerospace Corp
Plant 30
Bethpage LI, NY 11714
--Dick Henkel, Contract Mgr

International Environment Corp
129 Halstead Ave
Mamaroneck NY 10543
--RD Rothschild, Pres.

Currie Equipment Co*
1311 W 5th St
Lumberton NC 28358
--Bob Currie, Pres.

Ametek*
Hunter Spring Ave
Hatfield PA 19440
--John C Bowen

General Electric Co
Space Div.
PO Box 8661
Philadelphia PA 19101
--Bill Moore

State Stove & Mfg Co
Cumberland St
Ashland TN 37015
--Denver Collins

Intertechnology Corp
PO Box 340
Warrenton VA 22186
--GC Szego, Pres

*in addition to aluminum, these companies supply
ROLL-BOND copper panels.

EAST ALTON, ILLINOIS 62024

(618/258-2443)

Olin Manufactures 2 different sizes and
tube configurations of stock aluminum
ROLL—BOND collector plates (prices
around $1.15/sq ft. including connectors
and one side painted black) and one
type of copper ROLL—BOND (around
$3.18/sq ft.). The company advises
various protective measures which
should be taken to minimize corrosion
with the aluminum collectors.
Ultimately the use of Freon or high
viscosity oil as the heat transfer fluid
could provide an answer to this problem.

Econocoil SOLAR Collector Plates

STANDARD MODELS ARE AVAILABLE AS SHOWN BELOW

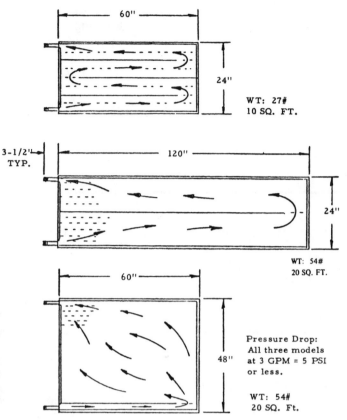

The "platecoil" is a quilted steel collector plate available in a number of different configurations. Prices, for the basic units with connectors — around $8.00/sq.ft. Tranter also makes a wide range of heat exchangers suitable for solar heating systems.

All above models are supplied in approx. 22 Ga. carbon steel, leaked tested at 125 psig, ready for painting and installation, fittings are 3/4" dia. threaded pipes. Other circuitry and sizes are available.

General Specifications:
1. Allowable operating pressure: up to 75 PSIG
2. Thickness: approx 22 ga. = approx. .029"
3. Material: carbon steel or stainless steel
4. Weight: approx. 55# for 2' x 10' size
5. Finish: supplied as welded with paint to be applied by others
6. Pressure drop: usually less than 5 PSI for usual low flow rates in this service
7. Carbon steel is generally considered suitable for closed recirculating systems using glycol or treated water
8. Stainless steel is ideal for swimming pool water and for once through systems such as heating tap water

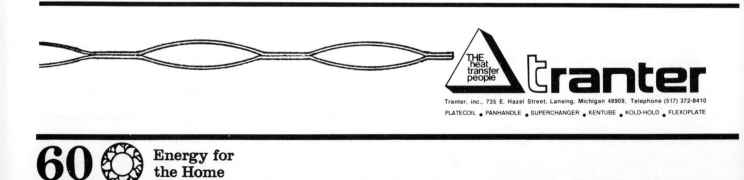

Tranter, inc., 735 E. Hazel Street, Lansing, Michigan 48909, Telephone (517) 372-8410

PLATECOIL • PANHANDLE • SUPERCHANGER • KENTUBE • KOLD-HOLD • FLEXOPLATE

p.p.g.

PPG manufactures a collector using an aluminum "roll-bond" absorber with a matte black painted surface, covered with a double layer of glass. The cost for a complete unit in a metal housing is around $7.20 per square foot. The photgraph shows a demonstration house in Columbus Ohio.

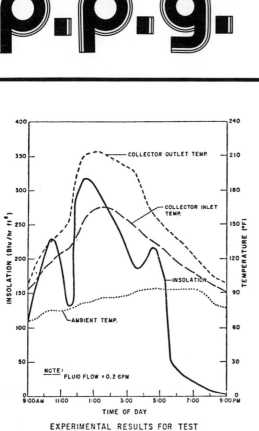

EXPERIMENTAL RESULTS FOR TEST AT MELBOURNE, FLA. - MAY 18, 1974.

Our collector is similar in design to our Twindow and metal pan spandrel unit which has several years of practical testing through exposure to the weather. The collector consists of two panes of 1/8" Herculite K glass, chosen to provide maximum resistance to windload, hail impact, snow load and vandalism and to provide maximum thermal shock resistance to the inner pane.

The absorber plate is aluminum Roll-Bond painted with a black PPG Duracron enamel which has an absorption of approximately 95%. The sealants used with the collector extend the operation of the collector to at least 300*F. Sealants to provide a higher temperature capability are being tested. The collector is vented through desiccant-containing chambers to prevent pressure build-up and the unwanted effects of moisture. The back of the absorber plate has a 2½" layer of exposed Thermafiber or fiberglass insulation. The collector thickness less insulation is 1 3/8" thick and weighs 4.8 lbs per foot without fluid.

We are attempting to standardize on approximately 34 3/16" x 76 3/16" outside dimensions of the unit for commercial applications. Cost of the unit is $6. to $7.20 per square foot, depending on whether the insulation is exposed or enclosed in a metal container. Quantities of 1 to 10 are $150. each with exposed insulation and $170. with enclosed insulation.

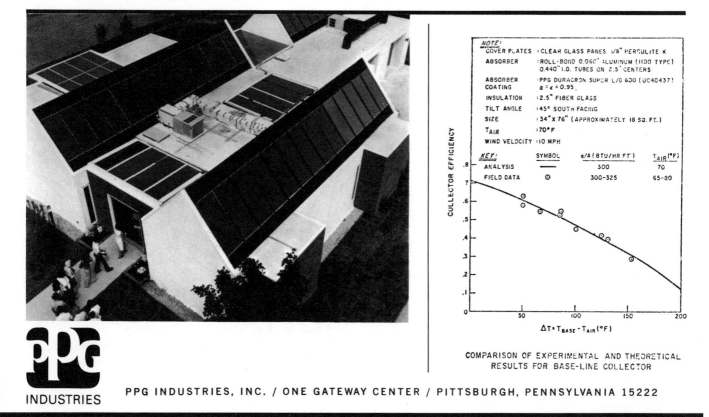

COMPARISON OF EXPERIMENTAL AND THEORETICAL RESULTS FOR BASE-LINE COLLECTOR

PPG INDUSTRIES, INC. / ONE GATEWAY CENTER / PITTSBURGH, PENNSYLVANIA 15222

Garden Way Laboratories

More than three years ago GARDEN WAY LABORATORIES began the research which offers our SOLAR PANEL to you today. In 1972, it looked as if solar energy was still a source of energy in the distant future, certainly not a resource for today. New materials, continued research, and your local power utility changed all that.

We are presently selling flat plate solar collectors which exhibit several advantages over earlier designs. They are more efficient thereby reducing the number required for space heating in new homes and allowing owners of older homes the advantage of immediately installing solar water heaters—— a major portion of any utility bill. They are less expensive (allowing a domestic hot water supply system to pay for itself in 4 to 8 years), they are easily installed (because they were designed specifically for use on older homes as well as in new home construction) and they are reliable (insuring long service life and low maintenance). How can we make such claims?

EXPERIENCE!

Our panels are presently heating many New England homes.

If you own an older home, now is the time to install a solar hot water heater. Hot water consumes approximately 20% of a person's yearly fuel bill or as much as 60% of your electrical bill. Solar hot water systems can be installed in any climate and on homes with roof areas facing in any direction except North. The 150 year old home pictured here contains a solar hot water system which supplies 90% of its yearly requirement with an Eastern exposure in Hinesburg VT. Furthermore, a hot water system can quickly pay for itself because of today's escalating fuel and electrical rates.

If you are presently thinking of building a new home and would like to install solar heat, or if you are interested in reducing your fuel bill immediately by incorporating a solar hot water system into your home, then write :

GARDEN WAY LABORATORIES
Dept 100W, PO BOX 66
Charlotte VT 05445

and ask for the Solar Panel Planning Guide-- ($1.00). This publication contains a wealth of information and explains how a Garden Way Solar Panel System can be used in your home.

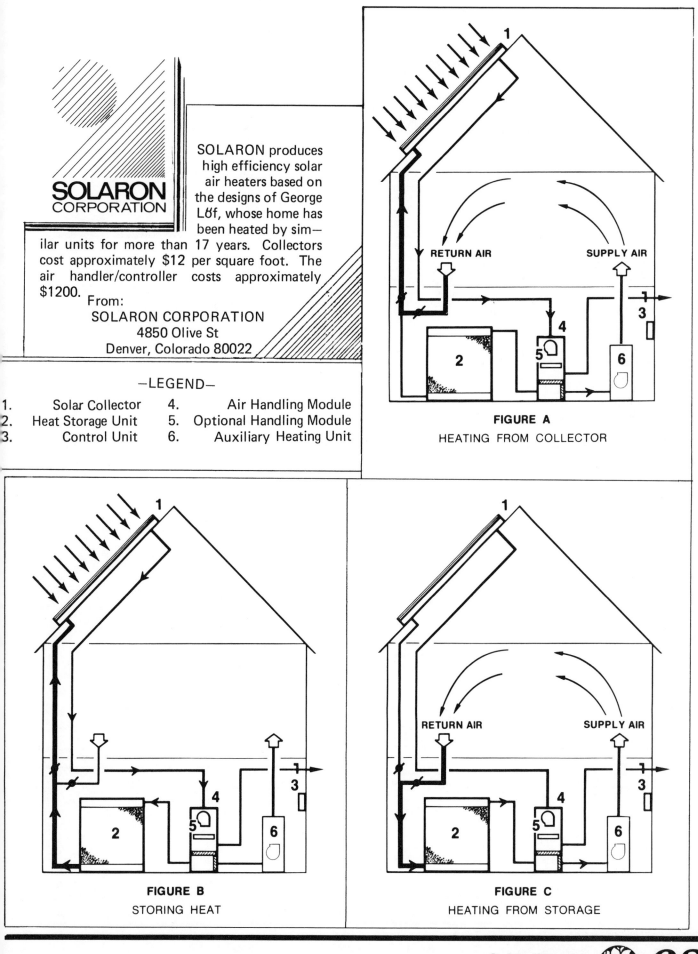

SOLARON produces high efficiency solar air heaters based on the designs of George Löf, whose home has been heated by sim—ilar units for more than 17 years. Collectors cost approximately $12 per square foot. The air handler/controller costs approximately $1200.

From:
SOLARON CORPORATION
4850 Olive St
Denver, Colorado 80022

—LEGEND—

1. Solar Collector
2. Heat Storage Unit
3. Control Unit
4. Air Handling Module
5. Optional Handling Module
6. Auxiliary Heating Unit

RETURN AIR   SUPPLY AIR

FIGURE A

HEATING FROM COLLECTOR

RETURN AIR   SUPPLY AIR

FIGURE B

STORING HEAT

FIGURE C

HEATING FROM STORAGE

Beasley Solapak solar absorber

(Reg'd Design No. 954—540)

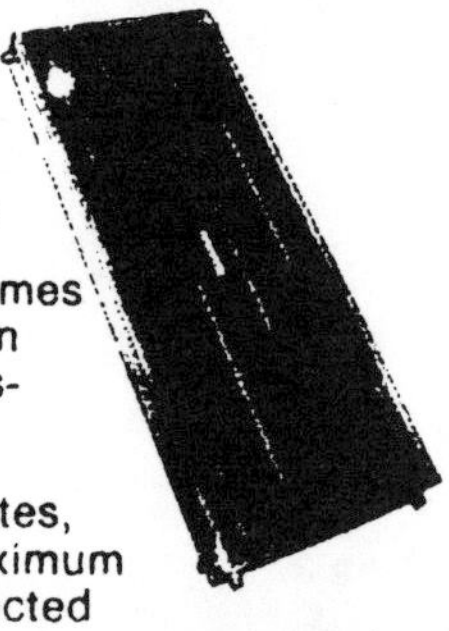

Beasley "Solapak" has been designed for maximum efficiency, long life, simplicity of installation, weights only 23 kilogrammes (50 pounds) and is carton packed to eliminate transport damage.

"Solapak" absorber plates, specially treated for maximum absorption, are constructed of copper with built-in water-ways, and tests throughout Australia have proved they provide Australian homes with an average of 70% of total hot water requirements all year round.

Each "Solapak" absorber, with a surface area of 0.75 square metres (8 square feet,) provides from 36-73 litres (8 to 16 gallons) of hot water a day at 57 C (135 F) average, depending on area of installation.

Beasley Solatank

Operates on the side fed displacement principle, which combines high standard performance with a very low overall height.

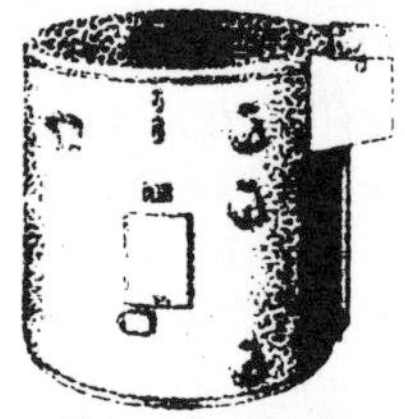

The inner cylinder is constructed of copper with all joints brazed and copper fittings — heavily insulated with fibertex wool which reduces heat losses to a minimum.

The outer casing is of rustproof galvabond. Installation is simplified as the Solatank has a factory fitted cold water supply tank (fitted with a ball valve and float) and built-in concealed pipe work.

Standard Solatanks are designed for installation where under cover, but weatherproofing is available as an optional extra for external installations.

A booster element and thermostat is recommended to ensure hot water supply for days when solar input is not sufficient and is fitted as an optional extra.

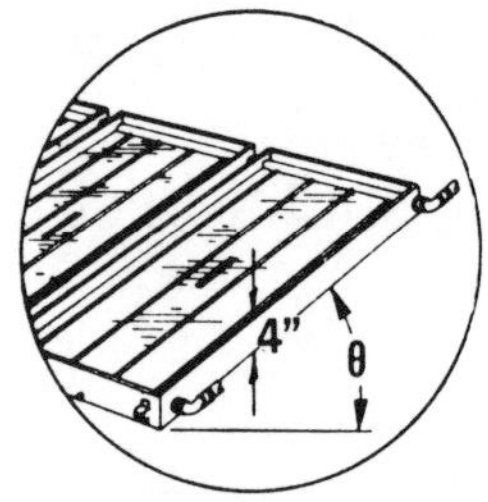
4"
θ

θ ANGLE OF INCLINATION EQUAL TO THE LATITUDE OF THE INSTALLATION AREA

Beasley solar hot water system

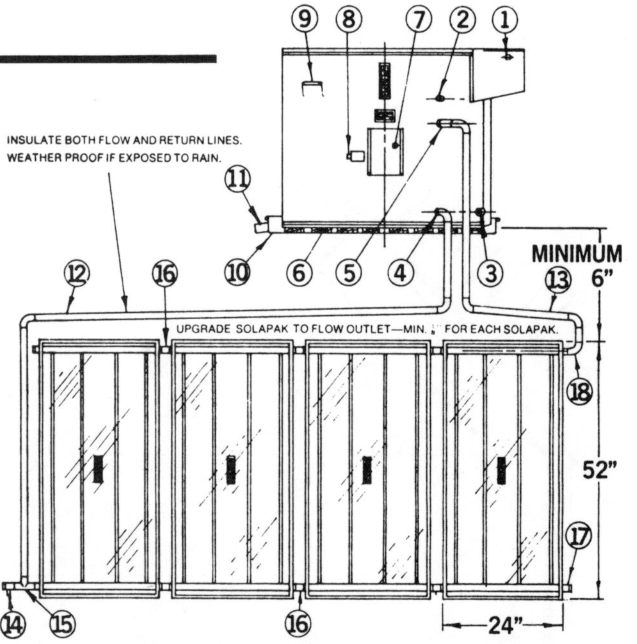
9 8 7 2 1
INSULATE BOTH FLOW AND RETURN LINES.
WEATHER PROOF IF EXPOSED TO RAIN.
11
12 16 10 6 5 4 3
MINIMUM 6"
13
UPGRADE SOLAPAK TO FLOW OUTLET—MIN. ½" FOR EACH SOLAPAK.
18
52"
17
14 15 16
24"

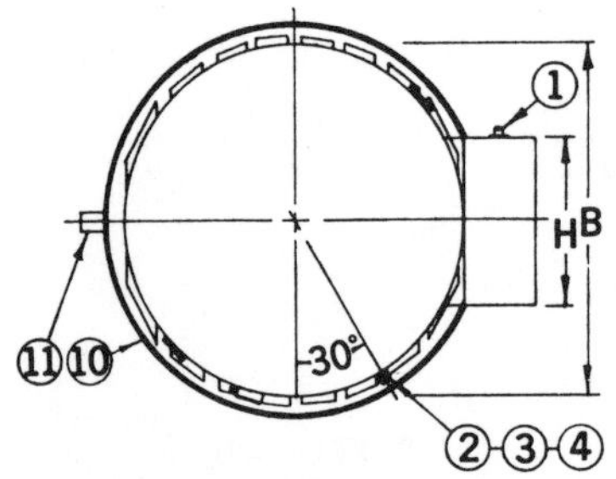
1
H
B
11 10
30°
2-3-4

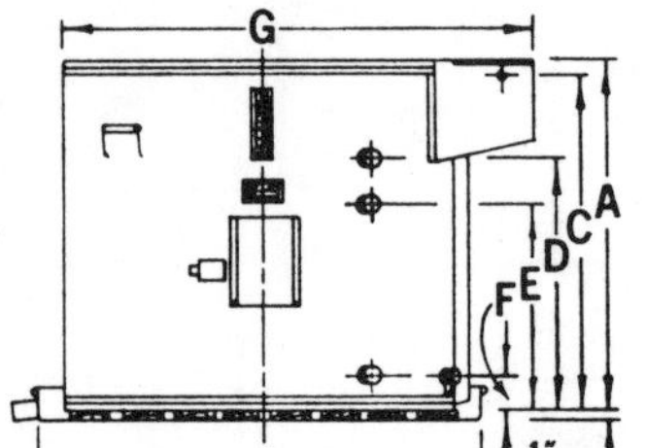
G
A
C
D
E
F
J
½" MIN

PARTS DESCRIPTION—SOLAR

1. Cold water inlet connection to ball-valve—½" B.S.P. male fitting.
2. Hot water outlet—¾" B.S.P. male tapered thread.
3. Drain cock.
4. Return line outlet—¾" B.S.P. male tapered thread.
5. Flow line inlet—¾" B.S.P. male tapered thread.
6. Water heater supports — minimum thickness ½".
7. Electrical access door — ('Solatank' fitted with booster element only).
8. Electrical junction box—entry ⅝" conduit diameter.
9. Lifting handles.
10. Galvanised iron safety tray.
11. Galvanised iron overflow pop—minimum diameter 2".
12. Return line—minimum diameter 1" copper tube.
13. Flow line—minimum diameter 1" copper tube.
14. Sola—Sludge cock.
15. Sola—Tee.
16. Sola—Connectors.
17. Sola—Cap.
18. Sola—Elbow.

WATER HEATER NOMINAL DIMENSIONS

Capacity—Gallons	20	30	40	60	80	100	120	140
A. Height—inches	35½	42	22½	30½	38½	48½	56½	64½
B. Diameter—inches	22½	22½	34	34	34	34	34	34
C. Height—inches	33½	40	21¼	29¼	37¼	47	55	63
D. Height—inches	25	32	14½	22½	30½	39	47½	55½
E. Height—inches	18	22¼	10½	17½	21	29¾	34	42
F. Height—inches	3	3	3	3	3	3	3	3
G. Length—inches	28	28	40½	40½	40½	43	43	43
H. Length—inches	17½	17½	17½	17½	17½	23½	23½	23½
J. Diameter—inches	26½	26½	39½	39½	39½	39½	39½	39½
Approx. weight lbs.	85	98	110	130	160	200	230	260
Booster element wattage	1000	1000	1000	1000	1500	2750	2750	2750

Beasley manufactures a high-quality water heater, sold widely in Australia. It will soon be available through distributors in this country. The collector consists of a copper absorber sheet with a selective surface, covered by one or two glass covers. It can be used for space-heating or domestic hot water heating. Beasley also manufactures a small "preheater" unit which can be linked to an existing hot water heating system and provide a considerable saving in fuel costs.

BEASLEY INDUSTRIES PTY. LTD.

Bolton Avenue, Devon Park,
South Australia 5008
Telephone 46 4871

METHOD OF INSTALLING WALL MOUNTING BRACKETS

'Solapaks' with mounting studs are supplied for installation with wall mounting brackets—specify when ordering if wall brackets are to be used.

Bolt wall bar (21) or (22) on to wall allowing correct gradient.

Remove nuts and washers on 'Solapak' top side, insert bolts through slotted hinge (24), replace nuts and washers and secure.

'Solapak' will hang with 'Solapak' base resting flush with wall.

Select correct location latitude and connect inner and outer telescopic tubes (25) and (27), and bolt together in selected hole.

Remove nuts and washers from 'Solapak' bottom side, swing 'Solapak' outward from wall and prop.

Insert bolt through slotted hinge (26), replace nut and washer and secure.

Adjust 'Solapak' until telescopic leg is horizontal, then bolt mounting plate (28) to wall.

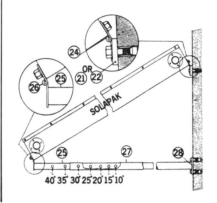

the Beasley
solar pre-heater
saves you money by using
energy from the sun to
provide hot water

SAV

The Unique 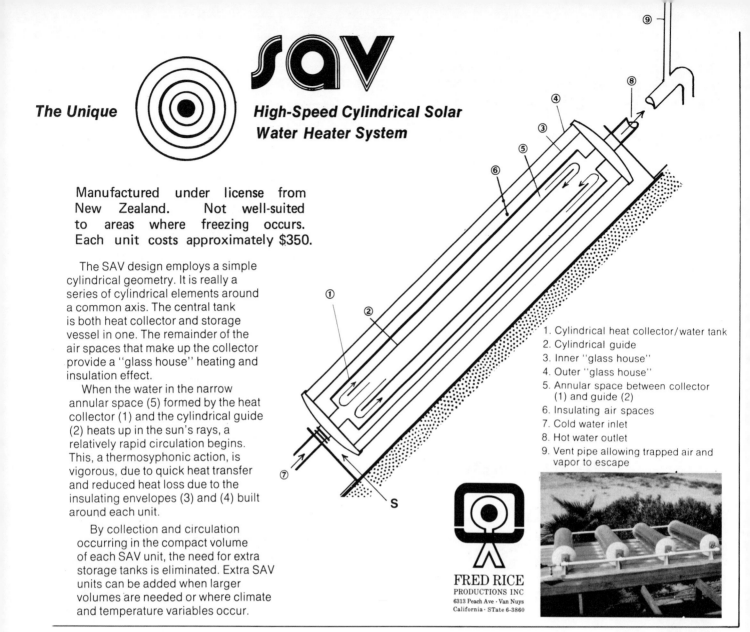 **High-Speed Cylindrical Solar Water Heater System**

Manufactured under license from New Zealand. Not well-suited to areas where freezing occurs. Each unit costs approximately $350.

The SAV design employs a simple cylindrical geometry. It is really a series of cylindrical elements around a common axis. The central tank is both heat collector and storage vessel in one. The remainder of the air spaces that make up the collector provide a ''glass house'' heating and insulation effect.

When the water in the narrow annular space (5) formed by the heat collector (1) and the cylindrical guide (2) heats up in the sun's rays, a relatively rapid circulation begins. This, a thermosyphonic action, is vigorous, due to quick heat transfer and reduced heat loss due to the insulating envelopes (3) and (4) built around each unit.

By collection and circulation occurring in the compact volume of each SAV unit, the need for extra storage tanks is eliminated. Extra SAV units can be added when larger volumes are needed or where climate and temperature variables occur.

1. Cylindrical heat collector/water tank
2. Cylindrical guide
3. Inner ''glass house''
4. Outer ''glass house''
5. Annular space between collector (1) and guide (2)
6. Insulating air spaces
7. Cold water inlet
8. Hot water outlet
9. Vent pipe allowing trapped air and vapor to escape

FRED RICE
PRODUCTIONS INC
6313 Peach Ave · Van Nuys
California · STate 6-3860

SOLARVAK™

SOLARSYSTEMS, INC.
1802 DENNIS DRIVE
TYLER, TEXAS 75701

Utilizing the sun's energy to heat fluids flowing through a collector module, the **SOLARVAK ENERGY COLLECTOR** efficiently heats these to more than 150*F above the surrounding air temperature through the use of a patented vacuum design. Due to this high temperature, Solar Energy becomes economically feasible for domestic hot water, space heating, air conditioning and low pressure steam for commercial and industrial applications. Therefore, before making a decision, consider the advantages a **SOLARVAK**, Flat Plate Type, offers.

— THE SOLARVAK ENERGY MODULE —

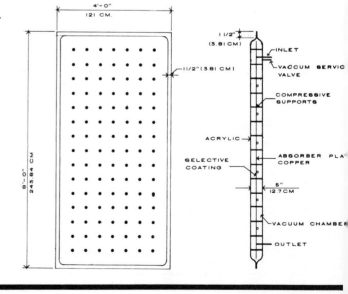

4'-0"
121 CM.

1 1/2" (3.81 CM)

8'-0"
245.84 CM

1 1/2"
(3.81CM)

INLET

VACCUM SERVIC VALVE

COMPRESSIVE SUPPORTS

ACRYLIC

SELECTIVE COATING

ABSORBER PLA COPPER

5"
12.7CM

VACUUM CHAMBER

OUTLET

66 Energy for the Home

UNITSPAN ARCHITECTURAL SYSTEMS, INC.

CREATIVE SPECIALISTS IN PRODUCTS FOR ARCHITECTURE

Swimming Pool Solar Collector

Material - All aluminum (treated) all copper
           or stainless steel. Integral headers.
           Low pressure drop.
Nominal Size - 4' X 6' - 8' - 10'
Approximate operating weight - 1.6 pounds per Sq.
                               foot.

Flat Plate Solar Panel - For domestic hot water
assist. Space heating hot water assist. Space
cooling assist.

Material - All aluminum (treated) or aluminum flat
           plate with copper or stainless steel water
           ways. Integral headers. Full insulation
           with sealed case. Single or double tempered
           glazing. Selective coatings.
Nominal size - 3' wide X 7' long X 4" deep.
Approximate weight - 110 pounds.

9419 MASON AVENUE   •   CHATSWORTH, CALIFORNIA 91311   •   (213) 998-1131
BRANCH OFFICES: SAN DIEGO   •   SAN JOSE   •   PHOENIX, ARIZONA

Edwards Completely Packaged SOLAR ENERGY SYSTEM

Edwards Solar Energy System consists of Solar Collector Panels thru which a heat transfer fluid is circulated in order to heat a storage reservoir containing water. In turn, the heated water is circulated thru valance terminal units for silent heating of the occupied spaces or zones. Auxiliary equipment is available as part of the entire system to supply domestic hot water and to maintain heating on cloudy days or extreme weather conditions. The auxiliary equipment can also furnish cooling and ventilation.

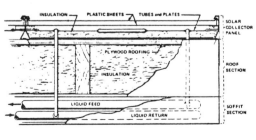

Edwards ENGINEERING CORP.
POMPTON PLAINS, NEW JERSEY 07444
ph. (201) 835-2808

Edwards Engineering manufactures all kinds of heating distribution systems, including a totally packaged solar heating system and auxilliary heat source.   Collectors have plastic covers. (durability?) --No evidence yet of one of these systems in operation.

Solar Collectors

The Solar Collector Panels are 2 feet or 3 feet in width and of any specified length to fit the building design. The Panels are so designed that they will take the place of the normal roofing material such as the shingles. The Panels consist of 1 inch of aluminum covered fibre glass insulation, heat absorbing aluminum plates, copper or aluminum tubes, one or two layers of transparent plastic sheeting, and an aluminum frame for fastening and holding the parts to the roofdeck.

Manufacturer of:

• BOX-FIN BASEBOARD RADIATION
• QUIET/SLIDE FINNED ELEMENT
• ZONE-A-MATIC BOILERS
• ZONE CONTROL VALVES
• INDUSTRIAL FIN-PIPE
• PACKAGED WATER CHILLERS
• VALANCE HEATING/COOLING
• COAXIAL CONDENSERS
• FINNED TUBING
• ELECTRIC HEATING
• EVEN-FLOW CIRCULATORS

SOLAR COLLECTORS

- Special blackened surface (Pyrene process) for efficient solar energy absorption.
- Insulation on back of collectors to reduce heat loss to a minimum.
- Rigid construction.
- Glass plates fixed in sturdy frames.
- Weather proof-treated galvanized sheets.
- Twin -- collector assembly insures sufficient heating of water.

HOT WATER SUPPLY

- Two energy sources. SOLAR and ELECTRIC to suit all weather. An automatic thermostat control determines source of energy used.
- The standard unit with one pair of collectors will heat approximately 50 gallons of water to a temperature of 120° to 150° F during a full day of sunshine.

GENERAL

- Collector dimensions   4" H x 32" W x 75" L.
- Tank dimensions   40" H x 24" Diameter.
- Tank storage capacity   32 gallons.
- Electric power supply   110 V, 60 Hz, 1500 W.
- High quality galvanized fittings and seamless pipes prevent water leakage.

Sol-Therm imports Israeli-built "Amcor" solar collectors and tanks, which can be installed as is, or adapted to an existing domestic hot water heating system. More collector area and storage is needed for a conventional U.S. family than provided with the standard unit (above). Prices: Standard unit $695, additional collectors $245 each

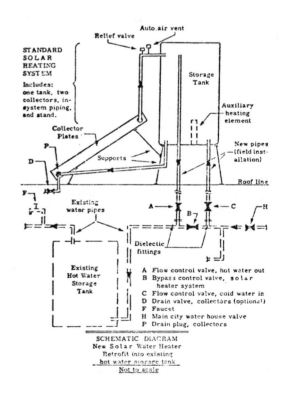

STANDARD SOLAR HEATING SYSTEM Includes: one tank, two collectors, in-system piping, and stand.

A Flow control valve, hot water out
B Bypass control valve, solar heater system
C Flow control valve, cold water in
D Drain valve, collectors (optional)
F Faucet
H Main city water house valve
P Drain plug, collectors

SCHEMATIC DIAGRAM
New Solar Water Heater
Retrofit into existing
hot water storage tank
Not to scale

SOL-THERM CORP.   7 WEST 14th ST, NEW YORK, N.Y. 10011   (212) 691-4632

RAYOSOL
Carretera De Cadiz, 32-D
Apartado 81
TORREMOLINOS
(Malaga) Spain

Rayosol makes a copper collector which is enclosed in a fiberglass container with a glass cover. The **Hart** unit (below) is a simple, well-packaged solar water heater, with an integral storage tank using a bronze absorber sheet.

TYPICAL INSTALLATIONS OF HART SOLAR-FLO WATER HEATER

Storage Capacity	Absorber Area
30 gal (136 lt)	20 sq ft (1.77 m2)
40 gal (182 lt)	30 sq ft (2.60 m2)
50 gal (227 lt)	30 sq ft (2.60 m2)

The Simplicity in design of the HART "Solar-Flo" enables the highest efficiency in installation on most dwellings without special structural or aesthetic provisions and comes ready for fixing to low or Mains Pressure Cold Water connections. The unit should be installed in a shadow free area, facing North at an incline equal to .8 times the geographical latitude at the place of fixing. e.g. Perth latitude 32 deg x .8 =

25 deg. Port Hedland latitude 20 deg x .8 = 16 deg. The incline angle should be no less than 15 deg and no more than 45 deg. A few degrees variation to suit the roof will not matter. Full installation instructions will be supplied with the "Solar-Flo".

"Solar-Flo" is also available in 60 gal (273 lt) storage tank by special order.

S. W. HART & CO., PTY. LTD.
112 Pilbara Street, Welshpool W.A. 6106
Phone 68 6211

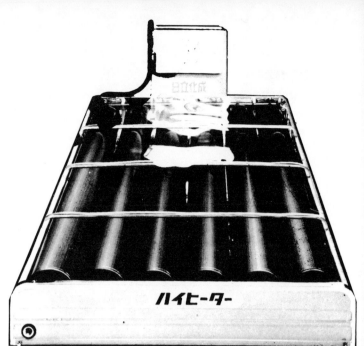

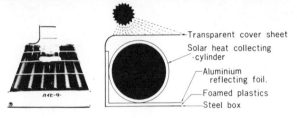

Transparent cover sheet
Solar heat collecting cylinder
Aluminium reflecting foil.
Foamed plastics
Steel box

FEATURES:

1. Properties of solar heat collecting cylinders
1. Heat resistance: Empty cylinderes are durable up to 100°C.
2. Humidity resistance: Up to 75%.
3. The cylinders are made of rigid polyethylene by extrusion method and durable against general weather conditions.

2. Excellent heat retaining properties
1. The steel box housing the cylinders is covered on the top with a transparent polycarbonate sheet, which allows extremely high permeation of solar energy and keeps warmth of hot water in the cylinders.
2. Heat is stored for many hours, thanks to alminium reflecting foil, foamed plastics, and snugly-enclosed structure.

3. Clean hot water
Water is always kept clean, free from incrustation and dusts, since the cylinders are made of polyethylene.

TEMPERATURE OF WARMED WATER OBTAINED BY "HI-HEATER" IS AS FOLLOWS:

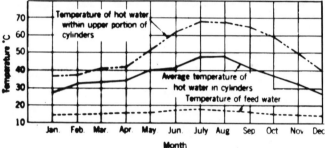

NOTE:
1. Temperature values are measured in Tokyo when the weather is fine.
2. Temperature of hot water is measured at 4:00 P.M.
3. Ground water is supplied to the cylinders at 8:00 A.M.

PRICE: US $390.00 per set
US 320.00 per set for orders more than 100 ur
(the above prices do not include installation.)

DELIVERY: Within 60 days after your order
Packing:
Net Weight	92.4 lbs.
Gross Weight	116.6 lbs;
Measurements	77" x 48" x 13"

Packed in wooden cases

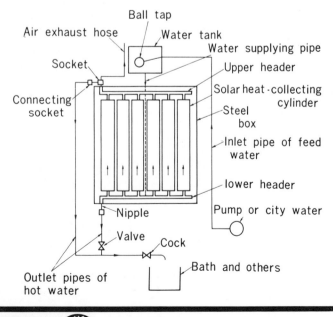

HITACHI

⊙ Hitachi Chemical Co.,Ltd.

437 Madison Avenue
New York, N.Y. 10022

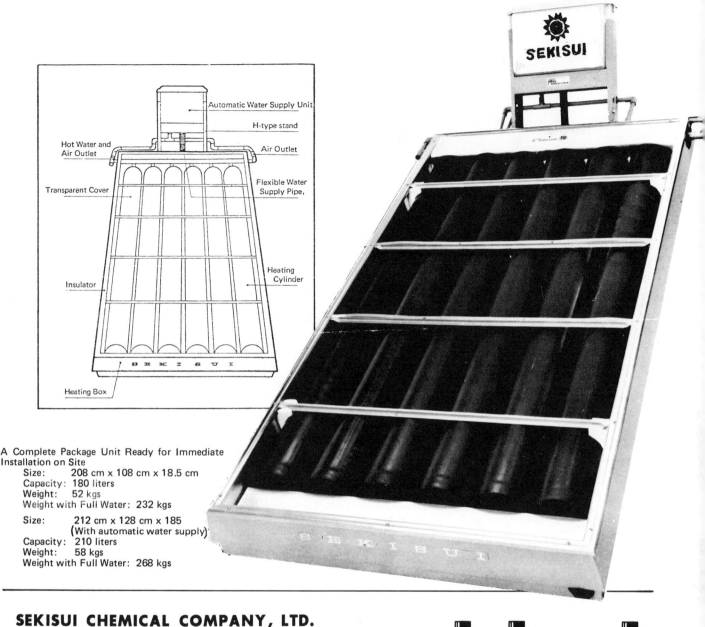

Automatic Water Supply Unit

H-type stand

Hot Water and Air Outlet

Air Outlet

Transparent Cover

Flexible Water Supply Pipe,

Insulator

Heating Cylinder

Heating Box

A Complete Package Unit Ready for Immediate Installation on Site

Size: 208 cm x 108 cm x 18.5 cm
Capacity: 180 liters
Weight: 52 kgs
Weight with Full Water: 232 kgs

Size: 212 cm x 128 cm x 185
(With automatic water supply)
Capacity: 210 liters
Weight: 58 kgs
Weight with Full Water: 268 kgs

SEKISUI CHEMICAL COMPANY, LTD.

INTERNATIONAL HEADQUARTERS

Osaka Sales Office: Dojima Kanden Bldg.
2, Kinugasacho, Kita-ku, Osaka, Japan

Tokyo Sales Office: Shinjuku Mitsui Bldg.
2-1-1, Nishi-Shinjuku, Shinjuku-ku, Tokyo, Japan

sekisui

Both the **HITACHI** and the **SEKISUI** water heaters are simple, packaged units suitable for installations where the roof of the building can take a concentrated load of about 500 lbs., in locations were temperatures are not likely to go below freezing. In most areas of the U.S, considerable auxiliary heating would be required to provide year-round hot water temperatures of around 140*F.

solarator

WHAT IS A SOLARATOR?

Solarator is a labyrinth of nearly 190 feet of tough, black PVC tubing that resists corrosion and chemicals. It is welded into a panel that is about three feet high and six feet wide. It has a flexible accordian action that prevents the formation of lime and scale. When the heat from the sun penetrates the Solarator the water is warmed.

HOW MANY SOLARATORS DO YOU NEED?

Every installation is different. A good rule of thumb is that one Solarator will heat 4,000 to 5,000 gallons of water to swimming temperature. If your pool is shaded or exposed to wind you may need additional Solarators. They can always be added with the simple parallel hookup.

Widely used for poolheating in many parts of the world, the "Solarator" is also advertised for domestic hot water heating. Its inability to withstand more than 4psi. is an obvious disadvantage. (Domestic water systems usually operate at 40 - 60psi) The long term durability of plastic is also questionable. However, the unit is cheap and can be installed very easily. Each "Solarator" costs $39.95. With a few valves and some plastic piping, you could install a small pool heater for around $100.

MANUFACTURERS
OF SOLARATORS ™

FUN & FROLIC, INC. ▪ P.O. BOX 277 ▪ MADISON HEIGHTS, MICH. 48071

fafco

FAFCO provides useful and very complete data on their plastic tube-sheet pool heaters. Ultraviolet inhibitors used in the plastic lengthen its life considerably. The simple modular collector system is easy to install and operate. Retail costs are around $100 for a 40 square foot panel. The well-written installation manual costs $4.

From:

FAFCO INCORPORATED
138 Jefferson Drive
Menlo Park,
California 94025

DIMENSIONS:
Length: 10 ′ or 8′, Area: 40 ft^2 & 32 ft, Width: 4′

PRESSURES:
Static:
Maximum Burst Pressure: more than 60 psi at 80° F
Maximum Design Pressure: 40 psi maximum at up to 120° F
Maximum Recommended Working Pressures:
20 psi at less than 100° F
5 psi at 200° F

TEMPERATURES:
Maximum of 210° F at 5 psi

ABSORPTIVITY:
.92 or greater to 50 microns

EMISSIVITY:
Same

CORROSION RESISTANCE:
Completely inert to virtually all materials

FREEZING RESISTANCE:
Not affected

WEATHERABILITY:
Extensive tests suggest minimum ten year life

<u>INSTALLATION MANUAL</u>

You have just received your FAFCO Solar Swimming Pool Heater and are probably very anxious to get it installed and operating, but let's start on a note of caution. <u>Please read the instructions carefully and fully plan how you are going to install your system before you begin work.</u>

<u>SITE SELECTION</u>

You should have between one-half and three-quarters of the pool's surface area in solar panels (e.g., 800 sq. ft. pool needs 400 - 600 sq. ft. of panel area). In terms of convenience and ease of installation, the ideal location for the solar panels is on a south-facing, sloped roof near the pool with enough space for mounting the required number of panels. However, as long as the conditions listed below concerning inclination and exposure are met, the panels do not have to be located near the swimming pool.

(1) You should have between one-half and three-quarters of the pool's surface area in solar panels (e.g., 800 sq. ft. pool needs 400 - 600 sq. ft. of panel area).

(2) The panels should ideally be inclined about thirty degrees from horizontal (or your approximate latitude) and should face south.

(3) The panels can be mounted on a flat, horizontal surface, but an angle of at least two (2) degrees is required to ensure proper flow and efficiency through the entire system.

Fortunately, the modular nature of the solar panel allows you to deal easily with these conditions and tailor your system to your site. Heating of the pool is in direct proportion to the number of panels used. In some installations the entire area of the pool is used.

<u>Southern Exposure and Required Panel Area</u>

The table below recommends the amount of solar panel area required for various orientatio These figures assume an installation on a normally sloped roof.

(1) All South facing: A minimum of 50% of the pool's area.

(2) All West facing: A minimum of 75% of the pool's area.

(3) East and West: Maximum on West and balance on East with a minimum of 75% of the pool's area.

zomeworks

Steve Baer and Zomeworks have developed many "Passive" solar collection systems,-- simple yet effective devices that allow for the collection of solar energy when it is available and provide insulation when it is not. Most devices are patented, but Zomeworks sells both plans and licenses at reasonable cost.

SOLAR BOOKLET..................................	$ 3.
SOLAR WATER HEATER PLANS.............	5.
DRUM WALL PLANS..............................	5.
BEADWALL PLANS & LICENSE..............	15.
GRAVITY DRIVERS.........................	$45-65.
SKYLIDS...	$241-425.

ZOMEWORKS CORP.
PO BOX 712
ALBUQUERQUE, NM 87103

drumwall

In the Baer structure south facing walls are made of 55 gallon drums filled with water in racks behind glass. The outside facing ends are painted black. The winter sun warms the water in the barrels through the glass and the heat radiates into the rooms. The large insulating doors are lowered in the mornings in the winter--they allow the sun to shine in and warm the barrels and act as reflectors to intensify heat from the sun. The doors are raised when the sun goes down to prevent heat loss. During the summer the doors are kept closed and the cool (c. 70*F) water in the drums acts as a sink for the heat in the air, keeping the room at a comfortable temperature. The drum wall is a specially satisfactory method of heating because the heater is an integral part of the structure of the house.

air heater

A bin of rocks - usually beneath or in front of the house - is heated by air flowing by convection through a collector. When heat is needed in the house, a vent is opened and the warm air rises into room.

In the summer the rock bin can be cooled at night and the cool air vented into the house during the day.

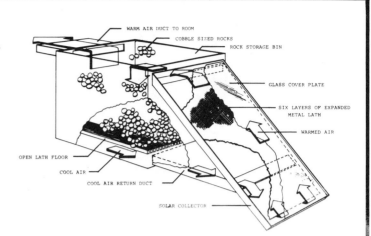

WARM AIR DUCT TO ROOM
COBBLE SIZED ROCKS
ROCK STORAGE BIN
GLASS COVER PLATE
SIX LAYERS OF EXPANDED METAL LATH
WARMED AIR
OPEN LATH FLOOR
COOL AIR
COOL AIR RETURN DUCT
SOLAR COLLECTOR

Diagram of warm air flow in Air Loop Rock Storage Convective Solar Heater.

skylid

The skylid is used with skylights or large windows. Insulated louvers open when the sun shines and close during nighttime and periods of heavy overcast. Freon moving from a warm cannister to a cooler cannister tips the balance of the louvers either open or closed. A manual override allows the skylid to be kept closed during the summer.

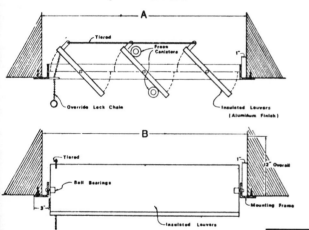

Standard Sizes: Length: 6'-10'.
                Width: 22"/panel.

Skylids are designed to be installed in finished openings. The finished opening dimensions should be;
        Length: Panel length + 2".
        Width: (# of units x 22") + 2".

Skylids can be ganged together in units of two or three as shown in the illustrations.

R Value: Between 2 and 10 depending on installation and orientation. Our tests are still incomplete.

Durability: Our first skylids have now been in operation for two years, opening and closing faithfully. We cannot see what will wear out in the mechanisms - all materials are sturdy and durable. The polyester cloth seals will eventually have to be replaced, but the louvers themselves should continue to function trouble free.

Construction:
        Aluminum skin curved over wooden ribs.
        Air foil cross section - 2" thick at edges, 5" at middle.
        Rotates on 5/16" guarded SKF ball bearings.
        Fiberglass insulation.
        Special polyester tube seal.
        Light - less than 2 lbs./ft.sq..

beadwall

The Beadwall (patent applied for) is an insulating window. Styrofoam beads are blown (left photo) between two panes of glass to prevent heat loss at night in the winter or heat gain in the summer. The beads are sucked out (right photo) to allow heat and light in. Three inches of styrofoam beads gives the wall a U factor of approximately .1.

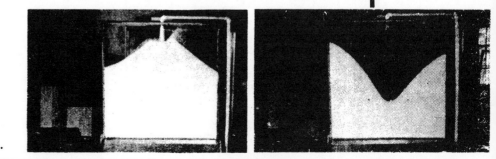

MOVABLE INSULATION

BAGS OF COOLED WATER

COOLS BY CONVECTION

OCCUPIED SPACE

DAY - SUMMER

HEAT ABSORBED BY WATER BAGS

MOVABLE INSULATION

HEAT BY RADIATION

OCCUPIED SPACE

DAY - WINTER

SPACE CONDITIONING
WITH MOVABLE INSULATION
BY HAROLD HAY

HEAT LOSS TO COOL NIGHT SKY

MOVABLE INSULATION

COOLS BY CONVECTION

OCCUPIED SPACE

NIGHT - SUMMER

MOVABLE INSULATION

WARMED WATER IN BAGS

HEAT BY RADIATION

OCCUPIED SPACE

NIGHT - WINTER

sky-therm
processes inc.

2424 **WILSHIRE BLVD.**
LOS ANGELES, CA 90057

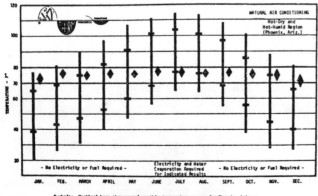

Harold Hay has developed a simple passive air-conditioning system using solar "ponds" (polyethlene bags of water on the roof of the building) to absorb, store or re-radiate heat as required.

Allowing for both heating and cooling, this system is most suitable for climates with large variations in temperature between day and night.

Two houses have already been built.

OPTICAL COLLECTOR OPEN
(SUMMER POSITION 35° ABOVE HOR.)

OPTICAL COLLECTOR OPEN
(WINTER POSITION 10° ABOVE HOR.)

DETAIL OF PYRAMIDAL REFLECTOR AND
EXPERIMENTAL FLAT-PLATE RECEIVER

wormser scientific

One of many ways in which solar energy can be concentrated onto a collector (to produce higher grade heat from a smaller collector area) using simple reflective panels. The Falbel system is fairly sophisticated, increases the radiation incident on the collector by 2 to 6 times, depending on cloud cover. Patented.

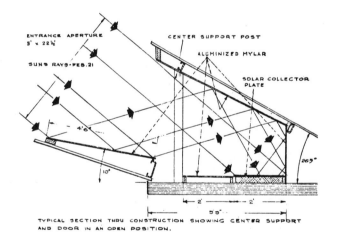

TYPICAL SECTION THRU CONSTRUCTION SHOWING CENTER SUPPORT
AND DOOR IN AN OPEN POSITION.

Contact:
Eric M. Wormser, President
Wormser Scientific Corporation
88 Foxwood Road
Stamford, Conn. 06903
Phone: (202) 322-1981

EXPERIMENTAL PROTOTYPE INSTALLATION OF

FALBEL PYRAMIDAL OPTICS SOLAR COLLECTION SYSTEM

edmund

Edmund Scientific has been involved in solar energy and its benefits since 1963. In addition to experimental solar cells, books and plans of Dr. Thomason's Solaris System Homes have been in the Edmund Catalog for quite some time.

In addition to these, Edmund provides solar panels, solar heat collectors, solar demonstrators, windmills, heat exchangers, solar furnaces, reflectors and a variety of other energy saving devices. You might call them "Solar Energy Headquarters USA".

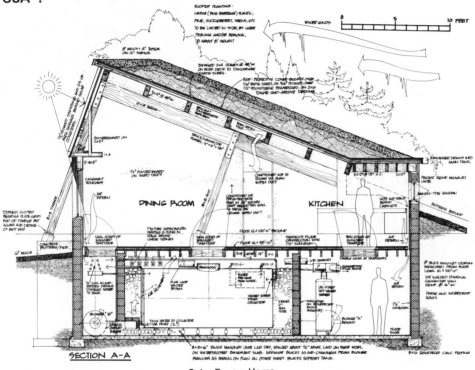

SECTION A-A

Solar Energy Home

Diagrams shown here are taken from one of these books and show various aspects of one of Dr. Thomason's designs built for Bob and Nancy Homan in Southern New Jersey.

Edmund's complete products and publications catalog is available by letter for $.50 from:

EDMUND SCIENTIFIC CO.
555 Edscorp Bldg.
101 E Gloucester Pike
Barrington NJ 08007

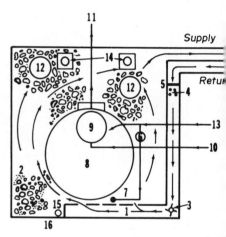

and diagram of its heat storage system

1. concrete blocks
2. stones
3. blower
4. A/C coil
5. air filter
6. humidifier valve
7. outlet for humidifier water
8. 2,000 gallon tank
9. 42 gallon tank
10. cold water in
11. warm out (to water heater)
12. flue pipe (water heater to chimney)
13. return from solar collectors
14. auxiliary heat pipes
15. pump suction line
16. use clear plastic pipe on outlet from for about 5 feet, to serve as sight ga check water level in 2,000 gallon ta

Thomason Patents:
- Solar Heat Collectors
- Solar Heat Apparatus
- "Solaris" Heating & Cooling Systems
- And Many More

thomason

"The Thomasons have patented more inventions than anyone else in the world in solar heating . . ."

Los Angeles Times: "In the do-it-yourself department of solar heating systems . . . Thomason reigns supreme."
Dr. M. L. Khanna: "I consider Thomason to be the Thomas A. Edison of Solar Energy."

University of Wisconsin: Tested one of the Thomason inventions in Patent No. 3,303,838 (solar heat collector with foam transparent cover) and reported very desirable characteristics for high temperature gains.

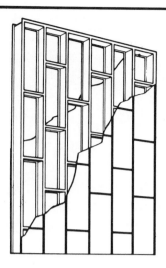

Kalwall makes fiberglass sandwich panels with various degrees of solar transmittance, used for cladding buildings. The company is developing a solar air heater, using a metal absorbing sheet between two layers of fiberglass. They also sell two grades of "Sun-lite"(shown here)--a highly transparent fiberglass sheet, suitable for low temperature collector covers. Ultra violet degradation is very slow.

Kalwall is a true sandwich panel—with rugged fiberglass reinforced face sheets permanently bonded to a supporting aluminum I-beam grid core.

kalwall
KALWALL CORPORATION
1111 CANDIA ROAD
P. O. BOX 237
MANCHESTER, N. H. 03105
TELEPHONE: A/C 603 627-3861

sunlite

Sun-Lite is the modern, lightweight, inexpensive answer to minimizing heat loss through and around windows. Sun-Lite was originally developed as a cover material for solar heat collectors. Its ability to transmit solar energy is equal to glass. But Sun-Lite, unlike glass, is shatterproof, extremely lightweight, and easily installed... thin gauges may be cut with tin snips, heavier gauges may be cut with a handsaw or light power saw.

Sun-Lite fiberglass reinforced plastic for slashing heat loss through windows and air infiltration around window areas offers the following immediate benefits:

* Shatterproof
* Superior Impact Strength-- 4 times stronger than acrylic. 10 times stronger than standard window glass.
*Lightweight-- adds no significant load to building or window frames.
*Easily Handled and Installed-- available in 50' rolls, either 4' or 5' wide, or cut to size.
*Low-Cost-- more economical than other safety glazing materials... 6 mil polyethelene costs nearly as much!!
*Insulating-- super energy savings compared to single glass.

UNTREATED PLASTIC — TREATED WITH SUN CLEAR

Polyethylene-covered greenhouse with transparent SUN CLEAR-treated and mirrored untreated panels.

Solar Sunstill, Inc.

Setauket, N.Y. 11733 U.S.A.   Telephone (516) 941-4078

NEW FORTIFIED FORMULA (200:1 Dilution): FOR BOTH FLEXIBLE AND RIGID PLASTICS				Price effective 2/1/75 (U.S. $)
SUN CLEAR (Conc. Vol.)	Av. Dil. Vol. (Gal.)	Coverage (av. sq. ft.)	Cost ($/sq.ft.)	
3 OZ. (88.7 ml)	5	1,000	.0027	2.70
1 PT. (0.473 l)	25	5,000	.0025	12.60
1 QT. (0.946 l)	50	10,000	.0023	23.40
1 GL. (3.785 l)	200	40,000	.0021	84.40
5 GL. (18.925 l)	1000	200,000	.0018	360.00

Solar Sunstill manufactures a wide range of products for sun control through glass and plastic. **Sunclear** is widely used in the greenhouse industry and could have certain applications in solar collectors. The **Vari-Shade** type of coating also has intriguing possibilities, but no information is given on its weathering characteristics.

SOLAR SUNSTILL, INC., specializes in products for the control of condensation and light. SUN CLEAR® no-drip coating is the first in a reputable line of products.

VARISHADE® A sprayable shade coating that limits the transmission of light when the coating is dry, but when wetted with water, becomes practically transparent and allows more light to be transmitted. VARISHADE can be applied to glass OR plastic, inside or outside.

SUN CLEAR-G FOR GLASS® A concentrated water dispersible liquid formula which, when diluted, increases light transmission, eliminates fogging and improves visibility on glass greenhouses and enclosures. SUN-CLEAR-G* can also be used as a second coating over SUN CLEAR for a longer-lasting "optical" effect on all plastics such as Lexan™ or Plexiglas.™

THERMOSHADE® A revolutionary new temperature sensitive film, is transparent below a certain temperature and becomes cloudy and shades above that predetermined temperature (80-100° F). Soon to be available in both plastic and glass forms. THERMOSHADE* will save energy in a method similar to VARISHADE.*

```
Ram Products,
1111 Centerville Rd.,
STURGIS, MI 49091.

Produces "plexi-view" acrylic
mirrors,-useful for reflectors
or parabolic focussing
collectors.
```

```
Enthone Inc.,
Box 1900,
NEW HAVEN, CT.06508.
```
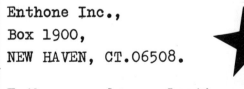
```
Enthone produce selective
surfaces with an absorbtivity of
0.9 and an emissivity of 0.1 on
steel and copper. Any quantities
accepted, sizes up to 3ft by 8ft.
```

 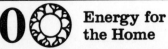

 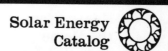

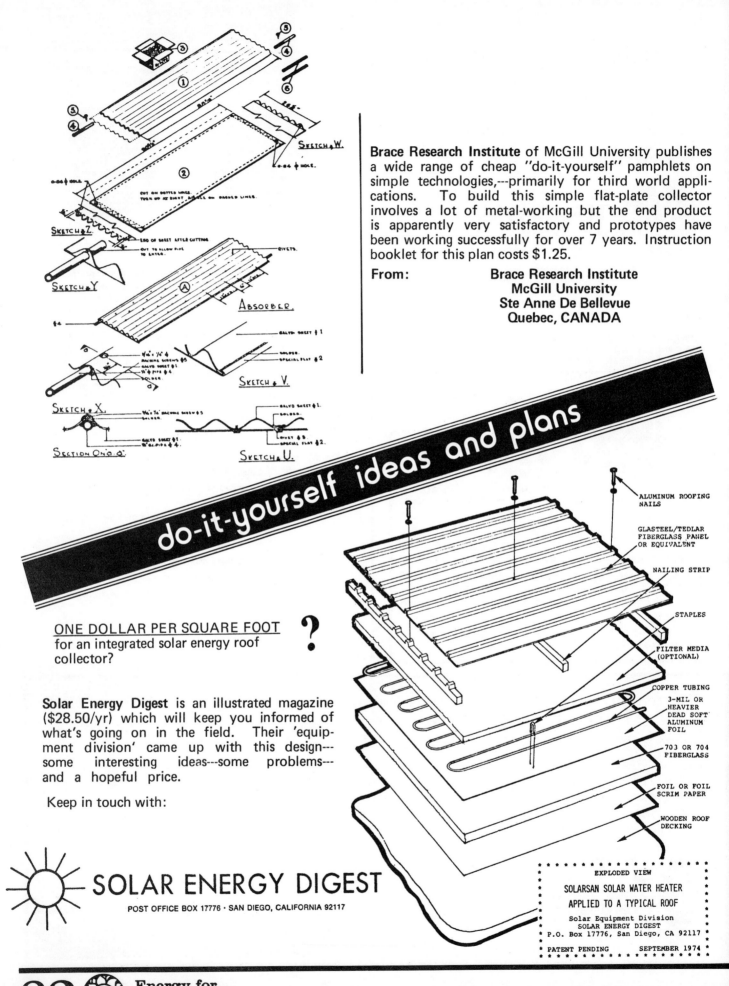

Brace Research Institute of McGill University publishes a wide range of cheap "do-it-yourself" pamphlets on simple technologies,---primarily for third world applications. To build this simple flat-plate collector involves a lot of metal-working but the end product is apparently very satisfactory and prototypes have been working successfully for over 7 years. Instruction booklet for this plan costs $1.25.

From:
    Brace Research Institute
    McGill University
    Ste Anne De Bellevue
    Quebec, CANADA

do-it-yourself ideas and plans

ONE DOLLAR PER SQUARE FOOT
for an integrated solar energy roof collector? **?**

Solar Energy Digest is an illustrated magazine ($28.50/yr) which will keep you informed of what's going on in the field. Their 'equipment division' came up with this design--- some interesting ideas---some problems--- and a hopeful price.

Keep in touch with:

SOLAR ENERGY DIGEST

POST OFFICE BOX 17776 · SAN DIEGO, CALIFORNIA 92117

ALUMINUM ROOFING NAILS

GLASTEEL/TEDLAR FIBERGLASS PANEL OR EQUIVALENT

NAILING STRIP

STAPLES

FILTER MEDIA (OPTIONAL)

COPPER TUBING

3-MIL OR HEAVIER DEAD SOFT ALUMINUM FOIL

703 OR 704 FIBERGLASS

FOIL OR FOIL SCRIM PAPER

WOODEN ROOF DECKING

EXPLODED VIEW
SOLARSAN SOLAR WATER HEATER
APPLIED TO A TYPICAL ROOF
Solar Equipment Division
SOLAR ENERGY DIGEST
P.O. Box 17776, San Diego, CA 92117
PATENT PENDING   SEPTEMBER 1974

prototype fibreglass collector

5/8 in
**half-round
beading
4in on center**

Make a mold (above) out of 5/8" half-round beading
glued to a sheet of masonite. Coat with paraffin
wax. Cover this with tight-weave fibreglass cloth
and soak with high-temperature resin. Let it set
remove the fibreglass and turn it upside-down. Sand
the ridges between the channels made by the mold.
Enclose the channels with another layer of fibreglass
cloth and resin,(layed flat) and incorporate two
nylon nipples at each end where the "tube" emerges
from the sheet. Let this set and you have a fibreglass tubesheet. Pass water through it and check for
leaks, -these can be patched by sanding and adding
another layer of resin. Spray with flat black paint.
The mold is reusable.

Efficiency Tests January 10th 1975. New Haven, Conn.

Cloudless day. Collector angle: 60° Time: 12 -12.30p.m.
Estimated incoming Solar radiation: 250 BTU/ft^2/hr.

Tube spacing on collector: 4". Area of collector: 10.67 sq.ft.
Single glass cover. Flow rate 3.75 gals/hour.

Inlet temperature: 70°F Outlet temperature: 110°F

Calculated Efficiency at 40°F temperature difference: 52.4%

Estimated Cost/sq.ft.

Fibreglass Cloth..........	85¢
Resin.....................	75¢
Fittings..................	5¢
Spray paint..............	15¢
Total....................$1.80¢	

(and a lot of work!).

Tony Fisher, John Goldman, Andra Georges, Chris Bartle, Yale University. '74.

do-it-yourself ideas and plans

Commercially available Flat Black
Spray Paints:

"Krylon" Velvet Black
$1.90 for an 8oz can, available
from auto suppliers
"Nextel" (manufactured by 3M)
$3.25 for a 6oz can.

Asphaltic undersealer for car
bodies (available in spray cans)
provides a thick absorbent layer.

Total Environmental Action
Box 47, Harrisville,
New Hampshire 03450.

Design, consultancy, research,
education and publication in the
field of energy conservation.

Homes *
Communities *
Life Support Systems *

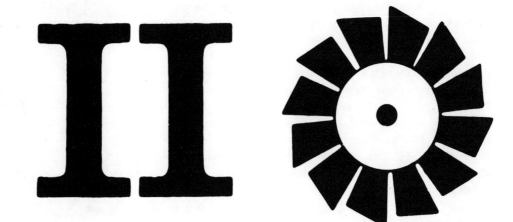

WIND
POWER

Wind Power

Windmills are thought to have existed in ancient Greece and may well have been in use before then. The wind turbine is one of the simplest machines which man devised to help him with mechanical tasks such as grinding grain and lifting water. It is based on the principle of using the wind to create a rotational force in a shaft by means of sails. Local variations in materials, skills and requirements led to the development of a wide variety of designs. A number of them have vertical shafts and sails which accept the wind from any direction. Others have horizontal shafts with the sails in the form of a propeller facing the wind. They all play a distinctive and vital role in their individual environments.

These traditional windmills do not produce electricity very efficiently. To achieve the high rotational speeds necessary for running a generator, the mill needs to be lighter and still more resistant to wear from the continuous and complex mechanical forces working on it.

a

b

The many and varied forms of traditional windmills:
a. 18th century timber frame mill at Cranbrook, Kent, England.
b. Windmills in Bessarabia, Russia (note how the whole building turns on its base).
c. A 17th century Dutch drainage mill.
d. Portuguese sail mill. The sound of the whistles attached to the sails indicates the windspeed.
e. Windmills for pumping water (like modern American mills) on the island of Cyprus.
f. Sail-type windmill on Crete.
These illustrations are taken from **Windmills and Watermills** by John Reynolds, Praeger 1970, an excellent account of the history of windmills.

Principles

A modern propeller-type electricity-generating mill, the Electro WGV5, 6kw model, blade diameter: 16 ft.

Wind Electric Systems

A wind-electric system consists of four basic components: a propeller, a generator, a means of controlling the current output, and usually some means of storing the energy. The rotational force of the propeller, transferred by the shaft, turns the armature of the generator. To produce a continuous and usable supply of electric current, the armature must be turning at a very high and fairly constant speed. This means that step-up gears are usually required between the shaft and the armature. It also means that the mill must generate the maximum torque (rotational force) at any particular windspeed in order to capture as much of the power of the wind as possible.

Propellers and Turbines

Aerodynamically shaped blades of propeller design produce more torque at high speeds than the traditional sails. The first reference to propeller-type blades for a windmill occurs in Belidor's work, "L'Architecture Hydraulique" written in 1737.

Most work on wind-electric generators is still based on this design. The aerofoil section of each blade develops its own rotational force as it moves around, much as a sailboat uses the wind passing round it to propel itself forward.

The theoretical maximum transfer efficiency, (from wind power in the swept area of the blades to rotational power of the shaft), has been calculated at 59.3%. In practice, however, most mills of good design reach approximately 40% efficiency. For producing electricity, a high tip-speed ratio (ratio of the speed of the extremities of the blades to the wind speed) is necessary in order to achieve high torque at high speeds. This entails a low blade-area to swept-area ratio. The tip-speed ratio of several common windmills is shown here. It should be noted that the traditional multivane waterpumping mill — very common in the United States — has a high torque at low speeds, but because of its weight and the area exposed to the wind, it becomes less efficient at high speeds.

The power available from the wind is approximately proportional to the cube of the wind velocity. This means that whereas an average windspeed of seven m.p.h. is seldom worth considering for running a windplant, velocities of 10-12 mph can often supply power economically.

and when the winds are low . . .

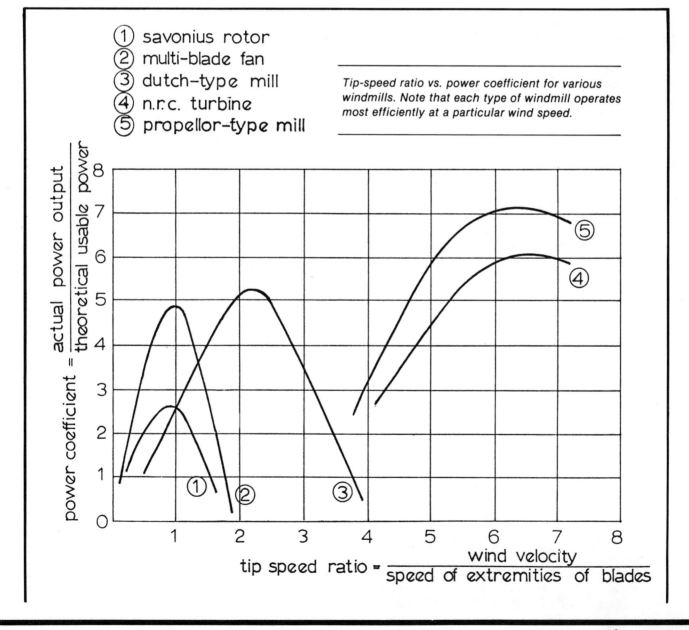

① savonius rotor
② multi-blade fan
③ dutch-type mill
④ n.r.c. turbine
⑤ propellor-type mill

Tip-speed ratio vs. power coefficient for various windmills. Note that each type of windmill operates most efficiently at a particular wind speed.

power coefficient = $\dfrac{\text{actual power output}}{\text{theoretical usable power}}$

tip speed ratio = $\dfrac{\text{wind velocity}}{\text{speed of extremities of blades}}$

Three-tier Savonius Rotor built by
Earthmind, Saugus, California.

All commercially-available windmills for generating electricity have horizontal shafts and propellers which need to be kept perpendicular to the wind direction. To do this, most windmills have a vane perpendicular to the propeller which causes them to turn back into the wind whenever it changes direction. Others have no vane but turn freely about the main support post until the propeller is perpendicular to the wind direction — downwind of the post. The latter design requires a careful balancing of the motor equipment on top of the support post, to ensure that rotation is very easy.

Vertical-shaft mills have the great advantage of being omnidirectional. They are also easier to construct, which would explain why they were in use long before the horizontal shaft machines. In the 1920's the Finnish engineer, S. J. Savonius, developed a more efficient version of the simple vertical shaft machine, using airscoops instead of sails. Lately, this design has been used for waterpumping, particularly in underdeveloped countries, but with a tip-speed ratio of only 1 to 1.5, it is not particularly suitable for generating electricity.

Another modification of the vertical axis mill uses aerodynamically shaped blades which curve up and around the central shaft, giving the mill the appearance of a large egg beater. The most recent research has shown that this mill can develop a **tip-speed ratio** of about 65, which compares favorably with propeller-type machines. Theoretically it could be produced for about one seventh the cost of a conventional electricity generating mill, which makes it particularly attractive for small scale power generation. Its main disadvantage is that it needs to be rotated manually before it begins to turn by wind alone.

Darreius Rotor (or N.R.C. turbine) prototype
built by N.A.S.A. at Langley Field,
Virginia. (see Reference 14.)

Energy for
the Home

VERTICAL AXIS

1A

1B

1C

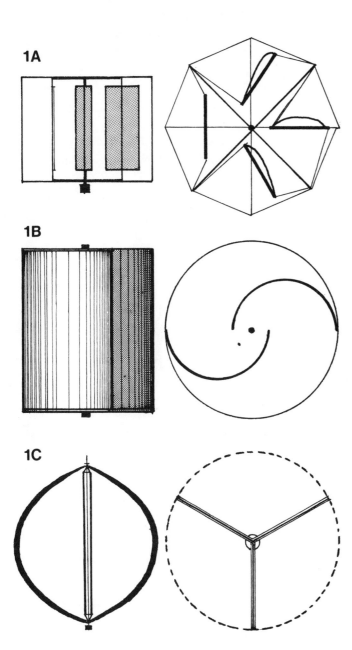

HORIZONTAL AXIS

2A

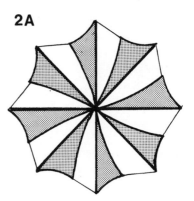

2B

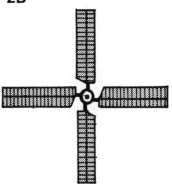

2C

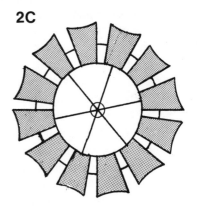

2D

Developments in windmill technology:
1a. Ancient vertical axis windmill.
1b. Savonius Rotor.
1c. Darrieus Rotor (vertical axis mill with
*   aerodynamically shaped blades, developed by N.R.C.)*
2a. Traditional mill with sails.
2b. Traditional Dutch and English mills with
*   canvas or wooden sails.*
2c. American multivane water pumping mill.
2d. Modern electricity generating mill, 2 or 3 blades.

Generators

The size of the generator is dependent on the wind speed available and the size of the propeller. Commercial windmills can generate 200 to 6,000 watts, and a windmill was once operated with a capacity of 1,250 kilowatts. Just as most automobile electric systems now use alternators instead of generators, so most commercially produced wind electric systems now employ alternators.

An alternator is merely a generator with the magnetic field in the armature instead of in the coil. It will normally produce "alternating current" (ac) though it can be wired to produce "direct current" (dc). The most suitable alternators for wind electric systems have permanently magnetized armatures which require no exitation from an existing current. This eliminates the need for brushes to supply the current to the electromagnetic armature and thus eliminates one of the weakest parts of a conventional generator. In good commercial wind plants a low-speed alternator is usually used. Anyone wishing to build a small wind generator can rewire a car alternator to start generating at a low rpm.

Using an alternator rather than a generator allows the choice of generating alternating or direct current. There are advantages and disadvantages to both systems. Almost all domestic electrical equipment uses ac. This is simply because the utility companies choose to generate ac which is much more *efficiently* transmitted. Direct current wired over long distances tends to lose energy in the form of heat (which is worth remembering when installing a wind power system), but dc does have the advantage that it can be stored in batteries, practically the only readily-available means of storing electricity.

The 1250 kW gargantuan windmill built during world War II on Grandpa's Knob, Rutland, Vermont. For the full story and sad fate of this wind machine, see Reference 4.

Often both ac and dc are used in different parts of a wind electric system, and therefore the cost and efficiency of the conversion becomes critical. Ac can easily convert to dc at virtually 100% efficiency by using a simple and cheap "rectifier." To produce ac from dc however, requires some form of "inverter" either an inefficient but fairly cheap mechanical type (called a "rotary inverter") which has an efficiency of around 60%, or an electronic "solid state inverter" which has an efficiency of around 80-85%. The loss in efficiency in either case is due to the power consumed by the inverter itself and is proportional to its capacity. Thus a simple 250 watt rotary inverter will consume around 100 watts even without a load running on it. Solid state inverters seem to be a better solution. They are more efficient and produce a steadier current. But they cost from 800 dollars upwards for a 400 watt model, suitable for a home.

Regulation and Storage

Regulating the unsteady output of energy from a wind turbine and storage of the power produced, are the two most difficult problems with a wind electric system. Since they can often be solved in conjunction, they will be discussed together.

Most commercially available windmills have some kind of governors operating on the blades themselves. A governor slows down the blades in high winds, either by a system of centrifugal weights or by turning the blades slightly out of the wind. In addition most mills need to be equipped with a brake or a means of turning the mill completely out of the wind (such as turning the vane through 90 degrees so that it becomes parallel to the propeller).

The alternator needs to be equipped with an appropriate voltage regulator (just as in an automobile electric system) which will maintain a steady voltage, but a fluctuating current. In order to produce a steady current some kind of "energy sink" is needed, where the fluctuations in the output of the mill can be absorbed. A battery bank is one way of achieving this; the electrolysis of water into hydrogen for fuel cells is another. Both of these are electro-chemical processes, but mechanical methods using pumped water, compressed air, or flywheels can also be considered.

At the moment, batteries are the most readily available and easily installed form of electricity storage. Conventional automobile batteries have a short lifetime, particularly when the chemical storage process (the eroding and depositing of lead on the plates) goes through a complete cycle in a very short time. Total discharge from a conventional battery will greatly reduce its lifetime.

Heavy-duty houselighting batteries have a longer lifetime (approximately 15 to 20 years!) and are not as affected by total discharge. They also cost more and are bulkier. The number of cells in a battery bank must be equal to the required voltage output. If the appliances operating off the system run on 110-115 volt current, the number of cells in the storage system must then be between 110 and 115 (or a multiple of that). In a single family house, a storage system with a capacity of three-day average demand would occupy about 40 cubic feet.

Other batteries are available that operate on different principles. For example, sodium-sulphur and nickel-cadmium batteries have both been developed to give longer life and a greater storage capacity per unit weight. However, these generally cost more and are not as easy to obtain as the lead-acid batteries.

Another energy storage system uses the current produced by the mill to electrolyse water into hydrogen and oxygen. The electrolytic process is relatively simple and can operate with a fluctuating current. The hydrogen gas produced would have to be stored, and could be used to power a fuel cell or an internal combustion engine in order to generate a constant output of electricity, or it could simply be burned to produce heat.

Hydrogen has one of the highest heat capacities per gram of any fuel gas; it is a clean, pollution-free source of energy which could well become more widely used as our reserves of natural gas decline. Using wind power to generate heat, however, is not really worthwhile. In most areas, solar power can be used more effectively. If it were necessary to produce heat from wind power, it would be simpler and more efficient to run alternating current direct from the mill to a resistance coil in a hot water tank, rather than generating hydrogen for fuel.

Of the mechanical means of storing wind energy, the flywheel seems to be the most promising for future use. A flywheel operates on the principle that a large rotating mass with very careful balancing and low air resistance will store most of the energy required to rotate it, for a very long time. In order to be economically feasible, the storage capacity of the flywheel must be very large in relation to its weight, its volume, and its cost. By enclosing the wheel in a vacuum-sealed container, the drag and the danger of failure can be minimized, while the efficiency is greatly improved.* Recent experiments on a "superflywheel", consisting of an array of steel rods radiating out from the metal hub, have resulted in storage capacities of 6 kilowatt hours per pound in a 1400 pound flywheel. This is a great improvement on past performances, and compares favorably with batteries at around 0.04 kilowatts hours per pound. But it is essentially a "high-technology" piece of equipment, and would be a very expensive investment for a single household.

*David Rabenhorst, "The Superflywheel," **Scientific American,** December 1973.

59.7%
THEORETICAL
MAX . . . . . EFFICIENCY

40%
ACTUAL
EFFICIENCY

Pumped water storage is used at present by utility companies for storing electricity at off-peak periods. It could also be used on a smaller scale with reasonable efficiency. A water-pumping wind mill (averaging around 50% efficiency) used in conjunction with a water turbine (modern turbines are about 90% efficient) could provide a practical system for generating electricity, as well as storing power. The windmill would pump water into a storage pond when the wind was blowing. The water turbine, equipped with an automatic governor, could use the stored water to generate electricity when needed.*

The main drawback would be the very high initial cost of the water turbine and governor, the pumping mill and the water storage dam. If one or more of these components were already in existence it might be worth adding the rest. Otherwise the installation would probably cost too much.

Finally, there is the possibility of using the mains of the electric utility network itself as a storage system. When a surplus of electric power is being produced by the mill, it would simply pass into the utility company's system. During periods without wind, the utility company would provide electricity in the usual way.

The difficulty here is that the period when an excessive amount of electricity is being produced often is during the night when there would be little or no load on the wind-electric system. At that time there would also be a much smaller load on the utility companies, which have indicated that this off-peak supply might be difficult to use.

*Figures taken from manufacturer's data on Aermotor mills, and The James Leffel and Company Water Turbines. The latter company is the only manufacturer of good small-scale water turbines in the USA and provides useful information for anyone considering installing a water turbine to generate electricity. See **Water Power Section**.

(OVERLEAF) The installation of a small Lubing wind-electric system (see Wind Catalog).

Wind energy storage systems showing estimated overall efficiency of each system. Data mainly from References 1 and 10.

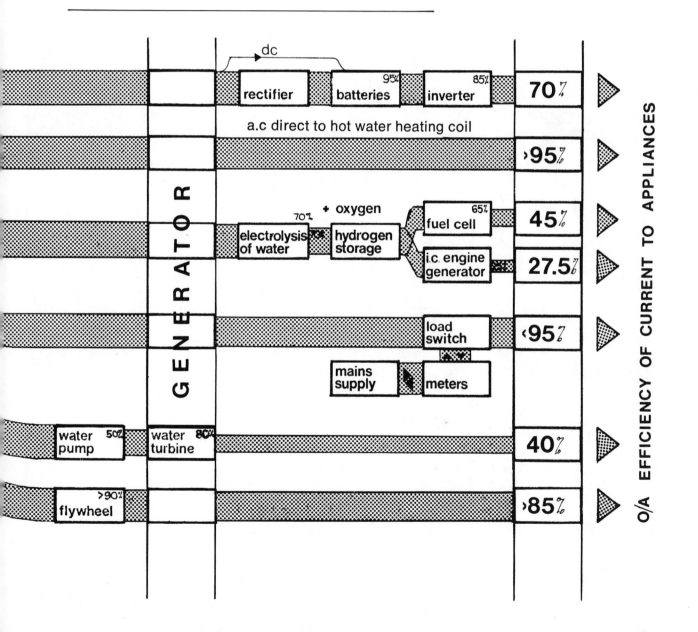

**HOW TO
ASSEMBLE
A WINDMILL
IN 22 EASY STEPS**

START ⬇ **HERE**

4

8

1

5

9

2

6

10

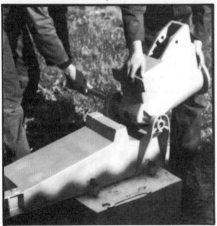

3

7

11

Energy for
the Home

12

16

20

13

17

21

14

18

22

15

19

CONGRATULATIONS

Not all mills are as easy to assemble and erect as the Lubing,— but this construction sequence does give an idea of the kind of work that is involved.

Available Energy

Air currents above the oceans in the Northern Hemisphere. Thickness of arrows indicates strength of wind. (From Reference 4.)

The selection of a site for generating electricity from the wind involves a series of complex and accurate measurements of wind speed and direction over a long period of time. Five years of research went into determining the site for the 1250 kilowatt generator on Grandpa's Knob near Rutland, Vermont. However, in assessing the suitability of sites for smaller mills a number of estimations can be made which give a fairly accurate picture of the patterns of air movement.

This table shows some yearly, average windspeeds throughout the United States and relates to the global patterns of air movement which are based on pressure differences between the equator and the polar regions,and the rotational path of the earth around the sun which causes the trade winds.

More detailed estimations of wind speed and direction are available from local metereological stations throughout the country. These stations supply accurate measurements of monthly and annual wind speed and direction, as well as maximum and minimum wind speeds over periods of many years. Thus depending on the distance from the nearest weather station, these statistics could provide a fairly accurate idea of wind patterns for a given site.

Wind speed is very much affected by local geographical conditions, such as terrain and height above the ground. Examine the increase in wind speed with height over different types of terrain. Above the sea, or on any flat, open land, the speed increases very rapidly with height, whereas obstructions near the ground such as buildings and trees will cause turbulence and lower the rate of increase. Over undulating terrain there is generally a concentration of wind power on exposed hilltops and ridges. On steep-sided hills, however, the wind current often breaks away from the edge of the slope causing turbulence which will lead to excessive wear on a windmill placed there.

	Mean hourly Windspeed mph	Prevailing Direction	Fastest recording mph.
January	12.7	NW	67
February	13.2	NW	52
March	13.1	NW	51
April	12.7	N	55
May	11.7	E	50
June	10.2	SW	38
July	9.6	SW	36
August	9.6	SW	42
September	11.0	NE	47
October	11.7	NE	51
November	12.5	NW	58
December	12.5	NW	53

Wind data recorded at Bridgeport, Connecticut. Similar comprehensive records are available from meteorological stations throughout the U.S.

Wind data recorded at various locations throughout the U.S.A. Documented by Automatic Power Inc. from weather data.

Here are listed the lowest monthly average wind velocity (LMV), highest monthly average wind velocity (HMV), average yearly wind velocity (AYV), yearly prevailing wind direction (YPD), and the highest recorded wind velocity (HRV), according to the U.S. Weather Bureau records.

STATE and CITY	LMV MPH	HMV MPH	AYV MPH	YPD	HRV
ALABAMA					
BIRMINGHAM	4.9 Aug	8.6 Mar	6.7	South	46
MOBILE	8. "	11. "	9.7	North	87
MONTGOMERY	5.8 "	8. Feb.	6.8	East	41
ARIZONA					
PHOENIX	5.1 Dec	6.4 Apr	5.8	West	40
YUMA	4.7 Oct	6.6 Mar	5.9	North	43
ARKANSAS					
FORT SMITH	5.5 Aug	9.2 Mar	7.2	East	57
LITTLE ROCK	5.7 "	9.4 "	7.4	South	49
CALIFORNIA					
EUREKA	6.1 Oct	8.8 Apr	7.4	North	46
FRESNO	5.3 Nov	8.7 Jun	6.9	N.W.	41
LOS ANGELES	5.7 Sept	6.4 Feb	6.1	S.W.	38
OAKLAND	7.3 Nov	11.8 Jul	9.3	West	50
RED BLUFF	4.5 Aug	6.7 Mar	5.8	S.E.	49
SACRAMENTO	6.1 Nov	8.6 Jun	7.5	South	65
SAN DIEGO	6.1 "	7.3 Apr	6.7	N.W.	43
SAN FRANCISCO	7.3 "	11.8 Jul	9.3	West	50
SAN JOSE	5.9 Oct	7.4 May	6.7	N.W.	38
COLORADO					
DENVER	6.6 Aug	8.4 Apr	7.4	South	53
GRAND JUNCTION	3.8 Jan	6.8 "	5.5	S.E.	—
PUEBLO	6. Aug	8.2 "	6.8	N.W.	64
CONNECTICUT					
HARTFORD	6.2 Sep	8.7 Apr	7.5	N.W.	58
NEW HAVEN	7.1 Aug	10.1 Mar	8.7	North	49
DIST. OF COLUMBIA					
WASHINGTON	4.8 Aug	8.5 Mar	6.4	N.W.	55
FLORIDA					
APALACHICOLA	6. Jul	9.3 Oct	7.8	North	59
JACKSONVILLE	8.3 Aug	9.3 Mar	9.1	N.E.	58
KEY WEST	8.3 "	11. Nov.	9.9	East	84
MIAMI	8.1 Jul	10.7 "	9.3	East	87
PENSACOLA	9.2 Aug	11. Mar	10.6	N.E.	91
TAMPA	6.7 "	8.6 "	7.8	N.E.	75
GEORGIA					
ATLANTA	8.1 Aug	11.9 Feb.	10.2	N.W.	51
AUGUSTA	5.4 "	7.1 Mar	6.2	N.W.	49
MACON	5.7 "	7.8 "	6.7	N.W.	46
SAVANAH	7.4 "	10.3 "	8.8	S.W.	60
THOMASVILLE	3.8 "	5.9 "	4.8	S.W.	—
IDAHO					
BOISE	5.4 Oct	7. Apr	6.	N.W.	43
POCATELLO	7.9 Aug	9.8 Mar	8.8	S.E.	46
ILLINOIS					
CAIRO	6. Aug	11.1 Mar	8.5	South	65
CHICAGO	10. "	13. "	11.	S.W.	
PEORIA	5.7 "	9.4 "	7.7	South	45
SPRINGFIELD	9.4 "	13.8 "	11.6	South	45
INDIANA					
EVANSVILLE	6.4 Aug	10.6 Mar	8.5	South	60
FT. WAYNE	7.6 "	11. "	9.6	S.W.	51
INDIANAPOLIS	8.5 "	12.1 "	10.5	South	63
TERRE HAUTE	7.2 "	11.7 "	9.4	South	47
IOWA					
CHARLES CITY	5.2 Aug	8.7 Apr	7.1	N.W.	48
DAVENPORT	7.1 "	10.2 "	8.7	N.W.	51
DES MOINES	6.1 "	9.5 "	7.8	S.W.	50
DUBUQUE	5.8 "	8.1 "	7.	N.W.	47
KEOKUK	5.7 "	9.1 Mar	7.5	S.W.	49
SIOUX CITY	9.9 "	13.2 Apr	11.6	N.W.	65
KANSAS					
CONCORDIA	6.5 Aug	9.8 Apr	7.8	South	60
DODGE CITY	9.9 "	13.2 "	11.	S.E.	58
WICHITA	11.1 "	14. Mar	12.1	South	68
KENTUCKY					
LEXINGTON	8.5 Aug	14.1 Mar	11.5	S.W.	55
LOUISVILLE	6.5 "	10.7 "	8.7	S.W.	58
LOUISIANA					
NEW ORLEANS	5.8 Aug	8.8 Mar	8.7	S.E.	66
SHREVEPORT	5.5 "	8.8 "	7.	S.E.	50
MAINE					
EASTPORT	7.3 Aug	12.5 Jan	9.9	South	—
PORTLAND	7.1 "	9.6 Mar	8.6	N.W.	48

STATE and CITY	LMV MPH	HMV MPH	AYV MPH	YPD	HRV
MARYLAND					
BALTIMORE	6.9 Aug	8.6 Mar	7.6	N.W.	54
MASSACHUSETTS					
BOSTON	12.2 Aug	16.5 Feb	14.3	West	60
NANTUCKET	11.6 "	16.3 Mar	14.6	S.W.	66
MICHIGAN					
ALPENA	9.3 Jun	12.7 Mar	11.5	N.W.	47
DETROIT	9. Aug	14. "	12.	S.W.	67
ESCANABA	8.2 "	10.1 Nov	9.3	South	45
GRAND HAVEN	8.3 "	13.4 "	11.3	West	60
GRAND RAPIDS	7.4 "	9.6 "	9.6	West	51
HOUGHTON	7.7 "	9.4 "	8.7	West	63
LANSING	4. "	7.8 May	6.	S.W.	45
LUDINGTON	8.9 Jul	12.6 Nov	10.7	South	46
MARQUETTE	8.4 Jun	11.4 Jan	10.2	N.W.	53
SAULT ST. MARIE	6.8 Aug	9.8 Mar	8.5	N.W.	56
MINNESOTA					
DULUTH	9.8 Jul	12.9 Apr	12.	N.E.	60
MINNEAPOLIS	10. "	12.3 "	11.2	N.W.	65
MOORHEAD	8.3 "	10.9 "	9.7	N.W.	58
ST. PAUL	7.9 Aug	10.7 "	9.4	S.E.	78
MISSISSIPPI					
JACKSON	4.9 Aug	8.1 Mar	6.4	S.E.	49
MERIDIAN	4.1 "	6.9 "	5.4	S.W.	49
VICKSBURG	4.9 "	8.1 "	6.4	S.E.	49
MISSOURI					
COLUMBIA	5.7 Aug	10.2 Mar	8.	South	50
HANNIBAL	7.5 "	10.8 "	9.2	S.W.	47
KANSAS CITY	9. "	14. "	11.	South	57
ST. JOSEPH	7.2 "	10.5 "	8.8	S.E.	51
ST. LOUIS	8.9 "	12.4 "	10.8	South	91
SPRINGFIELD	8.3 "	11.9 "	10.2	S.E.	52
MONTANA					
HAVRE	7. Aug	10. Dec	8.6	S.W.	57
HELENA	7.2 Nov	8.7 Apr	7.9	S.W.	54
KALISPELL	5.2 Nov	6.9 "	6.	N.W.	38
MILES CITY	5.3 Jan	7.5 "	5.6	South	47
NEBRASKA					
LINCOLN	9. Aug	12.1 Apr	10.4	South	62
NORTH PLATTE	8.3 "	10.7 "	8.7	West	73
OMAHA	7.5 "	10.3 Mar	9.	N.W.	53
VALENTINE	9.3 Jan	12.8 Apr	10.5	N.W.	59
NEVADA					
RENO	5.8 Dec	8.5 Apr	7.	West	46
WINNEMUCCA	6.8 Aug	8.8 "	7.8	S.W.	75
NEW HAMPSHIRE					
CONCORD	5.2 Aug	7.6 Apr	6.4	N.W.	40
NEW JERSEY					
ATLANTIC CITY	13. Aug	16.8 Mar	14.9	N.W.	—
CAMDEN	9.2 "	11.9 "	10.4	N.W.	68
NEWARK	12.4 "	17.8 "	15.2	N.W.	
SANDY HOOK	11. Jul	16. "	14.	N.W.	
TRENTON	8.9 Aug	12.4 "	10.6	N.W.	
NEW MEXICO					
ALBUQUERQUE	6.9 Jan	9.6 Apr	7.8	West	63
ROSWELL	5.7 Aug	9.3 Mar	6.9	South	64
SANTA FE	6. "	8.4 Apr	7.1	S.E.	42
NEW YORK					
ALBANY	6.8 Aug	9.2 Mar	8.	South	59
BINGHAMPTON	4.4 "	7.3 "	5.9	N.W.	37
BUFFALO	11.7 "	17.7 Jan	14.5	S.W.	73
CANTON	8.2 "	11.4 "	10.1	S.W.	62
ITHACA	7.6 "	12. "	9.9	N.W.	70
NEW YORK	12.4 "	17.9 Mar	15.2	N.W.	73
OSWEGO	8. "	12. Jan	10	South	59
ROCHESTER	7.5 "	10.8 Feb	9.2	S.W.	60
SYRACUSE	8.7 "	13.2 "	11.2	South	
NORTH CAROLINA					
ASHEVILLE	5.4 Jul	10.2 Mar	7.8	N.W.	40
CHARLOTTE	4.5 Aug	7.5 "	5.8	S.W.	49
GREENSBORO	6.2 "	9.6 "	7.6	S.W.	49
HATTERAS	10.8 "	15.4 "	12.8	S.W.	80
RALEIGH	5.6 "	8.6 "	7.	S.W.	53
WILMINGTON	6.4 Dec	9.3 "	7.7	S.W.	53
NORTH DAKOTA					
BISMARCK	8.3 Dec	10.9 Mar	9.1	N.W.	63
DEVILS LAKE	9.2 Aug	12. "	10.6	N.W.	
FARGO	8.3 Jul	10.9 "	9.7	N.W.	58
WILLISTON	8.3 Aug	10.5 May	8.9	West	56

STATE and CITY	LMV MPH	HMV MPH	AYV MPH	YPD	HRV
OHIO					
CINCINNATI	5.3 Aug	8.8 Mar	7.1	S.W.	54
CLEVELAND	10.9 Jul	15. Jan	13.2	South	60
COLUMBUS	8.2 Aug	12.4 Mar	10.4	S.W.	60
DAYTON	7. "	12. "	9.6	S.W.	51
SANDUSKY	9.7 Jul	13.6 "	11.9	S.W.	56
TOLEDO	9.4 Aug	12.5 "	11.2	S.W.	65
OKLAHOMA					
OKLAHOMA CITY	9.2 Aug	13.9 Mar	11.5	South	57
OREGON					
BAKER	6.6 Aug	7.5 Apr	6.9	S.E.	40
PORTLAND	6.1 Oct	7.5 Feb	7.	N.W.	43
ROSEBURG	2.4 "	3.8 Apr	3.3	N.W.	40
PENNSYLVANIA					
ERIE	9.3 Aug	13.2 Jan	11.4	West	55
HARRISBURG	5.1 "	8.6 Mar	6.8	West	54
PHILADELPHIA	9.2 "	11.9 "	10.4	N.W.	68
PITTSBURG	8.6 "	12. "	10.4	N.W.	55
READING	5.5 "	8.8 "	6.9	N.W.	70
SCRANTON	5.5 "	8.2 "	6.9	S.W.	41
RHODE ISLAND					
BLOCK ISLAND	11.9 Aug	18.1 Dec	14.7	S.W.	69
PROVIDENCE	9.3 "	13.4 Mar	11.6	N.W.	63
SOUTH CAROLINA					
CHARLESTON	9.2 Aug	11.6 Mar	10.5	S.W.	81
COLUMBIA	5.7 "	10.2 "	8.	South	50
GREENVILLE	6.6 "	9.6 "	8.	N.E.	50
SOUTH DAKOTA					
HURON	9. Aug	12.8 Apr	10.8	S.E.	56
RAPID CITY	6.8 "	10.4 "	7.8	West	—
YANKTON	6.2 "	10.4 "	8.2	N.W.	80
TENNESSEE					
CHATTANOOGA	5.2 Aug	8.4 Mar	6.6	S.W.	64
KNOXVILLE	5.6 "	7.9 "	6.6	S.W.	59
MEMPHIS	7.1 "	10.2 "	8.6	S.W.	58
NASHVILLE	7.2 "	11.9 Apr	9.1	N.W.	55
TEXAS					
ABILENE	8.2 Aug	11.9 Apr	9.9	South	51
AMARILLO	10.5 "	14. "	12.2	South	65
AUSTIN	6.6 Sep	9.4 Mar	7.7	S.E.	44
BROWNSVILLE	7.5 "	11.1 "	9.2	S.E.	80
CORPUS CHRISTI	10.4 Dec	14.1 Apr	11.9	S.E.	72
DALLAS	8.4 Aug	12.3 "	10.1	S.E.	63
DEL RIO	7.3 Dec	10.1 "	8.9	S.E.	57
EL PASO	8. Sep	11.6 Mar	9.3	East	60
FT. WORTH	9.2 Aug	11.6 "	10.2	South	55
GALVESTON	9.1 "	11.7 Apr	10.6	S.E.	71
HOUSTON	8.2 "	11.3 Mar	9.8	S.E.	63
PALESTINE	5.7 "	9.2 "	7.2	South	47
PORT ARTHUR	8. "	10.9 Apr	9.5	South	42
SAN ANTONIO	6.9 "	9.1 Mar	7.9	S.E.	55
UTAH					
SALT LAKE CITY	6.4 Dec	8.7 Apr	7.7	S.E.	53
VERMONT					
BURLINGTON	8.4 Jul	12.8 Jan	10.3	South	54
VIRGINIA					
CAPE HENRY	10.1 Jul	13.7 Mar	12.3	S.W.	80
LYNCHBERG	6.1 Aug	9.2 "	7.5	N.W.	49
NORFOLK	10.5 "	14.2 "	12.2	South	63
RICHMOND	6.1 "	9.1 "	7.3	S.W.	48
WASHINGTON					
NORTH HEAD	11.5 Aug	18.6 Oct	14.8	N.W.	126
SEATTLE	7. "	11.9 Jun	9.1	South	59
SPOKANE	5.9 Oct	7.4 Apr	6.5	S.W.	41
TACOMA	5.4 Aug	7.2 Mar	6.3	S.W.	41
TATOOSH ISLAND	9.9 Jul	21.4 Dec	15.	East	110
WALLA WALLA	4.6 Oct	6.4 Mar	5.5	South	53
YAKIMA	4.4 Nov	7.6 May	5.9	N.W.	34
WEST VIRGINIA					
ELKINS	2.6 Aug	5.1 Mar	4.5	West	44
PARKERSBURG	5.1 "	8.2 "	6.5	S.E.	—
WISCONSIN					
GREEN BAY	8.7 Aug	11.2 Apr	10.1	South	53
LA CROSSE	6. "	8.6 "	7.3	South	69
MADISON	7.6 Jul	11.2 Mar	9.7	N.W.	56
MILWAUKEE	8.7 "	12.2 "	10.9	West	49
WYOMING					
CHEYENNE	8.4 Aug	13.8 Apr	11.2	N.W.	63
LAUDER	3.4 Dec	5.5 Apr	4.5	S.W.	74
SHERIDAN	4.5 Aug	7.3 "	5.4	N.W.	58
YELLOWSTONE PK.	6.8 "	8.7 Mar	7.8	South	—

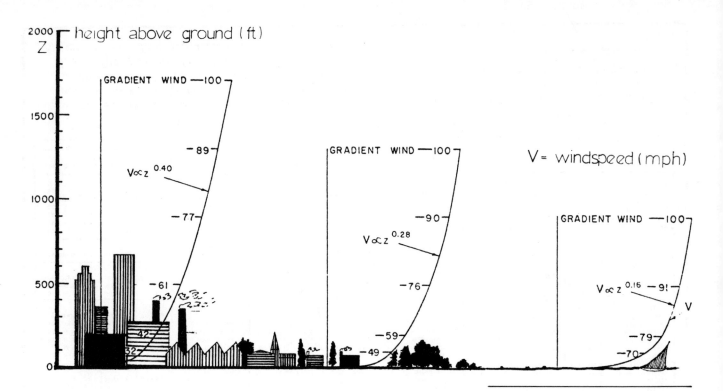

height above ground (ft)

GRADIENT WIND —100

$V \propto z^{0.40}$

—89

—77

—61

—42

—32

GRADIENT WIND —100

$V \propto z^{0.28}$

—90

—76

—59

—49

V = windspeed (mph)

GRADIENT WIND —100

$V \propto z^{0.16}$ —91

V

—79

—70

Concentration of windspeed over a hilltop. Reference 3.

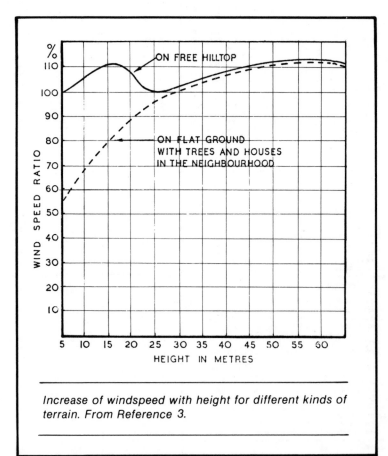

ON FREE HILLTOP

ON FLAT GROUND
WITH TREES AND HOUSES
IN THE NEIGHBOURHOOD

WIND SPEED RATIO

HEIGHT IN METRES

Increase of windspeed with height for different kinds of terrain. From Reference 3.

For more accurate estimates of wind power on-site measurements are necessary. These can be made intuitively by visiting the site frequently. The following Table shows the correlation between conventional descriptions of the wind and their approximate speed and force. Simple "anemometers" can be obtained cheaply, and used to make more accurate recordings. A number of readings taken over a period of many months will give a fairly accurate idea of average wind speeds on the site and can be adjusted, if necessary, to take into account the height of the proposed mill. It is worth remembering, however, that it is the velocities *higher* than average that are going to produce the most power — so "average" measurements can be misleading.

Once information on the wind speeds at the site is available, a windmill must be designed or chosen to operate most efficiently under those conditions. Most mills available for generating electricity are designed to put out maximum power in a 25 mph wind. This means that at

The correlation between Beaufort Scale number, wind force, windspeed, and conventional descriptions of the wind. Adapted from References 3 and 8.

Beaufort Number.	Windspeed m.p.h.	Mean Wind-force. lb/ft^2	Qualitative description of Wind.
0	0-1	C	Calm. Smoke rises vertically.
1	1-3	0.01	Light air. Smoke drifts but wind vanes do not turn.
2	4-7	0.08	Light breeze. Wind vane turns. Leaves rustle.
3	8-12	0.28	Leaves and twigs in constant motion.
4	13-18	0.67	Moderate breeze. Raises dust and loose paper.
5	19-24	1.31	Small trees in leaf begin to sway. Small crested waves form.
6	25-31	2.3	Strong breeze. Large branches move. Telephone wires whistle.
7	32-38	3.6	Moderate gale. Large trees in motion. Walking is difficult.
8	39-46	5.4	Strong Gale. Extreme difficulty in walking against wind.
9	47-54	7.7	Light rooves liable to blow off houses.
10	55-63	10.5	Hurricane. Even the strongest mills liable to be damaged.

around 9 or 10 mph the output of the mill is negligible. On the other hand, at wind speeds above 25 mph, this type of mill rapidly declines in efficiency, since the power available in the wind is increasing, but the mill has already reached its fixed, maximum output. Consequently for any particular site it is worth knowing not only the average and maximum wind speeds, but also the standard deviation from the mean. By looking at the variation in output of standard models with changes in wind speed, you are given some idea of the suitability of these machines at various locations.

The selection of the whole wind-electric system also depends on the amount of electricity required and on the storage necessary. An accurate study of the estimated consumption of various household appliances should be of use in determining the demand on the wind-power plant, and the size of the generator required.

APPLIANCE	POWER RATING watts	AVERAGE USE hours per month	POWER USED kWhrs / month
Air conditioner (window)	1566	74	116
hot climates		150	232
Blanket, electric	177	73	13
Blender	350	1.5	0.5
Clothes dryer	4800	17	81
Dishwasher	1200	25	30
Drill 1/4", electric	250	2	0.5
Fan, attic	370	65	24
Freezer (15 cu.ft.)	340	29	100
if frostless	440	33	147
Garbage disposal unit	445	6	3
Heat. Electric baseboard,			
ave. size home.	10,000	160	1600
Iron	1100	11	12
Light bulb, 75 watt.	75	320	2.4
Fluorescent tube, 2' long	20	320	0.6
Ave. household lighting	500	120	60
Oil burner, 1/8 hp	250	64	16
Oven, average size	2600		
with broiler	6100		
microwave type	800		
Range, four plates	8000		
Ave. household cooking	12,000	9	108
Refrigerator (14 cu.ft.)	326	29	95
if frostless.	615	25	152
Record Player	60	50	3
Skill saw	1000	6	6
Television (B&W)	237	110	25
Television (colour)	450	110	49
Toaster	1146	2.6	3
Vacuum cleaner	630	6.4	4
Washing machine, auto	512	17.6	9
Water heater	4474	89	400
Water pump, 1/3 hp	460	44	20
Ave. household without heating			800

Power requirements and average monthly consumption of various household appliances. From Reference 1.

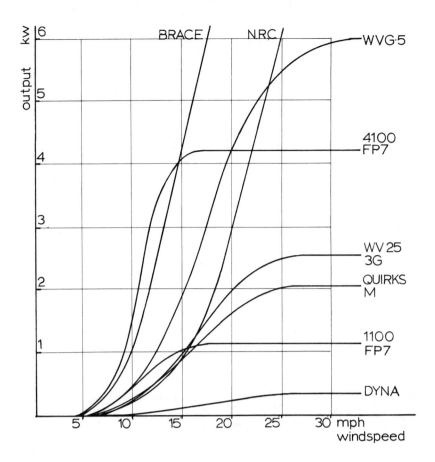

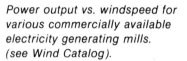

Power output vs. windspeed for various commercially available electricity generating mills. (see Wind Catalog).

Costing

To compete with the utility companies windmills must be able to produce electricity over a supposed 20 year investment period at a cost of around 5 cents per kilowatt hour. This cost is based on the initial investment amortized over the twenty year period at a given interest rate, plus the maintenance costs, which on many units are negligible. The projected rise in fuel costs must also be taken into account.

The table on the next page compares all the known commercially available windmills for producing electricity The table gives the cost of each mill, its output at various wind speeds, and an estimate of the cost of the electricity it produces. This last figure was derived by taking the cost of the equipment necessary for a complete wind-power plant and the installation costs. For

larger installations the estimated additional costs were computed as follows:

Solid-state Inverter 2 kilowatts	$1400
Batteries 19# 6 volt units. 15 kilowatt hours storage	$ 550
70 foot steel tower	$ 700
Miscellaneous, wiring, control panel, etc.	$ 350
Installation costs	$1000
Total costs (minus windmill)	$4000

The total cost of the installation was then amortized over 20 years at a 10% interest rate, and the result was divided by the total amount of electricity produced over the 20 years at an average windspeed of 15 mph. The overall power

efficiency was taken as 50%, to account for inefficiencies in the mill, the transmission, and the inverter.

It is obvious that there is a great variation in the cost of electricity from different installations. One of the best investments appears to be the *Elektro WGV5*, a windmill which produces electricity at 8 cents per kilowatt hour to which must be added the cost of maintenance, which will vary according to the type of mill. The proposed *nrc* vertical shaft wind turbine, which could conceivably be mass produced for less than 400 dollars, would provide 360 kilowatt hours per month at an average cost of 9 cents per kilowatt hour. This is much more than the *nrc* estimate because of the cost of the total plant.

At 8 cents per kilowatt hour, wind generated electricity seems to be a sound investment. This figure is very much dependent on the assumption of a 15 mph wind speed. At 10 mph the cost of electricity produced by the Elektro mill goes up to 26 cents per kilowatt hour. However, the cost of the initial investment could be cut by eliminating the need for an inverter (by using dc in all appliances) and by installing the mill yourself.

If the house is located a long way from the utility company's power lines, then the installation of a wind power plant becomes more feasible. The cost of installing power lines varies considerably from state to state. In Connecticut, for example, there was a charge of $2.50 a foot of buried cable over 150 feet from the utility lines. This does not include the cost of digging the trench and laying a bed of sand in it, which would probably add another dollar per foot. For a house 200 feet from the power line, the installation of an electricity

AVAILABLE EQUIPMENT

country	model	blade diam ft.	blade no.	generator type	generator output watts	volts	output in watts at 10 mph	output in watts at 15 mph	output in watts at 25 mph	weight	min windsp. for charging	type of governor	costs mill only	costs kWhrs/mo at 15 mph	costs cents/kWhr	
AEROWATT Automatic Power div. Navigational aids Pennwalt corp. P.O. Box 18738 Houston Texas 77023 (france)	24 FP7	3.3	2	a	28	24	14	27*	28	6	32	variable pitch propellor	1935	9.7	302[1]	especially designed for low windspeeds
	150 FP7	6.7	2	a	130	24	72	123*	130	6	110		3105	44.2	91[1]	
	300 FP7	10.7	2	a	350	24	184	335*	350	6	200		4565	120.6	43[1]	manufacturers discourage use of mills for domestic electricity on economic grounds
	1100 FP7	11.7	2	a	450	24/220	450	1100	1125	6	440		8375	396	28[3]	
	4100 FP7	30.7	2	a	4100	24/220	1500	4000*	4100	6	1600		18860	1440	15[4]	
BUCKNELL Bucknell Engineering 10717 E. Rush st. South El Monte. Ca. (us.)		5	2	a	220	12	15	60*	220	7	140		900 including tower	21.6	45 <1	available to order in kit form.
DYNA technology Ecological Science corp. P.O. Box 3263 Souix City. Iowa (us)	WINCHARGER	6	2	g	200	12	28	40*	200	7	134	centrifugal air brake type on rotor hub	395 including tower	14.4	35 <1	mainly for use in remote weather stations etc.
ELEKTRO winterthur agents: Henry Clews, Solarwind co. RFD. 2. East Holden Me 04429 also Budgen & ass see 'Lubing' (switzerland)	KSV 300	9.6	2	a	300	12	48	108	300	6.2		feathering blades & centrifugal governors	575	38	31[1]	
	WV 15.G	9.8	2	a	1200	12/115	180	650	1200	6.2			1045	234	17[3]	
	WV 25 3G	12.5	3	a	2500	115	350	950	2500	6.2			1435	342	15[4]	
	WVG 5.	16.5	3	a	6000	115	550	1800	5500	6.2			1785	648	8[4]	

⊙ calculated from manufacturer's data. 1-$1000, 3-$3000, 4-$4000, ~ assumed cost of installation less mill. (see text)

supply line would cost around 400 dollars. For distances over 250 feet overhead cables are generally installed. The material costs then become 45 dollars for every pole and 50 cents per foot for the cable. With labor costs this amounts to over $1.75 per foot (875 dollars for a 500 foot installation).* In very remote locations the cost of bringing a power cable to the house is often greater than the cost of a reasonably large power plant.

In Happytown, Maine, Henry Clews installed a 2 kilowatt power plant himself for 2790 dollars, less than the 3000 dollars which the power company would have charged to install a power cable. Clews has managed to run his household

electrical appliances on the 120 kilowatt hours per month which his Quirks mill produces in 8.6 mph average wind speeds.

Obviously the location has a great deal to do with the feasibility of installing a wind-electric power plant. As electricity prices escalate, wind power could provide part or all of the electrical demands of many suitably situated homes.

* All information on power line installation is specific to rural areas served by the Connecticut Light and Power Company who supplied all the information.

Comparison of available equipment, including economic analysis based on prices quoted by manufacturers and distributors in January 1974. Check the Wind Catalog or the manufacturers themselves for more recent prices.

	country	model	blade		generator			output in watts			min. windsp. for charging	weight	type of govenor	costs as of 1974			
			diam. ft.	no.	type	max output	volts	at 10 mph	at 15 mph	at 25 mph				mill only $	kW/mo at 15 mph	cents /kW	
LUBING agents: Budgen & ass., 72 Broadview ave., Pointe Claire, Quebec.	w. germany	Mo22 3-Go 400	7.2	3	a	400	24	45	190	400	7	324	feathering blades on rotor hub	1088[1]	68.4[1]	29[1]	downwind' type. also for water-pumping
SPERANDIO agents Budgen & associates as above	italy				g	100	12	16*	36*	100				1010	12.9	151[1]	other models also available
					g	1,000	48	160*	360*	1000				2648	129.6	40[1]	
QUIRKS dunlite agents Solarwind co. see "Electro"	australia	"L"	12.	3	g	1,000	32	160*	360*	1000	7	660	feathering blades & centrifugal govenors	1145	129.6	31[3]	
		"M"	12	3	a	2,000	24/115	320*	720*	2000	7	660		1675	2592	20[4]	
BRACE research McGill university, Ste Anne de Bellevue. Quebec. Canada.	canada		32	3	a	30,000 30kw		1,233	4,176	19,260				24,000	1,503.	18[4]	semi-commercial made for high winds. also for waterpumping
SMITH/PUTNAM grandpa's knob vermont	u.s.		175	2	g	1,250 kw	115						hydraulic pitch control flyball govenors				functioned as a supply for utility co. for 6 years
NRC canada Peter South & Raj Rangi National Research Council Ottawa, Canada	canada		15	3	a	8kw	115		1,000			750		375	360.	9[3]	'eggbeater' type vertical axis mill experimental only
AERMOTOR Broken Arrow Oklahoma 74012.	u.s.		8	10		90		30*	90*	90*	6	370	none off/on brake only	374	32.4	29[1]	standard 8' water-pumper 1/8 hp
			12	18	g	1490	32/110	218*	745	1490	8						12''electric aermotor discontinued 1918.

House Design

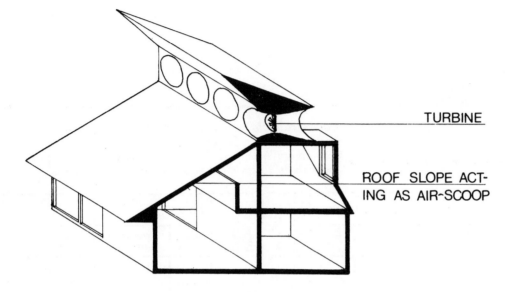

TURBINE

ROOF SLOPE ACT-
ING AS AIR-SCOOP

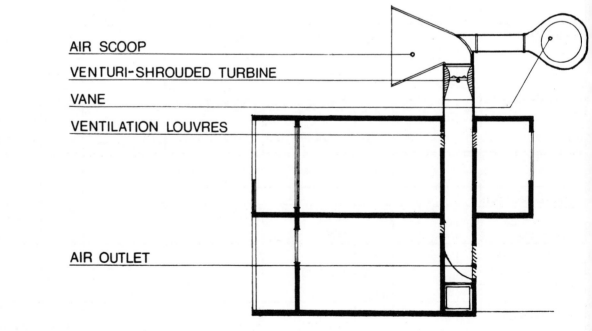

AIR SCOOP

VENTURI-SHROUDED TURBINE

VANE

VENTILATION LOUVRES

AIR OUTLET

*Wind power units incorporated
into the design of the house.*

The integration of a windmill and a building is very difficult because complex problems of noise and vibration arise. It has been suggested that mills could be attached to the leeward side of tall buildings where they would be operated by the suction force from the wind passing around the building, but it is doubtful whether this force would be strong enough to provide a worthwhile power output. It would, however, be possible to use the form of the building itself to direct the wind onto the mill providing, of course, that this did not cause undue turbulence. It should also be possible to funnel the prevailing wind through an airscoop and into a duct containing a wind turbine. Such a design would have to be very sturdily built to avoid noise and vibration, and would either have to face the prevailing wind or use a rotating funnel with a directional vane to guide it into the wind. By decreasing the diameter of the duct, the power of the wind on the turbine could be increased. Air scoops have long been used for ventilating houses in hot climates, but no research has been done on the speed of the wind entering the house. Whether sufficient power would be available in a reasonably sized duct to make electricity generation worthwhile remains to be seen.

In America the image of the windmill derives either from Dutch tourist posters or from photographs of mid-western farms. Both images have become romanticized, and are, therefore, publicly acceptable. But the modern two or three blade propeller-type mill is very different. It will no doubt be compared to the familiar but commonly detested utility power lines that it is intended to replace.

Tall spindly structures, open, insubstantial, and composed only of criss-crossing lines, detract, supposedly, from the beauty of the natural landscape. Both laymen and architects are conditioned visually to accept buildings, furniture, cars, solid objects of all kinds, but our television aerials, power lines, telephone poles and highway signs embarrass us.

If windmills become as popular as television aerials, they may be regarded with the same distaste. But, while a TV aerial can be hidden

One of Percy Thomas's wind power extravaganzas. Note the size of the mill relative to the houses beneath. Reference 2.

away at the back of the house, a windmill demands exposure to the winds — and therefore to public view. It is very difficult to hide a windplant from the neighbors. On the other hand, the windmill should not be considered an embarrassment or an engineering extravaganza, or the surreal fantasy of a Percy Thomas. It is a spectacular machine; it rotates; it follows the wind; it makes a pleasant low whirring sound; it is a strong visual statement of the link between man and climate.

The windmill is not a quaint romantic leftover from the past but an exciting and functioning machine with a valuable future, and it must once again assume its rightful place in the landscape.

References

1 **Electric Power from the Wind.** Henry Clews. Solar Wind Publications, Happytown, Maine, 1972.

2 **Electric Power From The Wind.** P. H. Thomas. U. S. Federal Power Commission, 1945.

3 **The Generation of Electricity by Windpower.** E. W. Golding. Electrical Research Association, London, 1955.

4 **Power From The Wind.** P. C. Putnam. New York, 1948.

5 "The Answer is Blowing in the Wind." J. B. Dekorne. **Mother Earth News.** Number 24, 1974.

6 "Wind." David Stabb. **Architectural Design.** March 1972.

7 **Windmills and Watermills.** John Reynolds (1970). Praeger Publishing Co. 111 Fourth Ave., New York.

8 "Windmills for Less-Developed Countries." Marshall Merriam. **Technos,** April-June, 1972.

9 **Windmills and Millwrighting.** S. Freese. London, 1968.

10 **U. N. Conference on New Sources of Energy.** Volume 7: Wind Power. Rome 1961. Published by the U.N., 1963.

11 **How to Construct a Cheap Wind Machine for Pumping Water.** Brace Research Institute, 1973.

12 **A Simple Electric Transmission System for a Free-Running Windmill.** T. H. Barton and K. Repole. Report Number T. 68, Brace Research Institute, 1970.

13 **Performance Test of A Savonius Rotor.** M. H. Simonds and A. Bodek. Report Number T. 10, Brace Research Institute, 1964.

14 **The Performance and Economics of the Vertical-Axis Wind Turbine Developed at the National Research Council, Ottawa, Canada.** P. South and R. Rangi. American Society of Agricultural Engineers, 1973.

15 **On-Site Wind vs. Central Station Power Generation, Nomograph for Economic Comparison.** E. M. Barber. Yale University School of Architecture, 1973.

16 **Wind Energy Systems Workshop,** June 11-13, 1973. Washington, D.C. Copies are available from the National Technical Information Service, Springfield, Virginia 22151.

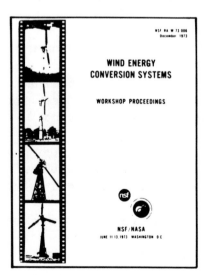

Further Readings

Standard Handbook for Mechanical Engineers. Theodore Baumeister and Lionel Marks. 7th edition. New York: McGraw-Hill Book Company. 1967.

The Design Development and Testing of a Low Cost 10 hp Windmill Prime Mover. R. E. Chilcott. Report Number MT 7, Brace Research Institute, 1969.

Climatic Atlas of the United States. (Gives wind averages, the strongest wind, and wind direction The atlas and a monthly wind report for each state are available from Environmental Data Service, National Climatic Center, Federal Building, Asheville, North Carolina 28801.

Proceedings of a Conference on Energy Conversion and Storage. Oklahoma State University, October 28, 1963.

"Low Drag, Laminar Flow Aerofoil Section of Windmill Blades." P. K. Ghosh. Brace Research Institute, Number CP20, May 1969.

"The Wind Shifts to Windmills." William and Ellen Hartley, **Popular Mechanics.** November 1974.

Potential for Wind Power Development. M. S. Kadivar. Report Number MT 10, Brace Research Institute, 1970.

"Wind Energy." Hans Meyer. **Domebook 2.** Available from Pacific Domes, Box 279, Bolinas, California 94924.

"Wind Generators." Hans Meyer. **Popular Science.** November 1972, pages 103 ff.

"A Report on Preliminary Testing of a Lubing Windmill Generator." H. L. Nakra, (MO22-3GO-400). Brace Research Institute, Number T. 75, 5 pages.

"Plowboy Interview with Marcellus Jacobs." **Mother Earth News.** No. 24.

"I Built a Wind Charger for $400.00!" Jim Sencenbaugh. **Mother Earth News.** No. 20.

"A Wind Tunnel Investigation of a 14 ft. Diameter Vertical Axis Windmill." P. South and R. S. Rangi. National Research Council of Canada, Laboratory Technical Report LTR-LA-105, September 1972.

"Helical Sail Windmill." VITA Publication, 3705 Rhode Island Avenue, Mount Ranier, Maryland 20822. Number 11131.1.

"Savonius Rotor Windmill." VITA Publication, Number 11132.1.

"Santa Barbara Fan Blade Windmill." VITA Publication, Number 11133.2.

"Fan Blade Windmill." (US/AID) VITA Publication, Number 11133.3.

"Low Cost Windmill for Developing Nations." VITA Publication Number 20. 1970.

Wind Energy Bibliography. A 64-page booklet, available from Windworks, Box 329, Route 3, Mukwonago, Wisconsin 53149.

Proceedings of the New Delhi Symposium on Wind and Solar Energy, 1956. Available from the United Nations Educational and Cultural Organization (UNESCO), c/o Department of State, Washington, D.C.

"Can We Harness Pollution-Free Electric Power from Windmills." **Popular Science.** November 1972.

"The English Windmill." Vincent Lines, illus. New York: Augustus M. Kelley. 1968.

"The Homemade Windmills." Bulletin of the U.S. Agricultural Experiment Station of Nebraska. The University of Nebraska. Bulletin Number 59. Volume XI, Article V. 1897.

WIND POWER CATALOG

Dear Reader,

The information appearing on the following pages was forwarded to us from the manufacturer or organization whose name appears in the book. We wrote to each organization requesting information about the work it was doing in the particular field of energy in question, explaining that they were welcome to send to us whatever copy they thought would represent them well.

Our goal was and is to make this helpful information available to you, the reader. Should you become interested in obtaining a product or further information from one of the companies displayed herein, we request that you **not** write to Garden Way Publishing Company but directly to that particular company whose product or research interests you.

Wind-power plants

with automatic control-propeller
Schaufelberger system

Since 1938 we have been occupied with the utilisation of wind power and build complete wind-driven generators in series. The parts are manufactured by the tolerance method of high-grade materials and are interchangeable. All types are constructed for the extremely severe requirements of mountain districts, and the great experience gained by us at high altitudes under rigorous service conditions have been considered in their desing.

Our wind-power plants run at low speeds, work quietly and have a long service life.

The generators also ensure reliable service in southern and tropical countries For these districts, our types can be constructed, if desired, with bearing sealing against desert sand, and also with the windings impregnated to prevent destruction by insects.

The plants are adopted for hotels in the mountains, solitary dwellings, club huts farms, electrically driven irrigation pumps, supplying electric energy to ultra shortwave relay stations, etc., etc. Various officiai bodies in Switzerland and other countries are among our clients.

The site of the plant should be accessible to main winds from at least two directions.

Elektro G.m.b.H. Winterthur (Schweiz)

St. Gallerstrasse 27
8400 Winterthur
Switzerland
Call 052 22 34 34

Electro produces the largest wind-electric generator currently available, a 6 kW unit, which in a suitable location should be able to produce enough power for the average home. They also produce smaller units, both horizontal and vertical axis mills. The larger mills are available in the USA through either of the following distributors:

Enertech Corporation
PO Box 420
Norwich VT 05055

Real Gas & Electric Co.
PO Box 'A'
Guerneville, CA 95446

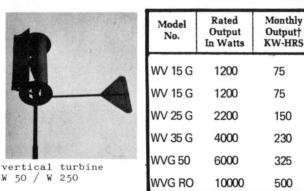

vertical turbine
W 50 / W 250

Model No.	Rated Output In Watts	Monthly Output† KW-HRS	Voltages Available	Propeller	
				Diam. Ft.	No. Blades
WV 15 G	1200	75	12V	9ft 10in	2
WV 15 G	1200	75	115V	9ft 10in	2
WV 25 G	2200	150	115V	12ft	2
WV 35 G	4000	230	115V	14ft 5in	3
WVG 50	6000	325	115V	16ft 5in	3
WVG RO	10000	500	115V	22ft	3

SW-63   6000 WATT, 115 VOLT D.C./3000 WATT, 115 VOLT A.C. SYSTEM

This system features the largest single wind generator currently in production anywhere in the world. With a storage capacity of over 5 days and a monthly output of 325 kw-hr. in 10 mph average winds, this system can supply adequate power for a refrigerator and freezer as well as other 115 and 230 volt appliances including shop tools, water pumps, oil burners, blowers and circulators. In good wind areas this system will provide sufficient power to meet all the electrical needs of a modern household (excluding cooking and hot-water heating, which can be done with gas). The components in this large wind electric system can be varied to meet your specific requirements. A typical system might include:

ELEKTRO MODEL **WVG50G, 6000** WATT, 115 VOLT WINDPLANT with automatic controls (auto-reset type) and voltage regulator suitable for unattended operation in winds up to 120 mph; 40 ft., ROHN guyed tower with tower top, 360 Amp-hr., 115 volt Mule storage battery set with connecting straps and charge indicators; 3000 watt Soleq sine wave automatic starting D.C. to A.C. inverter

Shipping weight 6000 lbs.   **F.O.B. Boston $13,820.00**

Energy for the Home

View of generator parts: Brush holder yoke, armature and pole casing.

Control-propeller hub of heat-treated non-corrosive light metal with regulating members, adjusting movement on taperoller and needle bearings, easy to lubricate, protected from weather, no risk of ice-building. **All stressed parts of ample size.** WVG 2 and WVG 5 with 3 blades, WVG 2 with 2 blades.

5 KW generator with gear, illustrated without casing.

Elektro G. m. b. H.
Winterthur (Schweiz)

(vormals Windkraft G. m. b. H.)

St. Gallerstrasse 27   Tel. (052) 2 34 34

Inhaber:
Kern & Schaufelberger
Dipl. Elektrotechniker

DUNLITE

BRUSHLESS
WIND DRIVEN

POWER PLANTS

TIME TESTED AND PROVEN FEATURES

* Rugged Construction

* Grease packed sealed ballraces on all rotating parts

* Slow speed aerofoil section propeller blades for efficient low wind performance

* Totally enclosed Brushless generator

* Five year operation without service or maintenance

* Solid state voltage regulator controls voltage to close tolerance and prevents overcharging of Batteries

* 60 years experience in design and manufacture of wind driven plants.

* Current available direct from generator when Batteries fully charged.

* WITH SOLID STATE DIOTRAN VOLTAGE CONTROL AND AUTOMATIC VARIABLE PITCH PROPELLER

YEARS AHEAD IN DESIGN!

DUNLITE ELECTRICAL CO. PTY. LTD. 21-27 FROME ST. ADELAIDE S.A.

114 Energy for the Home

SW-2A   2000 WATT, 115 VOLT D.C./300 WATT, 115 VOLT A.C. SYSTEM

This is the system which is described in the booklet **Electric Power from the Wind** and which powers the Solar Wind office. The Australian generator is simple and rugged and is ideal where minimum maintenance is desired. The system is completely automatic and suitable for unattended operation in areas where wind speeds seldom exceed 80 mph. This system can be expected to produce over 100 kw-hr of power per month with 10 mph average winds and is suitable for operating 115 volt lights, appliances, shop tools and a domestic water pump. (See booklet). Battery storage is sufficient for four windless days. A larger electronic inverter can be added to this system if more A.C. capacity is desired.

DUNLITE 2000 WATT, 115 VOLT, BRUSHLESS WINDPLANT complete with Diotran automatic control panel; 40 foot, 3-leg, self-supporting, Dunlite tower and top; 120 Amp-hour, 115 volt Mule storage battery set with connecting straps and charge indicators; 300 watt, D.C. to A.C. surplus rotary inverter for stereo, T.V., and small appliances requiring A.C.

Shipping weight 2900 lbs.   **F.O.B. Boston $5735.00**

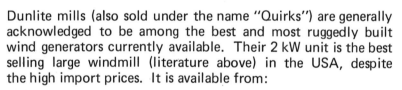

Dunlite mills (also sold under the name "Quirks") are generally acknowledged to be among the best and most ruggedly built wind generators currently available. Their 2 kW unit is the best selling large windmill (literature above) in the USA, despite the high import prices. It is available from:

Enertech Corporation   Real Gas & Electric Co.
PO Box 420   PO Box 'A'
Norwich VT 05055   Guerneville, CA 95446

as well as other major distributors.

Plants are designed to withstand wind speeds of 140 m.p.h. and will commence to charge in a 6-8 m.p.h. wind and deliver maximum output in a 25 m.p.h. wind.

All rotating parts are mounted on sealed, grease-packed ballraces, ensuring long life and freedom from maintenance worries.

An adjustable tower cap is supplied to ensure that the plant is perfectly level when installed.

Standard machine can be supplied in a voltage range of 24V-110V with an output capacity of 2 K.W. Other voltages and capacities can be supplied on request.

Quirk's exclusive automatic three-blade variable-pitch propeller. Simple, massively constructed, with blade arms mounted on sealed ball bearings. Completely weather proofed and in accordance with Quirk's practice, does not require lubrication for five years. All blades feather in the wind, thus reducing strain on plant and tower and preventing excess speeds of generator.

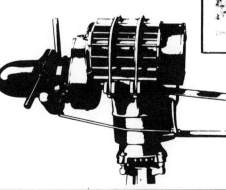

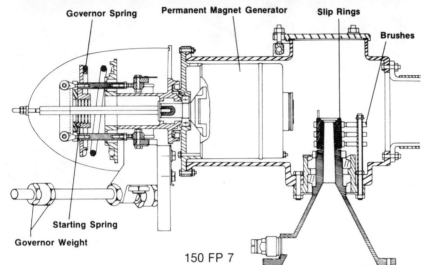

DESCRIPTION	LIST PRICE
24FP7	$ 2225.00
150FP7	3570.00
300FP7	5250.00
1100FP7	9630.00
4100FP7	21,690.00

Governor Spring

Permanent Magnet Generator

Slip Rings

Brushes

Starting Spring

Governor Weight

150 FP 7

TYPE 24

TYPE 300

TYPE 150

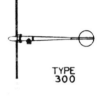

TYPE 1100

TYPE 4100

aerowatt

automatic power inc.

Automatic Power (a division of the Penwalt Corporation) specializes in all types of remote power generation. They import very expensive but ruggedly built French "Aerowatt" mills, – with power outputs ranging from 24 watts to over 4 kilowatts. These mills have the great advantage of being "rated" to produce maximum power at 16mph. (most mills are rated at 25mph.) so they are particularly suited to areas with low average wind speeds.

Automatic Power Inc, sells a wide range of power generation equipment, from solar cells to diesel generators. Most of it is not intended for homestead power generation, but for remote weather stations, radio relay installations etc. The economic feasibility study (below) gives a very approximate comparison of the various systems available. The assumptions for initial cost are fairly high however and the amortization periods very conservative.

Solar Cells:	Amortization	Cells, 5 years Batteries, 5 years Housings, 5 years
Primary Battery:	Amortization	Batteries, 1 year Housings, 5 years
Thermoelectric:	Amortization Fuel	Generator, 3 years Batteries, 5 years 25¢/gal
Wind Generator:	Amortization	Generator, 3 years Batteries, 5 years Housings, 5 years
Diesel Generator:	Amortization Fuel	Engines & Generators, 2 years Housings, 5 years 25¢/gal

Robert J. Dodge   NSF/NASA Workshop   Washington, D.C. June 1973

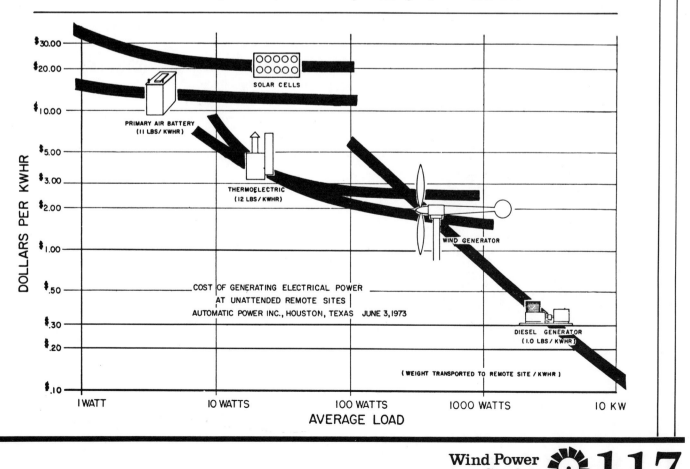

COST OF GENERATING ELECTRICAL POWER AT UNATTENDED REMOTE SITES
AUTOMATIC POWER INC., HOUSTON, TEXAS   JUNE 3, 1973

wincharger

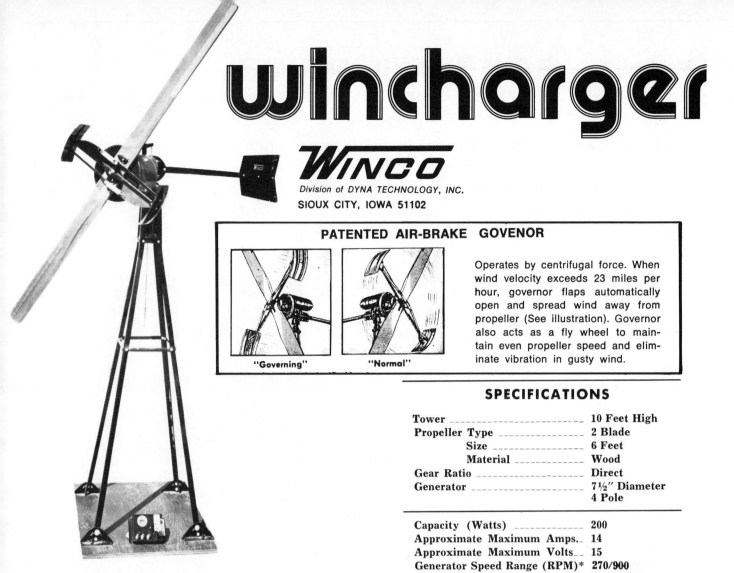

WINCO
Division of DYNA TECHNOLOGY, INC.
SIOUX CITY, IOWA 51102

PATENTED AIR-BRAKE GOVENOR

"Governing"   "Normal"

Operates by centrifugal force. When wind velocity exceeds 23 miles per hour, governor flaps automatically open and spread wind away from propeller (See illustration). Governor also acts as a fly wheel to maintain even propeller speed and eliminate vibration in gusty wind.

A small generator suitable for minimum lighting in a cabin or at a campsite. For $450 you get a generator, a 10 foot tower and a control panel.

SPECIFICATIONS

Tower	10 Feet High
Propeller Type	2 Blade
Size	6 Feet
Material	Wood
Gear Ratio	Direct
Generator	7½″ Diameter 4 Pole

Capacity (Watts)	200
Approximate Maximum Amps.	14
Approximate Maximum Volts	15
Generator Speed Range (RPM)*	270/900
Governor Type	22″ Air-Brake

WEIGHTS	Net	Domestic Shipping	Export Shipping	Vol. Cu. Ft.
Generator and Parts	61 Lbs.	67 Lbs.	93 Lbs.	32.6
Tower and Propeller	70 Lbs.	74 Lbs.	103 Lbs.	23.0
Governor Assembly	3 Lbs.	4 Lbs.	7 Lbs.	3.2

Propeller Speed Range (RPM)*	270/900
Wind Speed Range (MPH)*	7/23
Voltage Regulator	Not Available

Average Usable KWH per month	
10 MPH Average	20
12 MPH Average	26
14 MPH Average	30

Size Battery Recommended (Battery not included)	230 A.H.
No. Battery Cells	6
Volts per Cell (When fully charged**)	2.5

* Wind and Propeller and Generator speed ranges as given indicate first the speed that is required to begin charging the battery and then the speed required for the governor to begin operation.

For example: On Model 1222 the propeller begins charging the battery at 260 RPM which corresponds to a generator speed of 260 RPM and a wind speed of 7 MPH. Governing speed is reached at 700 RPM, which corresponds to a generator speed of 700 RPM and a wind of 23 MPH.

**For lead acid batteries only.

MASCHINENFABRIK LUDWIG BENING

LUBING Maschinenfabrik, 2847 Barnstorf, Postfach 110

lubing

Lubing manufactures wind machines suitable for a wide range of pumping applications, and for generating electricity. They provide 3, 4 or 6-blade rotors, depending on the load and the available windspeed. The propellor is a "downwind" type (without a tailvane). Maximum electrical power produced at 25 m.p.h. windspeeds is 400 watts.

LUBING M 022-3

7.2 FOOT DIAMETER

WATER-PUMPING MILL

Canadian Agents:
Budgen & Associates
72 Broadview Avenue
Pointe Claire, Québec
Canada
(514) 695-4073

MAX. 65' - 7½"

1. ROTOR VANES	8. GENERATOR
2. ROTOR HOUSING	9. CONCRETE PILLAR - SUPPORTING HANDWINCH
3. ALUMINUM GEAR AND GENERATOR HOUSING	10. GUY WIRE
4. SLIPRING ASSEMBLY - 2 RINGS	11. HANDWINCH
5. ALUMINUM TOWER	12. ELECTRICAL TWO CORE CABLE
6. ALUMINUM TOWER SWING HOUSING	13. CENTRAL PANEL
7. ALUMINUM TOWER BASE SUPPORT	14. BATTERIES

The windmill drive is made of a two step gear system, giving a ratio of 1 to 5.5 turning in an oil bath. The three aerodynamic blades made of fibreglass, can be rotated on their lengthwise axis so that they can turn out of the wind during stormy periods, thus avoiding excessive speeds. The main support tower of the windmill is 100 millimetres, 3.95 inches in diameter. The tower assembly is raised and lowered by means of simple hand winch (No. 11) connected by means of guy wires (No. 10). The windmill is equiped with a special long-life electric generator especially designed for continuous operation (No. 8). The generator produces three phase A.C. electricity. The generator does not have carbon brushes, or problems with collectors. The electric power is fed to 3 special brushes and 3 sliprings, then to the control panel, and passes through a silicone invertor which converts the A.C. into 24 volt direct current electricity. This is fed to the battery (No. 14) connected to the silicone invertor, which has a hand operated voltage regulator which governs the input to the battery, which has four settings: zero, weak, medium and strong. In this way it is possible to regulate the input of electricity to the battery. There is an optional automatic voltage regulator, costing an extra seventy dollars. This automatically regulates the input of the battery. This transistorized regulator limits the highest rate of flow of current to the battery from 0.8 to 1.0 amperes. If the power falls below this value, the windmill again begins to charge up the batteries. In order to allow four days without wind it is important to have a large capacity battery of from 100 to 250 ampere-hours.

CATALOG NUMBER	DESCRIPTION	LIST PRICE
6 Ft. Windmill	12	439.70*
8 Ft. "	12A	616.90*

MACHINE-CUT EQUALIZING GEARS work independently of each other on a steel bearing. Gears run in an oil bath. Machine cut gears and pinions give perfect bearing surface over full width of the cog—each gear carries its full part of the load.

SCIENTIFICALLY DESIGNED FANS utilize the full power of the wind. Fans are made from heavy gauge steel and securely fastened to circles to keep proper curvature and position. They cannot spring out of shape. Thoroughly galvanized wheel is not affected by atmospheric conditions.

INTERNAL EXPANDING BRAKE combines best features of both the steel band brake and cast shoe brake. Has heavy cast shoe and special steel brake lining.

BALL BEARING TURNTABLE allows quick response. Ball races are semi-steel, specially hardened and finished smooth to permit balls to roll freely. Enough balls are used to withstand five times the load they carry.

MAIN SHAFT ASSEMBLY should never wear out. Tapered roller bearings absorb the thrust and wear of the shaft. Provides quicker, smoother pumping starts.

dempster

DEMPSTER INDUSTRIES INC.
PO BOX 848
BEATRICE, NEBR.   68310

PHONE / 402 223 4026

AVERAGE WATER REQUIREMENTS FOR GENERAL SERVICE AROUND THE HOME AND FARM

Each person per day, for all purposes	.75 gal.
Each horse, dry cow or beef animal	12 gal.
Each milking cow	35 gal.
Each hog per day	4 gal.
Each sheep per day	2 gal.
Each 100 chickens per day	4 gal.

AVERAGE AMOUNT OF WATER REQUIRED BY VARIOUS HOME AND YARD FIXTURES

Drinking fountain, continuously flowing	50 to 100 gal. per day
Each shower bath	Up to 30 gal. @ 3-5 GPM
To fill bathtub	30 gal.
To flush toilet	6 gal.
To fill lavatory	2 gal.
To sprinkle ¼" of water on each 1000 square feet of lawn	160 gal.
Dish Washing Machine — per load	7 gal. @ 4 GPM
Automatic washer — per load	Up to 50 gal. @ 4-6 GPM
Regeneration of Domestic Water Softener	50-100 gal.

AVERAGE FLOW RATE REQUIREMENTS BY VARIOUS FIXTURES

(g.p.m. equals gal. per minute; g.p.h. equals gal. per hour)

Shower	3-5 g.p.m.
Bathtub	3-5 g.p.m.
Toilet	3 g.p.m.
Lavatory	3 g.p.m.
Kitchen sink	2 to 3 g.p.m.
½" hose and nozzle	200 g.p.h.
¾" hose and nozzle	300 g.p.h.
Lawn sprinkler	120 g.p.h.

pumping windmills

Aermotor and Dempster are the two major manufacturers of multi-blade waterpumping mills. They both produce high-quality, long-life equipment, and they are both relatively cheap. Select the size of the mill according to your water demand and the total height you have to lift the water. Consult both companies before making your choice, they will tell you all you want to know about water-pumpers.

SOLAR WIND

towers

A prefabricated windmill tower is not a cheap piece of equipment. If you are prepared to build your own you should look at the Windworks designs, or consider a simple telephone pole with guy wires. If you are good at scrounging look around for disused mill towers or motorway gas station poles. If you are prepared to pay for one then this page should give some ideas on sizes and prices.

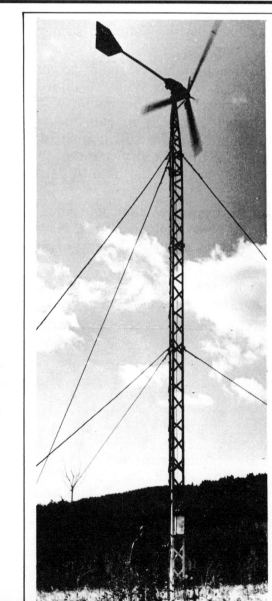

Solar Wind offers plans, kits and factory finished windplants in the 200 to 1000-watt range as well as many related wind power accessories. They plan to continue to enlarge their selection of simple, practical and affordable equipment. They are developing and will soon be manufacturing systems of their own design.

ROHN GUYED TOWERS

Heavily galvanized steel towers which come in 10-ft. pre-assembled sections can withstand windspeeds of 120 mph. Towers come complete with guyed cables, turnbuckle fittings and ground anchors. Tower heights listed are for the complete tower including a 9-ft. top section especially designed for the Sencenbaugh Kits. Because the Sencenbaugh model 750-14 Kit already includes this top section, our tower prices are listed less top section. Towers are shipped F.O.B. Peoria, Illinois.

Tower Height	Approx. Shipping Weight	Tower Less Top Section
30ft.	172 lbs.	$325.
40	265	490.
50	320	540.
60	365	590.
70	465	820.
80	520	875.

Tower top section separately $75.

inverters

SOLID STATE ELECTRONIC INVERTERS convert 12 volt D.C. to 115 volt A.C.

All inverters listed below are manufactured in the USA by TERADO and feature transistorized solid-state circuitry.

All units are protected by internal fuses and are guaranteed for 90 days. These inverters produce a modified square--wave output which is filtered to prevent excessive radio or T.V. interference; output voltage is nominally 117 volts, 60 cycles A.C. but may vary slightly depending upon conditions. Inverters with automatic frequency control will give steadier stereo and tape deck performance.

Model	Max. Output	Max. Continuous Output	Shipping wt.	F.O.B. Bangor
Galaxy	200 watt	175 watt	12 lb.	95.00
Gemini	750 watt	450 watt	18 lb.	175.00
Super Cemini	1500 watt	900 watt	38 lb.	445.00

Same as above, but with Automatic Frequency Control; gives steady 60 cycles for hi-fi, stereo, tape-deck, etc:

Model	Max. Output	Max. Continuous Output	Shipping wt.	F.O.B. Bangor
Chief	125 watt	100 watt	16 lb.	87.50
Continental	300 watt	275 watt	30 lb.	225.00

Standard (unregulated) inverters, but including built-in battery chargers. Can be used to charge 12-volt battery set from 115 V.A.C. auxiliary generator or power line:

Model	Max. Output	Max. Continuous Output	Shipping wt.	F.O.B. Bangor
Mark II	300 watt	275 watt	20 lb.	150.00*
Mark I	500 watt	450 watt	20 lb.	170.00**

*includes 15 amp battery charger
**includes 20 amp battery charger

For Complete Information on the subject, write to:

SOLAR WIND COMPANY
Box 7
East Holden, ME 04429

windspeed measuring equipment

After carefully evaluating these systems and selecting the one that will best suit your particular needs, we suggest you take some windspeed readings at the site you may choose to erect your tower. This is an important step as you may find there are other locations on your property where the windspeed is greater over a longer period. It is an obvious conclusion, but one worth repeating, that the more wind you have the more power you will get from your generator. To make an accurate determination of the winds at your particular site, you might be interested in one or more of the following instruments:

DWYER WIND METER

A surprisingly accurate **hand-held** wind meter with two ranges — 0 to 10 mph and 3 to 60 mph. Indispensable for judging windspeeds. Sent first class mail with case.   **$7.50** postpaid

Hand-Held Wind-Meter

DWYER WIND SPEED INDICATOR

Wall mounted indicator panel with roof-top pick-up and 50 feet of tubing. Range 0 to 60 mph, reads like a thermometer. Directions included.   **$30.95** postpaid.

TAYLOR WIND SPEED INDICATOR

A beautiful, self-contained precision instrument with 2 scales 0-25 and 0-100 in a mahogany case. Sold with 60 ft. of lead-in wire and instructions. Very accurate especially at the lower ranges.   **$95.00** postpaid.

FROM

SOLAR WIND COMPANY

FROM Dwyer Instruments Inc.
P.O.Box 373
Michigan City
Indiana 46360.

Taylor Instruments,
Arden,
N.Carolina 28704.

generators

SPECIFICATIONS

Duty: Continuous.

Operating Speed: Maximum of 6000 RPM. Nameplate gives exact speed for rated frequency. Many models have operating speeds within 1800 RPM.

Bearing Type: Ball bearings, sealed, lubricated-for-life.

Direction of Rotation: Either clockwise or counterclockwise.

Output Voltage: 115 volts, for single phase output. Three phase output models reconnectable for 115/200 (120/208) four-wire or 115 volts delta, line-to-line.

Output Voltage Stability: Within 1% for constant load and constant driving speed.

Temperature Rise: Nominal rating, 40 degrees C. Actual temperature rise within 30 degrees C.

R. F. Noise: May be considered zero for most applications.

Excitation: Internal, permanent magnet.

Regulation: Inherent—within envelope for unity p.f. loads. Regulator not required for most applications.

Wave Form: No sharp peaks or spikes. Total harmonics, single or three phase, within 4% for ratings 1 KVA or over; 4%-7% for ratings under 1 KVA, depending on model. Improved wave form on special order.

Operating Position: May be operated with shaft horizontal, vertical or at any angle.

Cooling: By internally mounted fan.

GEORATOR CORPORATION

ALTERNATOR
SERIES 36 • HIGH FREQUENCY TYPE

Georator Corporation (9016 Prince William St., Manassas, Virginia 22110) manufacture a wide range of permanent-magnet alternators. They require no electrical input to generate a magnetic field, and their power output varies directly according to the speed of the shaft.

distributors

— Some additional distributors not already mentioned—

Electo, Dunlight, Aerowatt

Automatic Power Co
205 Hutchinson St
Houston TX 77003

Environmental Energies
11350 Schaefer St
Detroit MI 48227

Independent Power Developers
Box 618
Noxon MT 11714

Complete wind power systems

American Wind Turbine
PO Box 446
St Cloud FL 32769

Kedeco Inc
9016 Aviation Blvd
Inglewood CA 90301

Zepher Wind Dynamo
PO Box 241
Brunswick ME 04011

Grumman Aerospace
Energy Programs Dept
Bethpage NY 11714

Surplus Inverters, motors, & controls

Electro Sales Co Inc
100 Fellsway
W Somerville MA 02145

Large selections of new inverters

Nova Manufacturing
263 Hillside Ave
Nutley NJ 07110

SEND A DOLLAR
$1
FOR
INFORMATION

 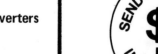

DAF wind turbine shown at Canadian National Exhibition, Toronto, Ontario.

DAF Ltd. in association with Canada's National Research Council has worked for several years on the development of a vertical axis wind turbine, and the research resulted in the first testing of a turbine in March 1971.

Vertical Axis Wind Turbine

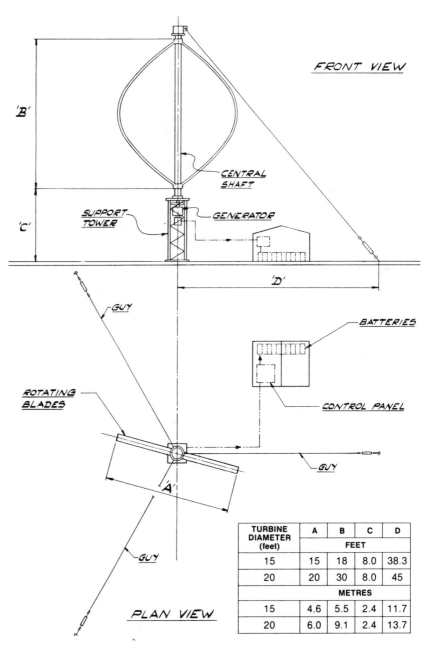

Since that time the firm has put two models on the market, and has a contract for the design, construction and installation of a giant turbine on Isle Magdalene for Quebec Hydro in Canada. The firm states the advantages of this design are that to generate electricity, the turbine does not have to turn to face the wind; the power is taken off at the base of the shaft, so that no heavy machinery is installed at the top of the tower, and the turbine can withstand wind velocities of 100 mph and gusts of up to 130mph. The turbine will generate electricity continuously at all wind speeds between 8 and 65 mph.

The 15 ft diameter turbine model has a 4 kilowatt output. This model, with related tower and control equipment, costs $3,500. The 20 ft model has a 6 kilowatt output and sells for $6,000. Battery storage systems, not included with the models, are also sold by the firm, with prices ranging from $138 to $14,000.

TURBINE DIAMETER (feet)	A	B	C	D
	FEET			
15	15	18	8.0	38.3
20	20	30	8.0	45
	METRES			
15	4.6	5.5	2.4	11.7
20	6.0	9.1	2.4	13.7

3570 Hawkestone Rd
Mississauga, Ontario
L5C 2V8 Canada

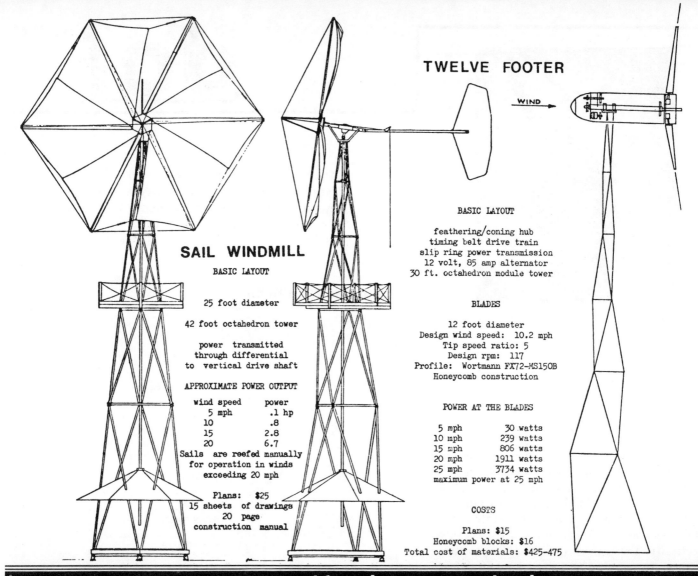

TWELVE FOOTER

WIND →

SAIL WINDMILL

BASIC LAYOUT

25 foot diameter

42 foot octahedron tower

power transmitted
through differential
to vertical drive shaft

APPROXIMATE POWER OUTPUT

wind speed	power
5 mph	.1 hp
10	.8
15	2.8
20	6.7

Sails are reefed manually
for operation in winds
exceeding 20 mph

Plans: $25
15 sheets of drawings
20 page
construction manual

BASIC LAYOUT

feathering/coning hub
timing belt drive train
slip ring power transmission
12 volt, 85 amp alternator
30 ft. octahedron module tower

BLADES

12 foot diameter
Design wind speed: 10.2 mph
Tip speed ratio: 5
Design rpm: 117
Profile: Wortmann FX72-MS150B
Honeycomb construction

POWER AT THE BLADES

5 mph	30 watts
10 mph	239 watts
15 mph	806 watts
20 mph	1911 watts
25 mph	3734 watts

maximum power at 25 mph

COSTS

Plans: $15
Honeycomb blocks: $16
Total cost of materials: $425-475

---

do-it-yourself ideas and plans

windworks

Windworks are experts in the field of low-technology do-it-yourself windmills. Among other things they sell plans for a 12 ft diameter "downwind" type mill with a very high rated output (above). The blades are constructed of fiberglass over a paper honeycomb material which in an unexpanded form (3" x 12" x 5") can be cut on a bandsaw to the shape of an aerofoil. The honeycomb is then expanded to 3" x 12" x 72", streched over a metal rod and coated with fiberglass.

WINDWORKS

BOX 329·RTE 3·MUKWANAGO, WISCONSIN·53149·AC 414·363·4408

SMALL TO MEDIUM-SIZED WIND DRIVEN GENERATORS

Windworks, under the sponsorship and direction of R. Buckminster Fuller, began working on wind energy conversion systems in 1970. It was decided, in view of the high cost per kilowatt output and the relative difficulty of construction of conventional or existing wind plants, that the first area of emphasis should be in making wind more accessible for experimentation and use.

With this in mind, we began working with paper honeycomb for the construction of conventional, propeller-type, windmill blades. Using fairly simple techniques and conventional power tools, it is possible to shape both simple foils (NACA 4415) and more complex foils (Wortmann FX-60-126 and FX-72-MS-150A) with or without tapered plan forms with or without varying profile. Still more complex geometries can be developed using router techniques developed by Hexcel Corporation.

For blade diameters up to 30 feet, typical costs are as follows:

```
Honeycomb . . . . . . . . . . . . . . . . . . . . . . . $ 0.14/ft² of blade
Fiberglass/resin  . . . . . . . . . . . . . . . . . . .    .90/ft² of blade
                                                        $ 1.04/ft² of blade
Construction time . . . . . . . . . . . . . . . . . . . . 8 to 12 hr/blade
Tolerances:
   Paper . . . . . . . . . . . . . . . . . . . . . . . . . . . . ± 1/32 in.
   Aluminum . . . . . . . . . . . . . . . . . . . . . . . . . . . ± 1/100 in.
```

SELL POWER TO YOUR UTILITY!!
--With the Gemini Synchronous Inverter from Windworks--

The Gemini Synchronous Inverter is a solid state device which when interposed between a variable voltage DC power source and an AC power grid converts the DC to AC at standard line voltages and frequencies. In operation all available DC power is converted to AC. If more power is available from the DC source than is required by the load, the excess flows into the power grid. If less power is available than is required by the load the difference is provided by the power grid in the normal fashion.

For any variable and intermittent power source that is small in comparison to the capacity of the power grid to which it is tied, use of a synchronous inverter eliminates the cost, maintenance and electrical compatability problems associated with storage sys

Features

Compared to a wind system using lead-acid batteries for storage and a conventional inverter to supply all or part of the load, a wind system using the synchronous inverter operates at higher efficiencies and uses all the power produced giving an increase in energy production over time. Voltage, current and current slope controls allow nearly perfect matching of the power demand curve of the inverter to the power available from the wind generator maximizing the power extracted from the air stream.

Interfacing

For a local utility, a wind system with a synchronous inverter appears as a decrease in load. This represents a fuel savings to the utility. Because of the nature of the service provided by the local utility, that of a storage medium, is different from their usual role, it will be important to establish the cost of the service provided. Utilities readily admit there are no technical problems, but the question of an equitable rate structure has to be resolved.

Specifications

AC Line Connection:	120/240 VAC
Rated DC Input Voltage:	0-200 Volts
Rated DC Current:	0-40 Amps
Maximum Conversion:	8kW
Efficiency at Maximum:	95%
Cost:	$1275 FOB Mukwonago

Sailwing Windmill Generator

A 1 kilowatt unit
designed for
amateur construction

SPECIFICATIONS

Power output . . . . . Nominal 1 kW in 20 knot
9.3 m/s wind

Voltage out . . . . . . depends on generator
or alternator

Rotor type . . . . 3-blade sailwing

Rotor Diameter . . . 10 ft. (3.05 m)

Maximum wind
strength . . . . . designed to withstand
100 mph (44 m/s) un-
tended; more if tethered

Support . . . . guyed tower recommended,
with anchors in concrete

CONSTRUCTION

Rotor consists of tubes fitted with patented sailwing. Materials are aluminum extrusions and sheet fastened with pop rivets. Rotor shaft connects internally with step-up power transmission to drive alternator or generator. A disk brake has been added to top the rotation when high winds are anticipated, thus reducing the horizontal forces on the tower. The rotor and support, as specified, are being designed for 100 mph winds.

A PATENTED DESIGN

The sailwing is protected by a U.S. patent owned by Princeton University which has licensed this application. The "Quixote" was designed at Princeton University by staff members of the Flight Concepts Laboratory, inventors of the sailwing, exclusively for Flanagan's Plans. All rights reserved.

Flanagan's Plans

61 Windsor Place
Brooklyn, N.Y. 11215

princeton sailwing

Plans for a three-blade "downwind" version of the Princeton "Sailwing" generator are available from Flanagan's Plans (address below). Full-scale testing of this prototype at Princeton indicates a very efficient conversion of windpower to shaft power. (C_p = 0.43.) Output equivalent of 1kW is reached at less than 20 knots.

The price for the plan is about $20 and includes several large sheets of blueprints, plus an offset printed instruction manual with photographs showing crucial steps. The manual includes lists of materials, suggested sources and some basics on the electrical side of the project.

For further information on their progress and inclusion on their mailing list, drop them a card.

Sencenbaugh Model 750-14 Kit

Model SWE 60B Mechanical Wind Odometer

sencenbaugh O₂ powered delight

FROM BOX 11174, PALO ALTO, CALIFORNIA 94306

Sencenbaugh Wind Electric is pleased to announce the Model 750-14 kit form wind driven generator. The Model 750-14 is a 750 watt 14 volt wind driven generator designed for battery charging applications. Design emphasis is centered on providing power for applications such as, remote repeater sites, small homes or cabins and is readily useable with 12-14 volt recreational vehicle equipment. Examples may be 12 volt refrigerators up to 6 cu. ft., 12 volt fluorescent and incandescent lighting, T.V.-radio and DC to AC inverters up to 500 watts.

Rugged, Simple Design

Emphasis has been placed on designing an extremely rugged, low maintenance plant with respectable performance characteristics and long life expectancy.

Simple Assembly and Installation

This unit is sold in a finished kit form only, with all machining, welding and fabrication of parts done at the factory. Only the assembly and installation must be done by the builder. The detailed instruction manual is outlined in a step by step fashion. Assembly steps are facilitated with photographs and 11 x 17 worksheets. Using a minimum of tools (sockets, open-end and box-end wrenches) any individual can assemble his plant with positive results in 25 to 30 hours. It is merely a bolt-together assembly that can be done by anyone with patience and the ability to follow instructions.

Examine our Manual

We invite you to examine our Assembly and Operations manual to get a better understanding of this unit's design and operational capabilities. This manual with worksheets is available at a nominal cost from the factory.

sencenbaugh wind electric

Send $ 1.00 for their catalog.

do-it-yourself ideas and plans

savonius rotors

Built from old oil drums, this rotor produces high torque at low windspeeds. Good for water pumping, unsuitable for generating electricity. For a complete listing of their many energy related project plans, write to:

BRACE RESEARCH INSTITUTE

Macdonald College of McGill University, 800 Ste. Anne de Bellevue Quebec, HOA 1CO Canada

V·I·T·A·

Volunteers in Technical Assistance (VITA) sell plans for a savonious rotor, like the Brace unit above, as well as the following:

LOW COST DEVELOPMENT OF SMALL WATER POWER SITES..........................	$2.00
LOW COST WINDMILL FOR DEVELOPING NATIONS.................................	2.00
DESIGN MANUAL FOR WATER WHEELS.................................	4.00
HANDPUMPS FOR VILLAGE WELLS..	1.50

All of these plans are designed for under-developed countries. Write to:

V.I.T.A.
3706 Rhode Island Ave
Mt Rainier MD 20822

About $1500 worth of materials, -including a disused aeromotor mill- and a lot of time and effort went into this remarkable structure. Built by Doug Gardner, Carl Pucci and Dan Quinto with the advice of Kent Bloomer and Ev Barber at Yale University. The windmill produced a.c. current to heat domestic hot water. The structure served as a playhouse and gazebo. The mill came to a sad end in a tornado shortly after it was built,- a warning to all prospective millwrights!

do-it-yourself ideas and plans

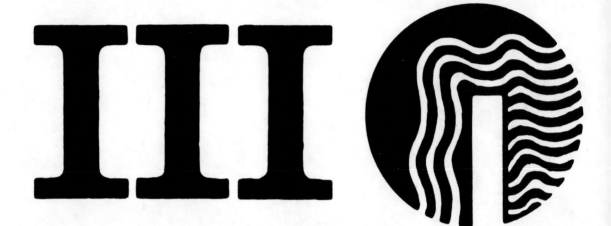

  Energy for
the Home

WATER POWER

Principles

Traditional Waterwheels

Watermills are one of man's earliest inventions. The first known reference to one is in 85 BC, but they were undoubtedly in use long before then. They fulfilled one of man's most basic needs — grinding grain to make flour.

Two basic kinds of early waterwheels can be distinguished, the vertical axis wheel, and the horizontal axis wheel.

The former was probably the first to be used and has become known as the "Greek mill", though it may have originated in the Middle East and was used throughout northern Europe. It is best suited to hilly country with small fast-flowing streams. The horizontal axis wheel became known as the "Roman mill" because it was used throughout the Roman Empire. It is suitable for larger, slower, streams and requires extensive gearing to transmit the force.

FIGVRE CXIIII.

The earliest horizontal axis waterwheels were *undershot,* that is, only the bottom paddles were submerged in the stream. However, during the later Roman period the more efficient "overshot" wheel was developed. The water was fed onto the top of the wheel so that both the weight of the water and the impact of the stream flow were used for turning the wheel. The overshot wheel requires a good *head* of water, that is, the supply of water falling onto the wheel must be significantly higher than the level of the water leaving the wheel (called the *tailwater).* The overshot design was common throughout Europe until the industrial revolution.

Although traditional waterwheels like these turn slowly and are best suited for pumping or grinding grain or driving machinery, it is possible to gear them up to turn the armature of a small generator to produce electricity.

The overshot wheel has the most efficient design of any traditional waterwheel, though undershot and breastshot wheels are quite useful for high rates of flow with low head. Overshot wheels have several advantages over the more sophisticated water turbines. They require little maintenance and operate well despite fluctuations in the rate of flow of the stream. They are not affected by trash and grit that may be

Above: Vertical-axis watermill from **Theatrum Machinarum Novum** *by G. A. Bockler, c. 1662. Left: Horizontal-axis watermill from* **Le Diverse et Artifciose Machine** *by Agostino Ramelli, 1588. Both illustrations reprinted from* **Windmills and Watermills** *by John Reynolds, Praeger, 1970.*

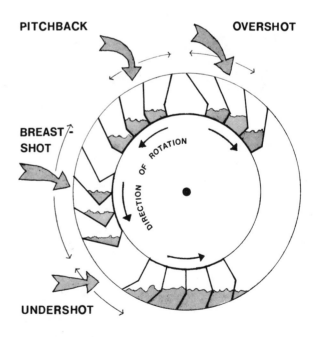

Horizontal-axis waterwheels. Where the water hits the wheel determines the design and the efficiency.

floating in the water (heavy objects like logs pass out over the wheel and fall clear by virtue of their own momentum). They are much easier to build than more modern turbines as they do not require machine tooling or accurate balancing.

The water must be brought to the top of an overshot wheel by a sluice (or "penstock") which should be about 6 inches above the wheel and should have a sluice gate to regulate the flow of water. The water should fall into the buckets just as they pass the top of their circuit. The buckets should hold the water until they reach the bottom of their circuit, thus deriving the maximum benefit from the water's weight. For optimum efficiency, with a limited amount of water, the buckets should be filled only about one-quarter full so that the water does not spill out until the last possible moment. The amount of water in the buckets is regulated by the sluice gate.

The buckets are held in place by a pair of wheels. These can be constructed from strong wood or steel. A drum type wheel is probably the

A Simple Overshot Waterwheel.

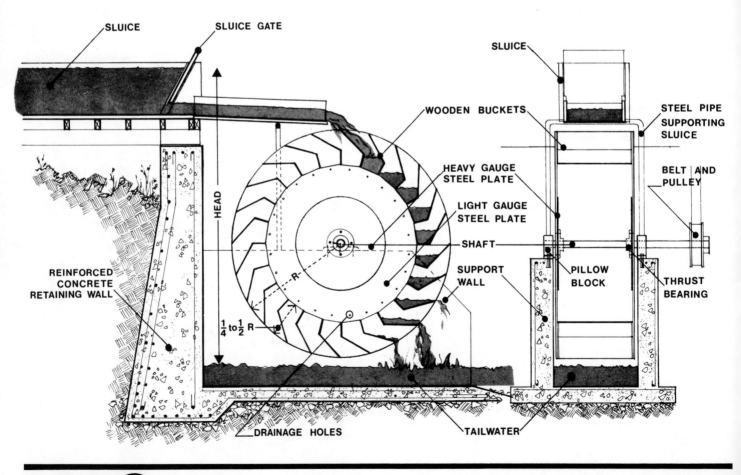

easiest to construct since it avoids the problems of making spokes.

Overshot wheels need at least enough head to clear the wheel (usually about 8 feet) and work well with heads of up to 30 feet. The *flow* of water, that is the amount and velocity of water passing a given point in the stream, is also important. Overshot wheels work best with a flow of 1 to 30 cubic feet per second. The power available in a stream is directly related to the head and the flow. The amount of that power an overshot wheel can capture is determined by the diameter and width of the wheel. At best, an overshot wheel can use up to 60-80 percent of the available power. But the wheel turns at between 2 and 12 revolutions per minute, which is much lower than the speed required by a generator, so for producing electricity an overshot wheel's efficiency is reduced by friction losses in the gearing and belting necessary to increase the rotational speed enough to power a generator.

Courtesy of David Abrams, Burlington, Vermont. Photograph of Shelburne Museum in Vermont.

A 16-foot high pitchback waterwheel built from scrap parts by Frank Gibson and Ben Duffy, installed in an existing millrace. It can generate up to 10 h.p. and is used for grinding grain as well as generating electricity for lights. Photograph, Courtesy **Vermont Life** *and Walter Hard.*

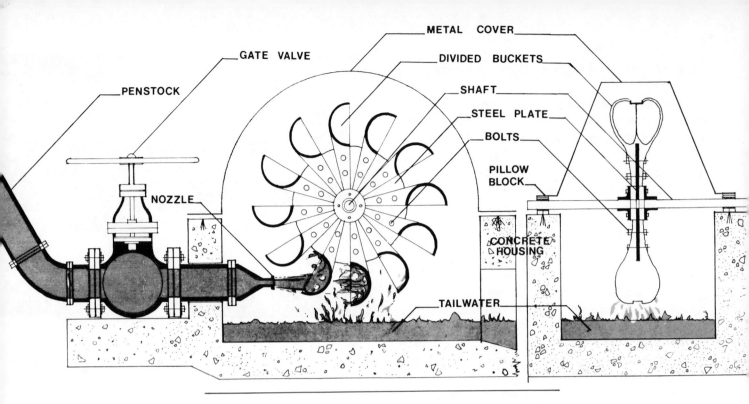

A simple Pelton wheel which can be built from sheet metal.

Modern Water Turbines

During the *Industrial Revolution,* careful study of the way water flows led to the development of turbines, which feed the incoming water through guide vanes onto the blades of the rotating wheel at a precise angle. The sophisticated design of both blades and guides causes the wheel to turn at the high speeds necessary for generating electricity. Modern turbines are so efficient that they often capture over 90 percent of the energy available in the water.

There are two kinds of turbines, impulse turbines and reaction turbines.

A simple impulse turbine, such as the Pelton wheel, uses a nozzle to increase the pressure of the incoming water. The water shoots out of the nozzle, hits a divided bucket and is deflected in a double curve. It then falls into the tailwater, having given up almost all of its momentum. The impulse turbine uses the force of the velocity of the water rather than its weight.

Very little water (a low flow-at least 1 cubic foot per second) but high speed and pressure (high head-at least 50 feet) are needed to run an impulse turbine efficiently. Above these levels, variations in rate of flow and amount of head do not significantly reduce its efficiency.

For impulse turbines, the head is measured from the level of the water supply to the level of the nozzle rather than of the tailwater. But this difference is small since the nozzle and wheel should be mounted as close to the tailwater as is possible without touching it even at times of high water.

The nozzle for an impulse turbine should be carefully aimed, so that the jet of water hits each bucket perpendicularly and is evenly divided by the centre ridge. A gate valve in the nozzle regulates the flow for maximum efficiency. A deflector can divert the water from the buckets if the wheel needs to be stopped suddenly. The buckets should be as smooth and evenly balanced as possible to minimize friction.

An impulse turbine is more difficult to build than a simple overshot wheel, but it is better suited for generating electricity since it rotates at higher speeds (approximately half the speed of the incoming jet of water). A certain amount of machine tooling is necessary to create an efficient impulse wheel. Because of the high pressure of the water, both the nozzle and the buckets will gradually wear down and should be made easily replaceable.

Reaction Turbines

Reaction turbines work on the same principle as rotating lawn sprinklers. Deflecting the force of the incoming water makes the blades begin to rotate. As the water is deflected along the curved blades it accelerates, increasing the speed of rotation which in turn increases the speed of acceleration.

The water entering a reaction turbine is guided through fixed passages onto the moving blades of the runner wheel.

The runner blades absorb the energy of the moving water so efficiently, that they turn at a speed approximately equal to that of the incoming water. Reaction wheels are considerably smaller than impulse turbines, which are in turn considerably smaller than traditional water wheels.

In the original reaction turbine, the water entered at the centre and was flung out the edges, just as in a lawn sprinkler. In 1849 J. B. Francis developed a reaction turbine with an inward flow — the water is fed in from the sides and flows out the bottom. Still used today, Francis type turbines are adaptable to a wide range of conditions. They can operate with anywhere from 10 to 3000 feet of head, though they work best with from 70 to 1000 feet. They require more flow than impulse turbines, but not so much as propeller turbines.

The other main kind of reaction turbine, a propeller turbine, works like a motor boat propeller in reverse. Instead of making the blades rotate to move the water, the moving water forces the blades to rotate. The propeller type of turbine spins very fast even with low heads of water (down to 10 feet), but it requires relatively high rates of flow.

Unlike impulse turbines, every reaction turbine is designed for maximum efficiency with a specific amount of head and rate of flow. Any variation reduces their efficiency substantially. Reaction turbines with adjustable blades can compensate for these variations but are substantially more expensive.

Reaction turbines have to be completely submerged in water. Some form of regulator is needed to adjust the amount of water entering the turbine so that it always operates at maximum efficiency, and in case of emergency can be gradually stopped (the flow of water cannot be shut off suddenly, because tremendous pressure builds up in the pipe leading to the turbine). Reaction turbines usually have gate valves at the bottom of the guide passages, in order to regulate the amount of water falling onto the runner blades.

Reaction turbines are so precisely made and designed that they are very difficult to build at home (though it is possible to convert centrifugal pumps and propeller-type pumps to work as turbines). They must be carefully installed and maintained to avoid leaks and minimize friction.

Because of vapour pockets formed by deflecting water at high speeds, corrosion is a big problem especially if there is grit in the water. The blades are usually made of cast steel, coated with stainless steel on the parts most subject to wear, but they still need to be resurfaced or replaced periodically in order to maintain their efficiency.

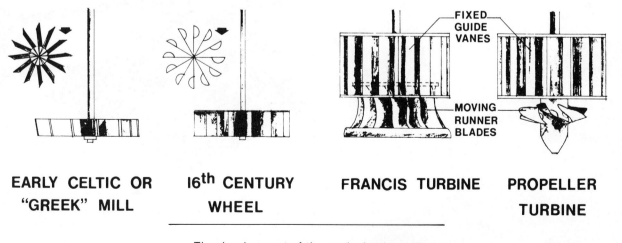

EARLY CELTIC OR "GREEK" MILL

16th CENTURY WHEEL

THESE CAN ALSO BE MOUNTED HORIZONTALLY

FIXED GUIDE VANES

MOVING RUNNER BLADES

FRANCIS TURBINE

PROPELLER TURBINE

The development of the vertical-axis turbine.

Gearing and Generators

Water mills generate electricity in much the same way that windmills do. The turbine provides a rotational force which is used to turn the armature of a generator. The generator must be carefully selected to match both the power output of the wheel and the electrical demands of the household.

Once the armature of a generator achieves its required rotational speed, it produces electricity at a constant rate. Most generators need very high rotational speeds (around 3000 rpm), but some start generating at speeds as low as *150* rpm. In other cases the output is directly proportional to the speed of the armature until its rated speed is reached, after which the output is constant.

The slower the speed of the water wheel or turbine, the more gearing will be required to run the generator, and consequently the greater the loss of power by friction. An overshot wheel might have to be geared up by a ration of 1 to 100, whereas a modern turbine might require no gearing at all. On the other hand, the slower the wheel turns, the easier it will be to build and repair.

Installing a slow-moving water wheel allows the stresses of high rotational speeds to be taken up by the gears or belts which are simpler and more easily replaceable than the wheel itself.

It is necessary to choose between a system which generates direct current and one which generates alternating current. Direct current can be stored in batteries and is easier to regulate. Alternating current can be transmitted over long distances and is more suitable for most modern appliances. If you should lack experience with electricity you will find DC easier to understand, and it would almost certainly be a cheaper system to install.

Courtesy of Irwin Abrams,
Burlington, Vermont.

An Ossberger Universal 5 h.p. turbine. The penstock is on the left, the belting and generator on the right. Courtesy of Ossberger Turbinenfabrik (see Water Power Catalog).

Available Energy

The amount of power available in a stream depends on the flow of the stream (volume and velocity of the water) and on the "head" (the vertical distance the water falls from the supply or intake to the water level at which the flow impacts on the generating unit, or rejoins the stream below the power plant). The flow is determined by nature, and the head by the location of the power plant.

Measuring the Flow

Before you decide on the location and type of your power plant, you will need to estimate the smallest flow that is available at a chosen site, and the largest flows you may have to cope with.

Unless 10-20 years of records are already available for your stream, to estimate the low and high flows it is generally essential to measure actual flows at several times in the year—particularly near the close of wet and dry periods, as in the spring and fall. These figures, together with the area of the drainage basin above your location, can then be related to the flows of another—usually larger—stream in your general area, on which a long record *is* available. For this purpose, unless you are yourself a hydrologist and have access to such records, it will be advisable to take your own measurements to your county or state office of engineering and ask their personnel to determine this relation and supply you with probable minimum and maximum flows for your stream and location. You should get acquainted with them anyway, because you may soon have to get a permit for the stream structure you will need to install, and may require advice on permissible designs for any necessary dam and spillway.

The easiest way to measure the flow of a larger stream is to toss in a floating object and measure the time it takes to travel a given distance. Do this several times and average the results for greater accuracy. Since water flows faster at the surface than at the bottom, multiply this result by 5/6 to obtain the average speed for the whole stream. Then calculate the cross section of the stream by measuring the width and the average depth (take several readings at approximately equal intervals). Multiply the average cross-sectional area (in square feet) times the average speed (ft. per second) to obtain the rate of flow (cubic ft. per second).

A much more accurate, though still approximate method of measuring flow is by use of a "velocity-head rod" at a firm, stable location in your stream. If no such location exists within a short distance of the proposed water intake location for your power plant, one can be made by installing a low, solid timber sill across the stream which will create a rectangular opening without appreciably constricting the flow. Then, if a velocity-head rod is not readily available to you, one can easily be made from a piece of one-inch finish lumber in accordance with the accompanying diagram.

In use, the rod is placed on the sill at each of a series of channel sections, preferably of uniform width (as one foot) (1) with the sharp edge upstream, so that you can read from the stick the actual depth (h_p) of water at that location; (2) with the flat (1-inch) side upstream so as to create a splash or "jump"; the height of this jump above the sill expresses the total hydraulic energy at that section,

$$H = h_p + v^2/2g = h_p + h_v,$$

where g is the acceleration due to gravity; and

$$H - h_p = h_v. \text{ Thence } v = \sqrt{2gh_v}, \text{ or } 8.02\sqrt{h_v}.$$

The following table shows velocities corresponding to observed values for velocity-heads (h_v) up to 1.50 feet.

Understandably, hydraulic jumps greater in height than 1.0 foot on the rod are accompanied by increasing errors in calculated velocities. For depths much over a foot, it would be wise to use a small current meter.

When depths and velocities have been obtained for each of a series of channel sections across the sill, the flow volume for each section can be calculated:

$$Q_s = d_1 w_1 v_1 + \ldots . d_n w_n v_n, \text{ where}$$

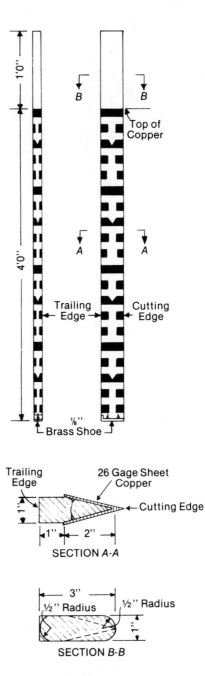

Fig. 1. Velocity-Head Rod Developed at San Dimas Experimental Forest

n = the number of sections across the stream; w = the width of each section; and Q_s = flow volume, in cubic feet per second.

Alternatively, you may prefer to install your channel-sill in the form of a "contracted weir," a temporary barrier "A" (see illustration) containing a rectangular opening which narrows or "contracts" the stream so that its cross-sectional area is not more than four-tenths of the normal stream cross-section. As shown in the illustration, the edges of the opening "B" should be beveled toward down-stream; and the water

Energy for the Home

Theoretical Velocities in Feet per Second, for Heads of 0.00 to 1.50 Feet. From the Formula $V_t = \sqrt{2gh_v}$

Head in Feet	0.00	0.01	0.02	0.03	0.04	0.05	0.06	0.07	0.08	0.09
0.0	0.00	0.80	1.13	1.39	1.60	1.79	1.96	2.12	2.27	2.41
0.1	2.54	2.66	2.78	2.89	3.00	3.11	3.21	3.31	3.40	3.50
0.2	3.59	3.68	3.76	3.85	3.93	4.01	4.09	4.17	4.24	4.32
0.3	4.39	4.47	4.54	4.61	4.68	4.74	4.81	4.88	4.94	5.01
0.4	5.07	5.14	5.20	5.26	5.32	5.38	5.44	5.50	5.56	5.61
0.5	5.67	5.73	5.78	5.84	5.89	5.95	6.00	6.06	6.11	6.16
0.6	6.21	6.26	6.31	6.37	6.42	6.47	6.52	6.56	6.61	6.66
0.7	6.71	6.76	6.80	6.85	6.90	6.95	6.99	7.04	7.08	7.13
0.8	7.17	7.22	7.26	7.31	7.35	7.39	7.44	7.48	7.52	7.57
0.9	7.61	7.65	7.69	7.73	7.78	7.82	7.86	7.90	7.94	7.98
1.0	8.02	8.06	8.10	8.14	8.18	8.22	8.26	8.30	8.33	8.37
1.1	8.41	8.45	8.49	8.53	8.56	8.60	8.64	8.68	8.71	8.75
1.2	8.79	8.82	8.86	8.89	8.93	8.97	9.00	9.04	9.07	9.11
1.3	9.14	9.18	9.21	9.25	9.28	9.32	9.35	9.39	9.42	9.45
1.4	9.49	9.52	9.56	9.59	9.62	9.66	9.69	9.72	9.76	9.79
1.5	9.82	9.86	9.89	9.92	9.95	9.99	10.02	10.05	10.08	10.11

flowing through it should fall free into the stream on the lower side.

To measure the depth of water flowing over the weir, drive a stake in the stream bed three or more feet upstream from the weir, to a depth such that a mark on the stake is exactly level with the bottom of notch "B." Measure the depth "D" in inches of water over the mark, and read the volume of flow in cubic feet per minute per inch of notch width from the table below. Multiply this volume by the notch width in inches, to obtain the total stream flow in cubic feet per minute. (Note that this dimension, cubic feet per minute, is used almost exclusively by turbine manufacturers; otherwise engineering usage speaks of cubic feet per second. For a weir five feet wide, the volumes shown in the accompanying table are exactly in cubic feet per second, or "second-feet.")

For very large flow volumes (which may even inundate your stable channel section or sill) you can get approximate estimates of the peak flows by use of the Manning formula. Date required are a detailed cross-section of the channel at or near your selected location and including the elevation of the highest flow (sometimes mapped after the storm, with peak heights obtained from silt marks

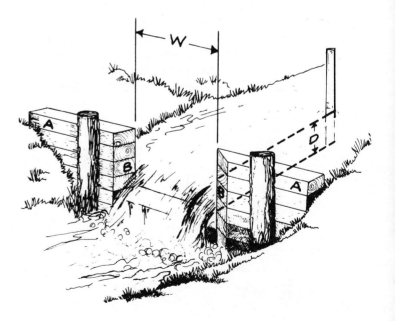

The weir method of measuring flow.

INCHES DEPTH ON STAKE D		⅛ Inch	¼ Inch	⅜ Inch	½ Inch	⅝ Inch	¾ Inch	⅞ Inch
1 Inch	.40	.47	.55	.65	.74	.83	.93	1.03
2 "	1.14	1.24	1.36	1.47	1.59	1.71	1.83	1.96
3 "	2.09	2.23	2.36	2.50	2.63	2.78	2.92	3.07
4 "	3.22	3.37	3.52	3.68	3.83	3.99	4.16	4.32
5 "	4.50	4.67	4.84	5.01	5.18	5.36	5.54	5.72
6 "	5.90	6.09	6.28	6.47	6.65	6.85	7.05	7.25
7 "	7.44	7.64	7.84	8.05	8.25	8.45	8.66	8.86
8 "	9.10	9.31	9.52	9.74	9.96	10.18	10.40	10.62
9 "	10.86	11.08	11.31	11.54	11.77	12.00	12.23	12.47
10 "	12.71	12.95	13.19	13.43	13.67	13.93	14.16	14.42
11 "	14.67	14.92	15.18	15.43	15.67	15.96	16.20	16.46
12 "	16.73	16.99	17.26	17.52	17.78	18.05	18.32	18.58
13 "	18.87	19.14	19.42	19.69	19.97	20.24	20.52	20.80
14 "	21.09	21.37	21.65	21.94	22.22	22.51	22.70	23.08
15 "	23.38	23.67	23.97	24.26	24.56	24.86	25.16	25.46
16 "	25.76	26.06	26.36	26.66	26.97	27.27	27.58	27.89
17 "	28.20	28.51	28.82	29.14	29.45	29.76	30.08	30.39
18 "	30.70	31.02	31.34	31.66	31.98	32.31	32.63	32.96
19 "	33.29	33.61	33.94	34.27	34.60	34.94	35.27	35.60
20 "	35.94	36.27	36.60	36.94	37.28	37.62	37.96	38.31
21 "	38.65	39.00	39.34	39.69	40.04	40.39	40.73	41.09
22 "	41.43	41.78	42.13	42.49	42.84	43.20	43.56	43.92
23 "	44.28	44.64	45.00	45.38	45.71	46.08	46.43	46.81
24 "	47.18	47.55	47.91	48.28	48.65	49.02	49.39	49.76

or entrapped grass or brush); and a careful estimate of the natural "roughness" of the channel to obtain a reasonable value for the channel-roughness coefficient n. Tables of n and details of the measurement and calculation procedures are given in any handbook of hydraulics.

Measuring the Available Head

Together with the expected minimum rate of flow in cubic feet per second (second-feet or *cusecs*), the potential electric power depends also on the available head: for example, a 1000-watt Hoppes hydro-electric unit requires a minimum of 3 cusecs flow with about 9 feet of head, or a little over 1 cusec with 25 feet of head.

In order to maximize the available head, locate the water intake for the power plant at the head of a steep reach of stream or a waterfall, and the power plant location itself as much lower than this level as possible. Then measure the vertical distance between these two elevations: most easily, by running a series of levels with a simple surveyor's level or even a Locke hand level and calibrated rod (see diagram) or one or more angles and distances with a surveyor's transit or an Abney hand level, and a measuring tape. if you don't have and can't borrow one, either of these simple hand-levels can be obtained from an engineering-supply firm or from a mail-order supply store such as Brookstone Company in Peterborough, New Hampshire.

Please notice particularly that any water-power plant requires a specified minimum flow and head to produce electric power: as suggested on page 137, an overshot wheel requires at least 8 feet of

Measuring the head of water with a carpenter's level. Several successive measurements are made and added together to give the overall head.

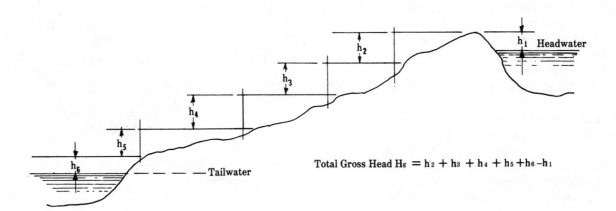

Total Gross Head $H_g = h_2 + h_3 + h_4 + h_5 + h_6 - h_1$

head and 1 to 30 second-feet of flow; and even the smallest (500 watt capacity) Hoppes Hydro-electric unit requires 8 feet of head and 1.6 second-feet or flow, or 12 feet of head and about 1 second-foot. And a 10,000-watt plant requires 16 second-feet at 12 feet of head, or 8 second-feet at 25 feet of head (see the Leffel Bulletin No. H-49). These statistics indicate the smallest stream and rate of fall that are practical.

Dams

Invariably your power plant will require damming the stream for one or more of these reasons: (1) to provide maximum head for the plant; (2) to divert a portion or all of the stream through the plant; (3) to protect the plant by making floodwaters bypass it; and (4) to store water in a pond so as to conserve the supply during times when the plant demands less than is in the stream, and then to supply water to the plant during times when it demands more flow than is in the stream. If the pond is large enough, such storage is of much benefit during periods of very low flow.[1]

Before entering seriously into plans for the investment of capital in a dam and power plant, you should by all means know what are the governmental requirements for such structures on or affecting a stream. First and most basic is the common-law doctrine of riparian rights in the East, under which stream-dwellers and users downstream from your plant have the right to stream volume and "regimen" (behavior pattern) substantially undisturbed by your activities. You may need to look into any effects you may have on your downstream neighbors; although, in the case of a comparatively small power plant, such effects

[1] See also Pamphlet "A" of the James Leffel and Company, Springfield, Ohio.

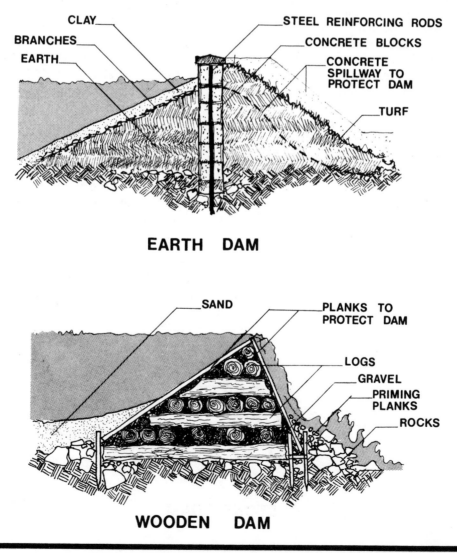

EARTH DAM

WOODEN DAM

are probably negligible. More important are any state requirements for permits. In Vermont, for example, any impoundment which stores more than 500,000 cubic feet must have a permit from a state agency. If you contemplate selling any electric power, the permit will have to be granted by the State Public Service Board; if the impoundment is for agricultural purposes, you will deal with the Vermont Natural Resource Conservation Districts. And if, as is most probably your case, you or any organization plans to develop electric power purely for your own uses and without sale or profit, the permits will be granted by the State Water Resources Board.

In any event, do check with your state government. Aside from permits, the appropriate agency will doubtless give you advice and perhaps technical assistance with your project. For example, its engineers doubtless will have, as in Vermont, statistics and analyses which will aid you in estimating the most probable minimum and maximum stream discharges at your proposed power-plant site; and advice on possible impoundments.

Dam sites are chosen primarily to maximize the available head, but ease of construction and effects on the landscape and natural ecosystems should also be considered. A dam is easier to construct if it is placed in a natural cut where the stream is quite narrow. Flooding the area behind the dam destroys some part of a natural ecosystem, but the pond created may improve the overall ecosystem by encouraging a greater variety of plant and animal life than would a fast running stream. Creating the pond may also change the water table nearby, and the dam may affect the course of the water much further downstream than expected.

The main difficulty involved in constructing a dam is preventing the water from seeping through or under it. Usually the dam is built around some sort of piling driven into the earth or bedrock below to prevent erosion from underneath. The stream bed should be cleared of all vegetation and loose material so that a firm seal can be achieved between the dam and its foundation. The land above the dam which will be submerged should also be cleared of vegetation so as to avoid polluting the water.

Dams may be built of earth, timbers, masonry, or concrete. (See Illustrations.) In an earth dam, the earth is built up in compacted layers around a central, impervious core which extends across the stream and into the foundation. The upstream, submerged side should be protected against waterlogging and wave action by a layer of clay, stone rip-rap, or even "gunite" sprayed concrete. Some ideas on earth-dam design and construction are given in Agriculture Handbook No. 387, *Ponds,* by the Soil Conservation Service; though this publication is primarily oriented toward farm ponds.

Timber dams are usually built of frames of heavy logs or timbers, filled with stones, logs and gravel or earth, and faced with protective planking. Sheet-piling of planking is sunk into the foundation material at the front and usually at the back of the dam to minimize seepage; and of course all of the wood materials should be treated against rot. For stability, the longitudinal width and height of timber dams should be similar to those of masonry and concrete dams.

"Gravity" dams built of concrete or masonry—stones, concrete blocks, or other stone-like material cemented with mortar—rely on their mass for stability, so that in general they should

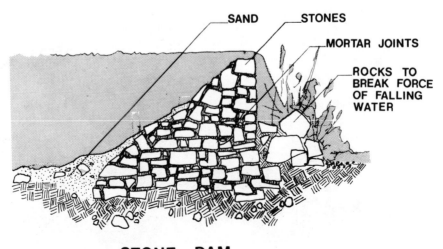

STONE DAM

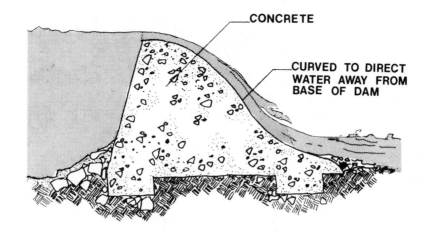

CONCRETE DAM

Labels in image: CONCRETE; CURVED TO DIRECT WATER AWAY FROM BASE OF DAM

be only about ⅔ as high as they are wide. More precisely, the overturn moment should fall within the middle third of the dam's cross-section. And of course, the base of the dam must be sealed by a cutoff wall extending into the foundation material. If the foundation and abutments of the dam site are strong—such as solid bedrock—material may be saved by employing a concrete arch or gravity-arch design; this, however, requires skilled engineering design and would be limited to comparatively elaborate water-power systems.

Whatever dam type is employed, it is exceedingly important to protect it and the rest of the hydropower equipment from damage or destruction by excessive flows. In the case of small dams and comparatively small maximum discharges, it may be permissible to design the whole structure as a spillway and to divert the water required for the power plant out of the stream and back into it below the plant. Thus excess water may be allowed to spill over the crests of small wood, masonry or concrete dams if measures are provided to break the force of the overflowing water or divert it away from the base of the dam. Large rocks placed at the downstream toe of the dam will serve the purpose, as will a channel design which will insure a substantial depth of "tail-water" submerging the toe during high discharges.

All earth dams, however, and any dams that are exposed to excessively high floods, require a solid spillway large enough to accommodate the greatest discharge expected. In addition, all earth dams with separate earth spillways should be provided with "trickle tubes" or other measures to prevent small, sustained excess flows from saturating the protective vegetation on the spillway. Earth spillways and trickle tubes for earth dams in comparatively gentle topography are well discussed in the Soil Conservation Service's Agriculture Handbook No. 387.

The Millrace

If the mill is not to be at the site of the dam, a millrace will be necessary to carry the water from the dam to the mill. The millrace can be either an open channel or an enclosed pipe. Often both are used, the open channel conducting the water almost horizontally to the pipe which carries the water at a steeper angle down to the mill. For traditional water wheels, however, the use of just an open channel is preferable. But the pressure building up in the pipe increases the efficiency of modern turbines.

The millrace should have a sluice gate to regulate the flow of water. A trashrack covering the inlet will prevent debris from clogging the machinery (more important for turbines than for traditional water wheels). The trashrack must be kept clean.

To reduce friction losses, the millrace should be as straight and smooth and short as possible. It should be well supported along its entire length as it will have to carry a great weight of water. If a pipe is used it must be large enough not to impede the flow of water.

If an open channel is used, it can be made of earth or gravel only if low water velocities are expected (less than about 5 feet per second), and with side walls sloped to an angle less than 30°. Wood, concrete, or masonry channels can tolerate higher velocities and, if necessary, can slope downwards more steeply; but always remember to retain as much head as possible for power generation.

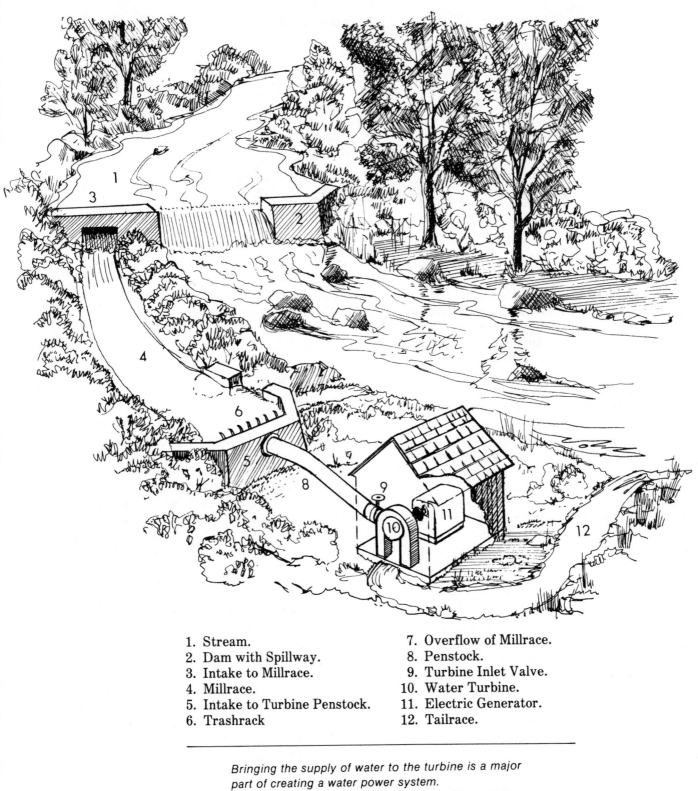

1. Stream.
2. Dam with Spillway.
3. Intake to Millrace.
4. Millrace.
5. Intake to Turbine Penstock.
6. Trashrack

7. Overflow of Millrace.
8. Penstock.
9. Turbine Inlet Valve.
10. Water Turbine.
11. Electric Generator.
12. Tailrace.

Bringing the supply of water to the turbine is a major part of creating a water power system.
The dam, millrace, penstock and sluice all have to be designed to withstand flooding.

Costing

There is obviously no point even considering building a water power plant unless a stream is available which has an adequate flow and head of water. Nor is it worth considering unless a lot of time and money can be devoted to the project. The construction of dams, sluices and waterwheels is complicated and exacting work, and however worthwhile doing-it-yourself seems, it may well be less frustrating and more efficient to pay the extra money for earth-moving equipment or for a modern water turbine.

The number of manufacturers of small scale turbines has dwindled to a few well-established companies dedicated to producing, installing and servicing equipment that really will last a lifetime. But naturally such products are expensive. A ½kw Leffel turbine, for example, costs about $4300, a 2kW model, $4850 and a 10kW model, $7300. Obviously the smaller units will take longer to pay for themselves. Investing in a water turbine may be expensive, but it is almost certain to give dependable service for many years.

With water wheels there is no alternative to doing-it-yourself, which means a lot of research as well as a knowledge of machinery and of welding techniques. If an old mill is available, a water wheel will be considerably cheaper and easier to install. Many old waterwheels (and mills) were abandoned as steam engines took over their work. Their junked parts are well worth hunting for. Nowadays most homebuilt watermill generators are made from junked parts installed in old mill races. Depending on the condition and price of the parts, building a waterwheel may be a relatively inexpensive way of producing electricity.

House Design

Watermills and Housing

Modern hydro-electric turbines have very little visual impact on the landscape. They are generally contained in small weatherproof shelters, located at some distance from the house. Remote controls or automatic governing devices can be installed which regulate the water entering the turbine according to the need for electricity.

A traditional waterwheel is a much larger, noisier and more cumbersome object. Before building a wheel alongside the house, it would be wise to consider what noise levels would be acceptable in the living room. A waterwheel makes at least as much noise as a small waterfall. Old watermills were carefully constructed with no metal parts touching, — the noise of pieces of metal banging, grinding and squeaking against each other would doubtless have proved too much for the poor miller and his family.

Another major consideration to take into account before rushing headlong into the construction of a watermill is the extraordinary power the mill will have to contend with in times of flood. At such times, any water power plant need be well protected, or else hours of hard work are likely to be washed away as the spillway overflows, the dam collapses, and the water wheel careens downstream. The potential outburst of a gentle little stream must not be underestimated.

Water has many uses besides generating power, and building a watermill automatically creates possibilities for improving a homestead. The pond behind a small dam can become a swimming pool and fishing hole. The water stored there can be used for irrigation. Water can become an integral part of the house, too. In hot, dry climates the water could be channelled through or around the house for cooling purposes. The still surface of a pond to the south of the house could be used to increase the efficiency of wall-mounted solar collectors — the water reflecting solar energy back onto the house.

Water is an exciting element for the home landscape designer and a very powerful one. Understanding the way water flows and the functions it serves is necessary before interfering with the natural course of a stream.

The waterwheel as a landscape feature. This wheel, built by Thomas Oakes, is described in Reference 7.

References

1. **Low Cost Development of Small Water Power Sites.** Hans W. Hamm. V.I.T.A. Publications, 1967. V.I.T.A. also has plans for a 1 kw power generator, available for 75¢ from V.I.T.A., 3706 Rhode Island Ave., Mt. Ranier, Maryland 20822.

2. "Power from Small Streams." C.A. Crowley, in **Popular Mechanics** September, 1940 (Part I) and October 1940 (Part 2).

3. **Power from Water.** T.A.L. Paton. London, 1961.

4. **Water in the Service of Man.** H.R. Vallentine, Penguin Books, 1967.

5. "Build Your Own Water Power Plant," C.D. Basset in "Popular Science," 1947. Reprinted in **The Mother Earth News Handbook of Homemade Power,** 1974.

6. "Water Power," Thomas Oakes in **Mother Earth News,** Number 24, November, 1973. Also reprinted in **The Mother Earth News Handbook of Homemade Power,** 1974.

7. **Windmills and Watermills.** John Reynolds (1970). Praeger Publishing Co. 111 Fourth Ave., New York.

8. Hydroelectric Power Bul. No. 49, the James Leffel and Company, Springfield, Ohio. **Also,** see Leffel's Pamphlet "A."

9. **Ponds for Water Supply and Recreation.** U.S. Dept. of Agriculture, Soil Conservation Service, Agri. Bul. No. 387 (1971).

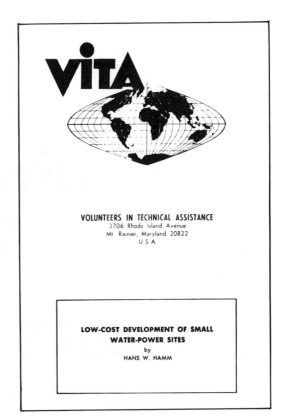

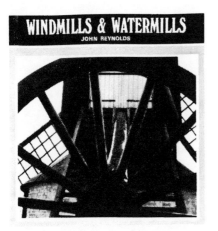

Further Readings

East Riding Water Mills, K. J. Allison, East Yorkshire Historical Society, 1970.

Sensitive Chaos, Theodore Schwenk, Rudolph Steiner Press, 1965. (A beautifully written book on water as the lifeblood of the earth.)

Hydro-Electric Handbook, W. P. Creager and J. D. Justin, New York, 1950. (A good reference book.)

Hydro-Electric Engineering Practice, J. Guthrie Braun, 1968, (A long and complete treatise).

Established in 1862

THE JAMES LEFFEL & CO.

VITA

RIFE RAMS

RIFE HYDRAULIC ENGINE MANUFACTURING CO.
RIFE RAM AND PUMP WORKS

OSSBERGER-WASSERTURBINE

WATER POWER CATALOG

Dear Reader,

The information appearing on the following pages was forwarded to us from the manufacturer or organization whose name appears in the book. We wrote to each organization requesting information about the work it was doing in the particular field of energy in question, explaining that they were welcome to send to us whatever copy they thought would represent them well.

Our goal was and is to make this helpful information available to you, the reader. Should you become interested in obtaining a product or further information from one of the companies displayed herein, we request that you **not** write to Garden Way Publishing Company but directly to that particular company whose product or research interests you.

the james leffel

Leffel manufactures all kinds of turbines, and will provide engineering and consulting services for any size of water power installations, down to ½kW. Their experience in the field, and their literature, is the source of information for many recent publications on water power. They manufacture the only small hydro-electric unit sold in the USA---the Hoppes Unit,--- which comes in sizes from ½ to 10kW. The first thing to do if you are planning an installation is to send off for the pamphlet 'A' and bulletin 'H49'.

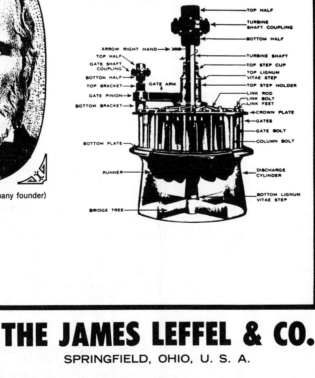
The Hoppes Hydro-Electric Unit has been specially designed to provide an economical source of electricity and power for people in locations where otherwise it would not be possible to enjoy it. This unit will give continuous service. It will operate without noise and require no further service than for a small amount of lubrication.

This unit being of the efficient vertical design permits the generator and electrical equipment to be carried above flood water. This unit is direct connected. Troublesome and power absorbing gears and belts are eliminated.

The instrument board is equipped with voltmeter, switch, fused cutout, rheostat, and porcelain bushings to protect the wiring. The generator, instruments and governor are protected from the weather by a steel housing and the compact unit is furnished with an I beam foundation frame. A worm gear operated butterfly valve at the inlet permits shutting down the unit when desired. A tapered steel draft tube is furnished.

The turbine governor is mounted on the power shaft and regulates the speed of the unit. The interior view of the unit, Fig. 4, shows the stream line water passage, free from gates, links and other obstructions, which might cause it to clog with leaves and interfere with the water flow.

HOPPES HYDRO-ELECTRIC UNIT

Switchboard

Generator

Governor

Water Inlet

Draft Tube

Cutaway Section Showing Governor Control Valve. Fig 4

ELECTRICAL CAPACITY	Head in Feet	Style	Water in Cubic Feet Per Minute
½ KILOWATT OR 500 WATTS	• 8	HL	104
	• 9	HJ	92
	• 10	HJ	82
	• 11	F	74
	• 12	F	68
1 KILOWATT OR 1000 WATTS	• 8	IL	190
	• 9	HL	175
	• 10	HL	155
	11	HL	140
	12	HJ	127
	13	HJ	118
	14	HJ	110
	15	HJ	105
	16	HJ	100
	17	HJ	94
	18	HJ	90
	19	F	84
	20	F	80
	21	F	76
	22	F	74
	23	F	72
	24	F	70
	25	F	68
2 KILOWATTS OR 2000 WATTS	• 8	JP	330
	• 9	JP	290
	• 10	JP	260
	• 11	HL	245
	• 12	HL	225
	• 13	HL	215
	14	HL	190
	15	HL	178
	16	HL	166
	17	HL	156
	18	HJ	153
	19	HJ	148
	20	HJ	140
	21	HJ	133
	22	HJ	127
	23	HJ	120
	24	F	116
	25	F	110
3 KILOWATTS OR 3000 WATTS	8	LR	470
	9	JP	415
	10	JP	370
	11	JP	340
	12	JP	310
	13	JP	280
	14	JP	260
	15	IL	250
	16	IL	240
	17	HL	225
	18	HL	210
	19	HL	200
	20	HL	190
	21	HL	180
	22	HL	170
	23	HL	165
	24	HJ	162
	25	HJ	158

ELECTRICAL CAPACITY	Head in Feet	Style	Water in Cubic Feet Per Minute
5 KILOWATTS OR 5000 WATTS	8	OT	760
	9	OT	600
	10	LR	590
	11	LR	535
	12	LR	490
	13	JP	470
	14	JP	435
	15	JP	400
	16	JP	365
	17	JP	340
	18	JP	330
	19	JP	320
	20	JP	315
	21	HL	300
	22	HL	290
	23	HL	285
	24	HL	275
	25	HL	260
7½ KILOWATTS OR 7500 WATTS	11	OT	800
	12	OT	740
	13	LR	680
	14	LR	630
	15	LR	590
	16	JP	550
	17	JP	515
	18	JP	490
	19	JP	480
	20	JP	450
	21	JP	430
	22	JP	410
	23	JP	400
	24	JP	390
	25	JP	380
10 KILOWATTS OR 10000 WATTS	12	OT	980
	13	OT	900
	14	OT	840
	15	OT	780
	16	LR	715
	17	LR	670
	18	LR	650
	19	JP	610
	20	JP	580
	21	JP	550
	22	JP	525
	23	JP	500
	24	JP	490
	25	JP	480

Style refers to various sizes of Hoppes Hydro-Electric Units.

Quantity of water the unit will use at full rated capacity is listed above in cubic feet per minute.

*Units marked with * furnished in direct current only.

Standard rating for alternating current units is 3 phase 60 cycle and either 120 or 240 or 480 volts. These Hoppes Hydro-Electric Units may also be furnished for 50 cycle current.

When you write us, please give full particulars on your electrical requirements.

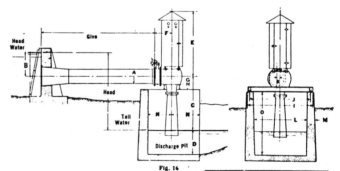

Fig. 16

Dimensions of various sizes of Hoppes Hydro-Electric Units are indicated in the above diagram and listed in the chart. Minimum distance from head water level to center of inlet pipe is given. Diameter of inlet pipe to connect with the unit is given. This inlet pipe should be short as possible.

In addition to the examples of complete Hoppes Hydro-Electric Units illustrated and specified herein, many other styles of turbines may be furnished, see page 11. Our Engineering Department will gladly assist and advise you regarding any details relating to the installation of Hoppes Hydro-Electric Units or Leffel turbines. For over three quarters of a century we have specialized in the designing and constructing of hydraulic turbines of all kinds. With this background of experience we are prepared to furnish designs to meet your requirements.

GENERAL DIMENSIONS
Style Sizes

	F	HJ	IL	JP	LR	OT
A	6"	10"	12"	16"	18"	20"
B	18"	24"	24"	36"	36"	36"
C	60"	60"	60"	60"	60"	60"
D	24"	30"	30"	36"	42"	48"
E	58"	72"	72"	88"	90"	90"
F	20½"	18"	18"	22"	23"	27"
G	5½"	8½"	9½"	11¼"	11½"	14½"
H	5"	5"	5"	6"	6"	7"
I	72"	72"	72"	84"	84"	96"
J	66"	66"	66"	78"	78"	90"
K	3½"	4½"	4"	4"	4"	4½"
L	60"	60"	60"	72"	72"	84"
M	8"	8"	8"	9"	10"	10"
N	30"	30"	30"	36"	42"	48"
O	73½"	73½"	75½"	78½"	84½"	86½"

ossberger

Ossberger is a specialized manufacturer of small-sized water turbines from 1kW to 1MW of output. They developed the **Michell-Ossberger Cross-Flow Turbine** now in use throughout the world. Their **Universal** and **Hydro-Light** units are particularly suitable for small-scale power sites (1.5 to 8kW) and low heads of water. Remote control is possible by means of cable and pulleys.

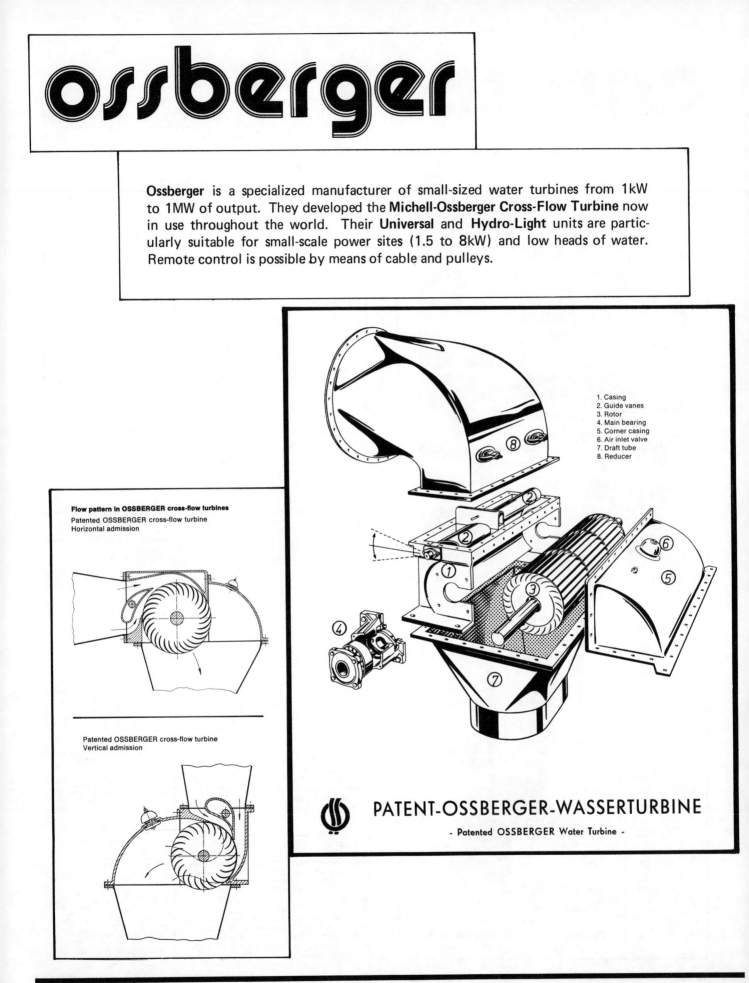

1. Casing
2. Guide vanes
3. Rotor
4. Main bearing
5. Corner casing
6. Air inlet valve
7. Draft tube
8. Reducer

Flow pattern in OSSBERGER cross-flow turbines
Patented OSSBERGER cross-flow turbine
Horizontal admission

Patented OSSBERGER cross-flow turbine
Vertical admission

PATENT-OSSBERGER-WASSERTURBINE
- Patented OSSBERGER Water Turbine -

TYPE UNIVERSAL A/B

Both UNIVERSAL types A and B specially are suitable for utilization of small waters (22 to 80 litr/sec.) under heads of 4 to 30 metres. The outpout ranges between 2,1 and 12 HP (see tables). The favourable speeds (380 to 1070 r. p. m.) permit to directly drive generators or transmissions by means of suitable belt pulleys. The hand-wheel of the manually regulated turbine either can be fitted on the turbine or at every other place to remotely control the plant by means of wire rope and rope rollers.

UNIVERSAL A/B

OSSBERGER-TURBINENFABRIK · WEISSENBURG/BAYERN

GERMANY - ALLEMAGNE - ALEMANIA - TELEFON 40 97

HYDRO-LIGHT

OSSBERGER-TURBINENFABRIK

WEISSENBURG/BAYERN

GERMANY — ALLEMAGNE — ALEMANIA

Schliessfach - P. O. Box - B. P. - Apartado 32 — Telefon 40 97

HYDRO-LIGHT, the miniature power plant accommodated in a neatly designed housing of about 1 cubic metre volume supplies energy for smaller premises where water is available in quantities of about 30 to 80 litres per second. An economic substitute for diesel units and other power generators which are costly to run continuously. Unit construction requires a minimum of foundations. Only needs connecting to the pressure and draft tubes and electrical gear for starting.

TECHNICAL DETAILS:

Prime Mover: Divided Patent-Ossberger Draft Tube Turbine with a guaranteed efficiency of 80% over a wide load range of 1/1 to 1/6 of the full water volume (see main catalogue). Mounted on rigid bed frame.

Regulation: by hand, infinitely variable over the whole range of utilisation.

Generator Drive: by special flat belts running on replaceable generator belt pulley.

Electrical Gear: Self-acting three-phase constant voltage generator working on a swivel base, incl. steel fly-wheel. Control panel with generator safety switch and instruments for measuring current, voltage and frequency.

Remote Control: Manual long distance control of the turbine by a cable drive. The initial cable pulley is attached to the manual adjusting gear on the turbine. The alternately drawing and drawn length of cable is conducted over rolls to the masts of the overhead line to the point of maximum current consumption, where a second handwheel is mounted along with a voltmeter. As the current consumption increases, which is indicated by the reduction in voltage, open the turbine by means of handwheel and cable line wide enough for the normal working voltage to be reached. For cutting out the electrical equipment reverse the procedure. Small load variations (switching incandescent bulbs off and on) do not as a rule require any re-adjustment. This form of manual regulation is ideal for installations of this power class and has given complete satisfaction in practise. Rugged design of the unit ensures cost free running practically without maintenance for a great number of years. The propellant water is free of charge.

● Range of application

with generator of $\begin{cases} n = 1500 \text{ U/min.} \\ \text{r.p.m. - t/min.} \\ 50 \text{ Hz. - C. - Pér.} \end{cases}$

H =	4	5	6	7	8	9 m
Q =	49	55	60	66	70	75 l/sec.
N =	2,1	2,9	3,8	4,9	6,0	7,2 PS - HP - CV
n =	364	410	450	485	520	550 U/min.-r.p.m.-t/m.

For heads 4 to 6 m: with 3 kVA-Generator; exceeding these heads: with 5 kVA-Generator.

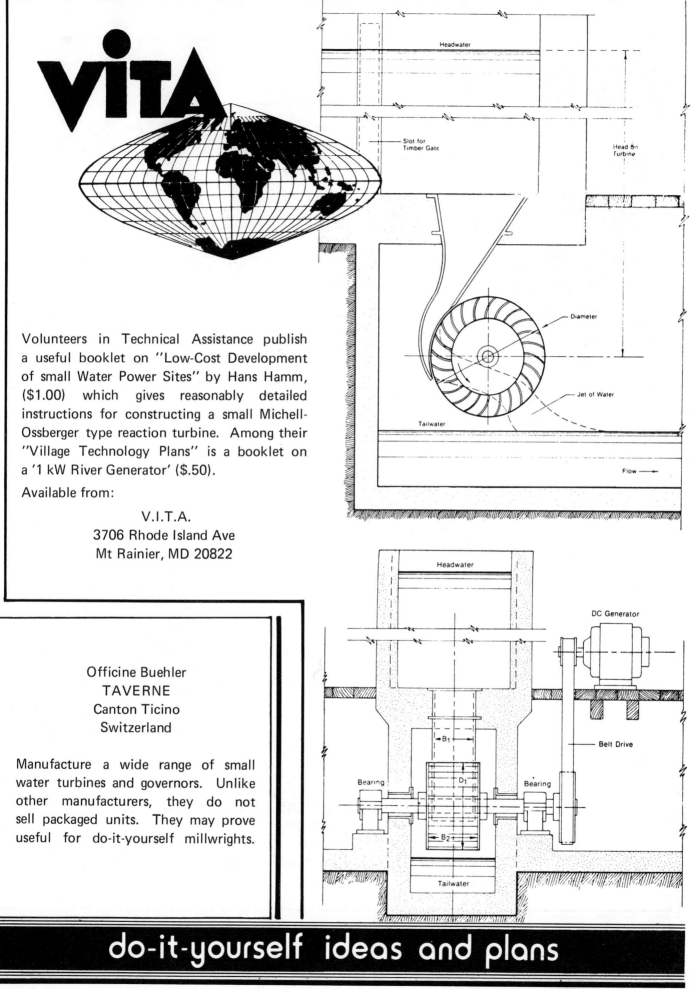

Volunteers in Technical Assistance publish a useful booklet on "Low-Cost Development of small Water Power Sites" by Hans Hamm, ($1.00) which gives reasonably detailed instructions for constructing a small Michell-Ossberger type reaction turbine. Among their "Village Technology Plans" is a booklet on a '1 kW River Generator' ($.50).

Available from:

V.I.T.A.
3706 Rhode Island Ave
Mt Rainier, MD 20822

Officine Buehler
TAVERNE
Canton Ticino
Switzerland

Manufacture a wide range of small water turbines and governors. Unlike other manufacturers, they do not sell packaged units. They may prove useful for do-it-yourself millwrights.

do-it-yourself ideas and plans

rife
hydraulic rams

ALSO MAKE
"DAVEY"
◀ **RAMS**

RIFE RAMS
What They Are and What They Will Do

A RIFE HYDRAULIC RAM is a device for pumping water by means of water-power, connected with a Spring, Creek, or Artesian Well, with a flow of 1½ gallons per minute or more. It is necessary to have a Fall or "Head" of 20 inches or more. When so located, it will automatically pump a good volume of the water to a height of 25 feet for each one-foot of Fall available. (For example, if there is a Fall of 3 feet, the Ram will pump a good volume of water 75 feet high).

RIFE HYDRAULIC RAMS are built on the "HIGH BASE" Principle, embracing a Positive and Automatic Air Feed which maintains indefinitely, the all-important "Air Cushion" in the Air Chamber preventing the Air Chamber filling up with water. They are the last word from the standpoint of efficiency and freedom from service interruptions. They use NO GASOLINE, NO ELECTRICITY, NO POWER BILL. *A RIFE RAM will pump a continuous flow of water day in and day out, year in and year out, without one cent operating cost. THE FLOW AND FALL OF YOUR OWN WATER DOES THE PUMPING!*

RIFE RAMS have been manufactured continuously since 1884 and since that time more than 30,000 have been sold in every State of the Union and in many foreign countries.

Rife is the major manufacturer of hydraulic rams in this country. Most of their installations are made to supply water for agricultural purposes. Their "double acting" ram (below), however, makes it possible to use the power in an ordinary stream to supply your home with pure spring water (provided you have both the stream and the spring!). The Rife installation manual ($.50) is the most valuable piece of literature available on rams. Rife now owns and sells Davey Rams, slightly cheaper and less efficient than the Rife units.

RIFE'S DOUBLE ACTING RAM is used where there is not sufficient Pure Spring Water available to operate a Ram, but where there is a nearby creek with sufficient water and Fall to operate the Ram. In this instance the creek water is used to furnish the power to operate the Ram, and pump the Pure Spring Water. It is possible for a RIFE RAM to pump two-thirds of the Pure Uncontaminated Spring Water. The other one-third mixes with the creek water and is wasted through the Outside Valve.

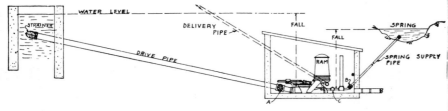

Layout of Double Acting Ram Installation. Spring Water connections can be brought into Ram from any direction. Delivery Pipe can likewise be led away from Ram at any desired angle. A minimum fall of 18 inches is required from Spring to Ram location. Take advantage of all fall possible of Creek Water.

RIFE HYDRAULIC ENGINE MANUFACTURING CO.
RIFE RAM AND PUMP WORKS

TRADE MARK:
RIFE
REG. U. S. PATENT OFFICE

CABLE ADDRESS:
"RIFENGINE" MILLBURNNEWJERSEY

BOX 367

MILLBURN, NEW JERSEY 07041

FOUNDED 1889

NEW JERSEY TELEPHONES
AREA CODE 201
379-4994
786-5230

THE HYDRAULIC RAM

RIFE HYDRAULIC ENGINE CO.

Rife rams will operate with a fall of between 2 and 50 ft. and a flow of between 1½ and 400 gpm. This table will give you the specifications for the model you need.

A TYPICAL RIFE **FARM** INSTALLATION

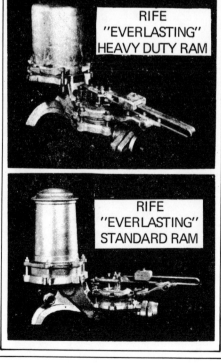

RIFE "EVERLASTING" HEAVY DUTY RAM

RIFE "EVERLASTING" STANDARD RAM

SPECIFICATIONS OF RIFE HYDRAULIC RAMS
New High Capacity Models

RAM NO.	INTAKE (drive) PIPE SIZE	DISCHARGE (delivery) PIPE SIZE	INTAKE CAPACITY (Gals. per min. used) Min.	Normal	Max.	MINIMUM VERTICAL FALL required in feet	CRATED WEIGHT (SINGLE-ACTING) in pounds (approx.)

RIFE "NEW MODEL" SERIES B RAMS (4 Bolt Design)
Maximum Vertical Fall 15 ft. - Maximum Vertical Lift 150 ft.
Unit includes iron gate strainer for intake end of drivepipe

RAM NO.	INTAKE	DISCHARGE	Min.	Normal	Max.	FALL	WEIGHT
10B	1-1/4"	3/4"	1½	6	7	2	94
15B	1-1/2"	3/4"	6	10	13	2	102
20B	2"	1"	8	18	20	2¼	150
25B	2-1/2"	1"	12	28	35	2½	202
30B	3"	1-1/4"	20	40	55	3	263

RIFE "EVERLASTING" STANDARD RAMS
A more rugged development of the previous Series "A" 6 Bolt Design
Maximum Vertical Fall 25 ft. - Maximum Vertical Lift 250 ft.
All steel and iron parts zinc coated or plated
Unit includes special steel strainer for intake end of drivepipe

RAM NO.	INTAKE	DISCHARGE	Min.	Normal	Max.	FALL	WEIGHT
10S	1-1/4"	3/4"	3	7	10	3	160
15S	1-1/2"	3/4"	5	11	15	3	171
20S	2"	1"	10	20	25	3½	249
25S	2-1/2"	1"	15	30	45	3½	273
30S	3"	1-1/4"	25	45	70	4	339
40S*	4"	2"	35	90	125	4	565
60S*	6"	3"	75	225	350	4	1325
80S	8"	4"	Repair parts only				

* #40S and #60S equipped with steel air chamber. #60S includes special welded pipe nipple to assemble inclined drivepipe to level ram.

RIFE "EVERLASTING" HEAVY DUTY RAMS (equipped with steel air chamber)
Maximum Vertical Fall 50 ft. - Maximum Vertical Lift 500 ft.
All steel and iron parts zinc coated or plated
Design generally similar to Standard Ram, but with steel base and **valve chamber, and other special parts**
Unit includes special steel strainer for intake end of drivepipe

RAM NO.	INTAKE	DISCHARGE	Min.	Normal	Max.	FALL	WEIGHT
10HD	1-1/4"	3/4"	3	8	12	3	145
15HD	1-1/2"	3/4"	5	12	18	3	145
20HD	2"	1"	10	25	35	3½	208
30HD	3"	1-1/4"	25	55	85	4	302
40HD	4"	2"	35	100	150	4	565
60HD**	6"	3"	75	250	400	4	1325

** Unit equipped with special welded pipe nipple to assemble inclined drivepipe to ram.

ACCESSORY EQUIPMENT

Plug Valves, quick opening and closing, self-lubricated.
Gate Valves, Check Valves and Pressure Relief Valves.
Double-Acting Attachments, factory installed, to equip any ram to pump from a pure water source (spring), using power from an impure water supply, such as stream or lake.
NOTE: We recommend that the following auxiliary equipment be included in installations of RIFE Hydraulic Rams:
Series "B" - Gate valve at discharge end; also at intake end of 30B.
Standard - Plug valve at intake end - and gate valve at discharge end.
Heavy Duty - Plug valves at both intake and discharge ends.

Edward Barberie, of

The Whole Mother Earth Water Works
Green Spring, West Virginia 26722

Offers free advice on the construction of home-built Hydraulic Rams and also distributes the DICOA Netafim-Blass hydraulic ram, (the only patented and proven drip irrigation system in the world).
---Their Home Garden Kit (HGK 1000) supplies irrigation for a 1000 square foot garden and costs $79.95 + postage. Please enclose self-addressed, stamped envelope with your inquiries.

IV

WATER/ WASTE SYSTEMS

Principles

Water-Waste Systems

Sewage treatment and disposal is one of the least effective and most polluting of our service industries. In 1969, 10 percent of all the communities in the United States served by sewers had no effective sewage treatment at all. Another 30 percent had only primary treatment which produced highly toxic residues. The resulting damage to soils and waterways is inestimable.

The more centralized our service systems become, the greater the risk of large scale pollution. The natural processes of digestion, excretion and decomposition constitute a very important part of the cycling of the earth's nutrients. In small quantities, carefully treated and returned to the soil, human waste is a valuable source of fertilizer and energy. When collected in large amounts and mixed with vast quantities of water (containing detergents, industrial wastes, etc.) it can actually harm the earth, and biological treatment becomes much more difficult. Rarely is sewage treatment carried so far that the effluent has no damaging effects on the natural systems into which it is released. Even more rarely are any of the valuable nutrients in the effluent returned to the earth in a usable form.

On-site sewage treatment facilities minimize the disruption to natural ecosystems caused by sewer lines and centralized treatment plants. But the conventional on-site treatment, the septic tank, often fails to function properly.

The vast quantities of water consumed by the average household often overload the system — causing it to break down, resulting in ground water supplies becoming polluted and existing vegetation being killed.

We have come to regard water as a "free commodity," but we are rapidly approaching such a crisis in water consumption that large cities are considering desalinization plants or melting icebergs for their water supply.

Any discussion of waste treatment systems must include reduction in household water consumption. The two problems are interlocked.

The amount of water used for various purposes in an average household is shown in the illustration. We use the same quality of water for drinking, washing, and toilet flushing (the latter consuming over 40 percent of the household water supply). Many of the problems with our present water/waste systems stem from using one waste treatment system and one standard of water quality. The key to a decrease in household water consumption and a more effective waste system is the use of separate systems for different purposes.

Toilet wastes have a very high biochemical oxygen demand (**bod**), which means they require an input of oxygen to break down the harmful intestinal bacteria present in human excreta.

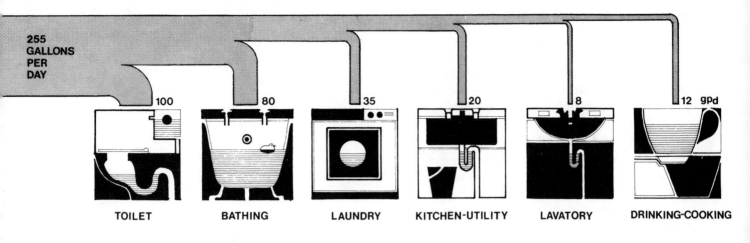

255 GALLONS PER DAY

100   80   35   20   8   12 gPd

TOILET   BATHING   LAUNDRY   KITCHEN-UTILITY   LAVATORY   DRINKING-COOKING

Average amount of water used in a four person household in the U.S. in 1968. Reference 8.

Wastes from bath, sink and laundry have almost no **bod**, but do have a large quantity of substances, suspended or dissolved, which could be harmful if released into natural waterways. Some of these substances can be removed by oxidation, some by bacterial or chemical action and some by filtration.

At present, of the many potential solutions to the problems of treating sewage, very few are economically viable. Technological research could ultimately produce systems suitable for the single family house. Chemical toilets are available, but they require continual replacement of the active chemical agent and do not produce an effluent that can easily be absorbed by natural ecosystems. We have chosen to concentrate mainly on biological waste treatment systems which are suitable for private utility systems and homes. These processes use various kinds of naturally-occurring bacteria which operate under certain environmental conditions to degrade the toxic substances in the sewage.

Aerobic bacteria only exist in the presence of air or dissolved oxygen. They are fast-acting, and not susceptible to rapid changes in the consistency or temperature of the input material. Aerobic digestion yields large amounts of carbon dioxide, ammonia, and sulfurous gases.

Anaerobic bacteria only exist in an oxygen-free environment. The acidity, consistency and temperature of the waste material is critical. If the correct conditions are maintained, however, anaerobic digestion will yield high quality fuel gas. Both aerobic and anaerobic bacterial digestion take place in nature. The object of a waste treatment system is to create the right environmental conditions for these natural processes to be accelerated.

Most sewage treatment relies on natural processes of bacterial decomposition. A simple septic tank uses both anaerobic and aerobic bacterial digestion. In the tank itself, which is enclosed and airtight, anaerobic bacteria break down the human waste into simpler and less harmful substances. Then the waste flows into gravel-filled trenches in the leach field where it comes into contact with oxygen. Aerobic bacteria then break down the remaining wastes into products which can easily be absorbed by the soil. Recent developments in household septic systems have shown that aeration of the sewage can speed up detoxification, and produce a more stable and efficient system. For further details of aerobic sewage systems see Catalog.

Waste Transport Systems

The average waterflush toilet uses around five gallons of water per flush. In order to produce fuel gas from waste material, a solid to liquid ratio of about one to ten is required; the water flush toilet produces a solid to liquid ratio of approximately one to five hundred. Therefore, some other method of collecting and transporting human wastes must be found if we are to consider generating fuel gas.

An old-fashioned privy design can be economical and effective, but many people today would probably find it objectionable. Alternatively, the solid waste could be separated and filtered off from the transport water, but then much of the nitrogen in the urine would be lost, and another treatment system would have to be installed for the transport water. A better solution is a vacuum system.

Vacuum systems use negative pressure of between 7 and 10 pounds per square inch to suck the waste material in liquid "plugs" along the drainage lines. The pressure is maintained by a vacuum pump which is activated only when the pressure seal is broken by flushing the toilet. About three pints of water are required per flush, instead of the usual four or five gallons. The material collects in a holding tank at the end of each vacuum line where it can either be treated or transferred to a positive pressure sewer line or conventional septic tank. The vacuum pump[6] needed for a mobile rest room with four toilets, two urinals and four lavatory basins is run by a 1½ horse power motor. In a single family house, the pump, which only runs intermittently, would consume much less power.

The vacuum system offers many advantages to offset the additional power consumption and extra capital costs. It is less susceptible to blockages, even over long drainage lines. It allows for a smaller pipe diameter and for such flexibility that the pipes can even be laid on an upgrade. It prevents leaks at joints or even cracks. It eliminates the manholes and lift-stations of a positive pressure sewage system. In addition the volume of water consumed by the average household would be reduced by approximately ninety gallons a day, and the possibility of separating *black water* (toilet wastes) from *grey water* (other water wastes) allows for more efficient treatment of both.

[6]Manufactured by Envirovac division of Colt Industries.

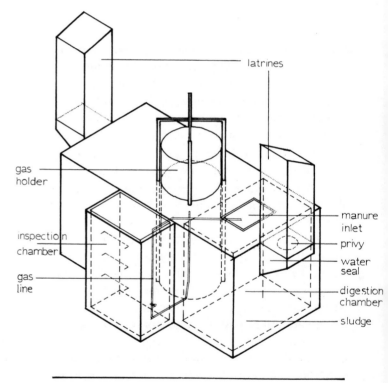

Outdoor privies built above methane digester and composting unit. Adapted from Reference 11.

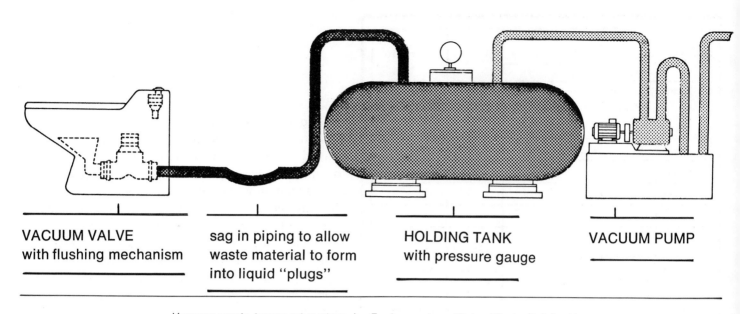

VACUUM VALVE
with flushing mechanism

sag in piping to allow
waste material to form
into liquid "plugs"

HOLDING TANK
with pressure gauge

VACUUM PUMP

Vacuum waste transport system, by Envirovac (see Water-Waste Catalog).

Methane Digesters

Once the toilet waste material has been collected in an airtight container without the addition of large amounts of water, anaerobic digestion will start to take place. Initially there will be some aerobic digestion yielding carbon dioxide, but the aerobic bacteria die as soon as they have used up the available dissolved oxygen. Then anaerobic digestion will begin. The series of highly complex bacterial processes leading to the production of methane can be simplified into two basic anaerobic stages. First, acid-producing bacteria convert most of the digestible waste (fats, proteins and most starches) into simpler compounds and volatile acids. In the second stage, another kind of bacteria feeds on the volatile acids and converts them into certain basic compounds, mainly methane, carbon dioxide and water.

Anaerobic digestors must maintain the correct environmental conditions for the bacteria to live. The acid-producing bacteria can exist in a wide range of conditions, but the methane-producing bacteria are more delicate. They work best at about 90-95 degrees Fahrenheit and will die if the temperature goes below 50 degrees Fahrenheit or above 115 degrees Fahrenheit. They also need a Ph level between 7.5 and 8.5 (relatively neutral). Excessive alkalinity or particularly acidity will kill the methane-producing bacteria.

In an efficient digester, the carbon to nitrogen ratio must be about thirty to one, though digestion can take place when the ratio is about sixty to one. In experiments with paper pulp added to raw sewage solids, it was found that the degradation of the cellulose content was as much as 90%, and that using paper for up to 60% of the total solids in the digester was feasible (or a C/N ratio of 45:1). Digester failure occurred when the C/N ratio reached 52:1. Many digesters are fed with farm manure which contains a considerable amount of bedding material (straw, hay, etc.). Since bedding material is very high in carbon, it balances the high nitrogen content of the animals' excretions. Human waste, however, has an even higher nitrogen content and therefore requires the addition of a great quantity of carboniferous (cellulose, for example newspaper, straw, etc.) material.

Organic wastes from the kitchen and garden, which decompose very easily, or cellulose material could provide the additional carbon. The cellulose, such as newspaper or paperbags, would have to be shredded and mixed in with the human waste.* If machinery were installed to shred cellulose waste products for use in the digester, the solid waste output of the house could be reduced by over 50 percent. Such a machine need not be much more expensive or complex than the conventional garbage disposal unit in the kitchen sink.

*G.E. Johnson has patented the idea of using coal to stabilize the digestion of sewage solids. See "The Production of Methane by Bacterial Action on a Mixture of Coal and Sewage Solids." G. E. Johnson, **Chemical Abstracts.** (1972).

Material	Production/day		% N	C/N ratio
	A	B		
Humans. Urine	2.2	0.13	18	
Feces	0.5	0.14	6	6-10
Cows	72.0	10.0	1.7	18
Horses	44.0	7.0	2.3	25
Pigs	11.5	1.5	3.8	
Sheep	4.5	0.5	3.8	
Chickens	0.3	0.1	6.3	15
Hay			2.5-4.0	12-20
Straw			0.5-1.1	48-150
Non-legume vegetables			2.5-4.0	11-19
Sawdust			0.1	200-500

A. Production/day in lbs. Total material
B. Production/day in lbs. Total solids
%age of Nitrogen measured from dry weight
  (Total solids)

Production per day and constituents of various animal and plant wastes. Reference 6.

Digesters can be fed either in batches or continuously. In batch-feeding, the empty digester is filled with raw material and sealed for three or four months while digestion takes place. Gas output begins after about two weeks, reaches a maximum after two more weeks, and then gradually declines until all the material has been digested. This system is equivalent to an aerobic compost heap where the organic material is allowed to ferment by itself. Batch-feeding is more suitable for vegetable matter which is often collected in large quantities and would not move easily through a continuous-feed system.

For sewage treatment however, a continuous-feed digester can more easily cope with the continuous production of waste and can recycle it faster. The size of the digester tank should be chosen according to both the rate at which waste material is produced and the length of the required "detention period" (the time the material remains in the digester). No more than two pounds of material per cubic foot of tank space should be added in one day, otherwise the bacteria will not be able to cope with the acidity of the raw material.

The detention period should be approximately forty days for complete digestion. At higher temperatures within the acceptable range, the detention period can be shorter; at lower temperatures it should be longer. Diluting the input material will also result in a shorter detention period, though an excessive amount of water will seriously hamper the methane-producing bacteria.

In an efficient continuous-feed digester more than half of the gas will be released in the first two weeks after the raw material is added. The rest of the gas is produced at a slower rate over the remaining weeks of the detention period. This pattern of fermentation has led to the development of two-stage digesters, which make use of the different rates of digestion.

The raw material is pumped into the bottom of the first tank. During the first stage of fermentation, it rises and overflows into the second tank. During the second, slower stage of fermentation it becomes more dense. It then sinks to the bottom of that tank. From there it is forced out by the pressure of the input material — ready for use as fertilizer.

*A two-stage anaerobic digester and gas collection system.
The main feed line from the holding tank
is shaded. The complex arrangement of valves and
feed pipes allows the pump to remove scum, to stir
the material in the digester or the holding tank,
and to empty the digester, all as separate operations.*

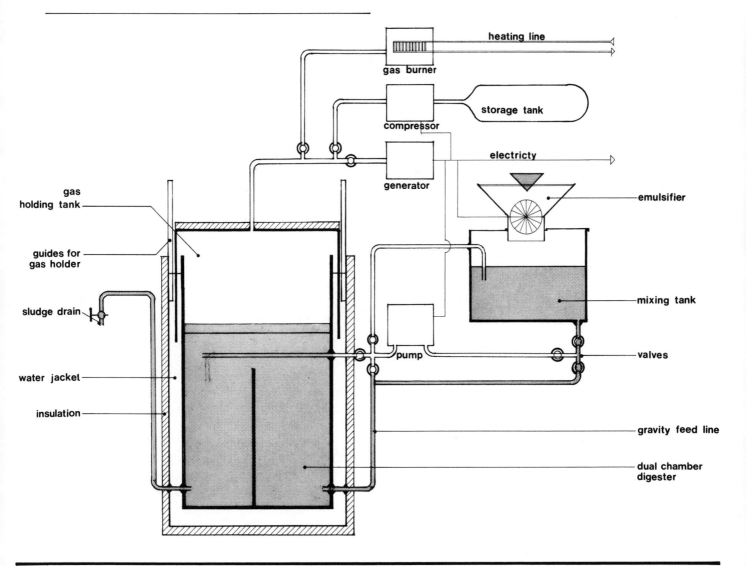

heating line

gas burner

storage tank

compressor

electricty

generator

emulsifier

gas
holding tank

guides for
gas holder

mixing tank

sludge drain

valves

pump

water jacket

insulation

gravity feed line

dual chamber
digester

Alton Eliason and Joe Pellicio with the methane digester they built on Alton's homestead in Northford, Connecticut. The digester, fed on chicken manure, produces gas to heat the greenhouse for a winter vegetable crop.

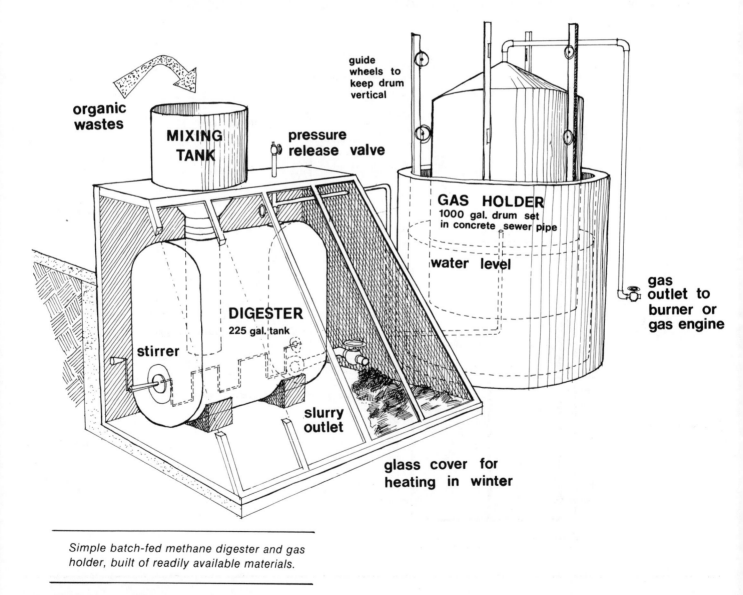

organic wastes

MIXING TANK

pressure release valve

guide wheels to keep drum vertical

GAS HOLDER
1000 gal. drum set in concrete sewer pipe

water level

gas outlet to burner or gas engine

DIGESTER
225 gal. tank

stirrer

slurry outlet

glass cover for heating in winter

Simple batch-fed methane digester and gas holder, built of readily available materials.

Gas Collection

The gas collected from a waste digester contains between 60 and 70 percent methane, about 30 percent carbon dioxide, and traces of oxygen, ammonia, nitrogen, etc. It burns with a clean flame and produces around 550-650 BTUs per cubic foot (methane-based natural gas produces about 1000 BTUs per cubic foot).

The rate of gas production depends on the nature and amount of input material and on the efficiency of the digestion process. One pound of input material normally produces just under one cubic foot of gas.

Ram Bux Singh suggests that vegetable matter can give up to seven times as much gas per pound if seeded with nitrogen, although the carbon dioxide content is higher. The Table opposite gives the rate of gas production for various experimental digesters.

The gas can easily be collected by bubbling it through water into an inverted tank, but storage for long periods of time could be difficult since the gas occupies a great deal of space. It can be compressed and stored in tanks, but this consumes both time and energy. It seems more reasonable to put the gas to use as it is produced, either by burning it to produce heat, or by using it to run a gas-powered motor or generator. If stored in compression tanks, the gas could be used to fuel an automobile with only slight alterations to the carburation system. Much of the gas could be used for running the various pumps and motors required by the sewage system itself. The amount of methane gas required for various uses is shown in the illustration.

Fertilizer

The "slurry" emitted from the digester is as valuable a bi-product as the gas. It contains more available nitrogen, fixed mainly in the form of ammonium salts, than the fertilizer from an aerobic compost heap made up of the same raw materials. It contains carbon and valuable trace elements — phosophorous, potassium, magnesium, iron, etc. — which are essential to plant growth. Storage need not present much of a problem. The residue from the digester is reduced to about one-third of its original volume and is largely solid. It can be piped from the digester to a suitable storage area until needed.

Available Energy

Material	Amount	Gas produced in cu.ft./lb A	B	% CH^4 in gas
Chicken manure	100%	5.0	0.8	59.8
Chicken manure Paper pulp	31% 69%	7.8	1.25	60.0
Chicken manure Newspaper	50% 50%	4.1	0.66	66.1
Chicken manure Grass clippings	50% 50%	5.9	0.94	68.1
Steer manure	100%	1.4	0.20	65.2
Steer manure Grass clippings	50% 50%	4.3	0.69	51.1
Pig manure	100%	7.5-10	1.2-1.6	
Cow manure	100%	4.0-6.0	0.6-0.9	
Chicken manure	100%	7.5-17	1.2-2.7	
Conventional sewage	100%	7.5-12	1.2-1.8	

A. Measured in Cu.ft./lb of volatile solids (i.e. potential digestible materials)
B. Measured in Cu.ft./lb of the total weight of input material.

Volume of gas produced from various digesters. The first six examples are laboratory experiments, the last four are working digesters.

Appliance	CU.FT.	Rate of Consumption.
Lighting	2.5	per mantle per hour
Cooking	8-16 12-15	per 2# 4"burners per hour per person per day
Gas Refrigerator	1.2	per hour per ft^2 of refrigerator space
Gasoline Engine at 25% efficiency	11.0	per hp hour

The consumption of gas by various appliances. 1 cubic foot of methane yields 950 BTUs. From Reference 6.

Water Recycling

The technologies for recycling the domestic water supply and for treating sewage are at similar stages of development. Many systems have been developed which are cost prohibitive. Some of the simpler filtration processes could be used efficiently, however, if the demand arose.

At present the recycling of water for domestic use is difficult because one water supply provides all the water for drinking, washing and toilet flushing. So far, little work has been done on the physiological and psychological effects of using recycled water for drinking, and many companies are understandably cautious about marketing the equipment. However, if drinking water came from another source, then the recycled water could be reserved for washing and toilet-flushing.

A small, enterprising community in Alaska recently installed a sewage treatment plant which returns water to each house only for toilet flushing. The returned water is the chlorinated effluent from a conventional secondary sewage treatment plant It is warmed by a heat exchanger from the incoming sewage and flows back to each house along an insulated duct which also contains the sewage pipe. Consequently, neither the sewage nor the return water is likely to freeze. In Alaska the shortage of water and the likelihood of freezing pipes justified the extra capital costs of the system.

The re-use of grey water for toilet flushing in homes could probably be economically justified by the savings in water costs over a long time period. Such a system would require some simple filtration equipment to prevent the build-up of impurities in the toilet tanks and would require a pump to raise the water from the small filtration plant to the toilets.

The recycling of grey water for washing and bathing requires more treatment and also the understanding that not every faucet would provide potable water. The main elements to be removed from grey water are scum, grease, suspended solids, and dissolved salts — particularly phosphates from soap and detergents. A grease trap, which is a standard plumbing fixture, can cope with both the scum and the grease. The addition of alum (or other metallic salts) as a "coagulant" will precipitate up to 95 percent of the dissolved phosphates which can then be filtered out.

There are various types of filters available for industrial use which could also be employed in domestic water treatment. A filter capable of removing suspended solids would be required. This could be provided by a standard vertical pressure filter along with an "in-depth" filter bed of sand or anthracite. If necessary, a second filter of

Vertical pressure filter suitable for large scale water filtration. Manufactured by Crane Co. P.O. Box 191, King of Prussia, Pa. 19406.

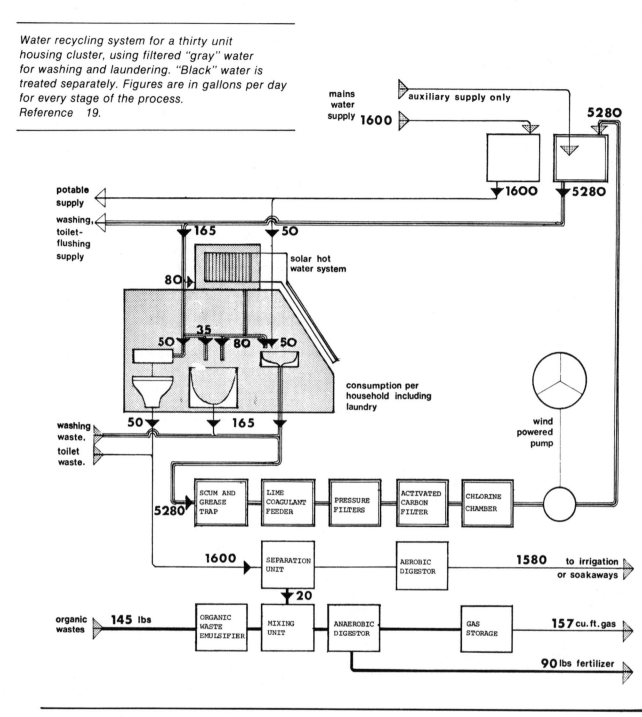

Water recycling system for a thirty unit housing cluster, using filtered "gray" water for washing and laundering. "Black" water is treated separately. Figures are in gallons per day for every stage of the process.
Reference 19.

mains water supply 1600   auxiliary supply only   5280

1600   5280

potable supply

washing, toilet-flushing supply

165   50

solar hot water system

80

35
50   80   50

consumption per household including laundry

washing waste.
toilet waste.

50   165

wind powered pump

5280

| SCUM AND GREASE TRAP | LIME COAGULANT FEEDER | PRESSURE FILTERS | ACTIVATED CARBON FILTER | CHLORINE CHAMBER |

1600   SEPARATION UNIT   AEROBIC DIGESTOR   1580   to irrigation or soakaways

20

organic wastes   145 lbs   ORGANIC WASTE EMULSIFIER   MIXING UNIT   ANAEROBIC DIGESTOR   GAS STORAGE   157 cu. ft. gas

90 lbs fertilizer

activated carbon could be installed in the same unit to oxidize dissolved organic substances and remove odor. The sand filter would require backwashing regularly to remove the collected solids; this would be accomplished automatically at times of low flow. The carbon would have to be either replaced every few months or regenerated by "burning" — a fairly simple operation. Filtration equipment is available with automatic coagulant feeding and surface backwashing.

Gray water could be recycled for washing and toilet flushing in a cluster of 30 houses, using the procedures already mentioned. In such a situation the benefits of cost-sharing, the greater efficiency of large scale water treatment, and the savings in water consumption (approximately an 80 percent reduction in average household consumption) could offset the extra capital and maintenance costs of the system.

Costing

So far small scale methane digesters have only been constructed to deal with farm manure. A number of large scale, sewage treatment plants use the methane they generate to run the plant; they burn off any excess gas because the gas is uneconomical to collect and store.

Ram Bux Singh, director of the Gobar Gas Research Station in Ajitmal, India and one of the world's experts on methane digesters, is partly responsible for the 2500 methane generators currently working in various parts of India. He has suggested that the same principles of decentralized waste treatment, using the low impact technology employed in India, could be modified to suit the single family house in the United States.

A small scale digester, run on household wastes and human excrement, could produce a valuable amount of gas. The heat for the digester could be provided by the warm waste water from the kitchen and bathroom. Pumps would be needed to force the raw material through the digester. A shredder to grind up the cellulose and organic wastes and an agitator, to keep the digestion material moving, could also be added. These energy consuming additions to the basic system would reduce maintenance and make the digester virtually automatic.

This system, which sounds ideal for dealing with household wastes, is not overly practical. Amount and content of human excretion varies considerably according to diet. In a normal household, the amount of toilet waste will vary from day to day according to the number of occupants present, but a digester, to run efficiently, requires a regular input of digestible material. The smaller the digester the more likely the cessation of bacterial action due to disturbances in the temperature, acidity, or consistency of the input

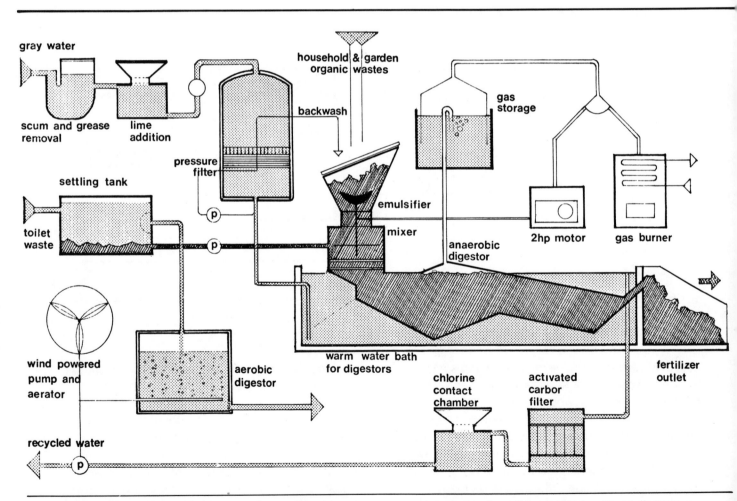

Waste treatment and water recycling system for a thirty unit housing cluster. A continuous-feed methane digester treats solid wastes. A simple filtration system recycles 80% of the water used. From References. 19.

material. It is even more likely that the volume of gas produced per day — a maximum of twelve cubic feet — will not be worth the money to collect. For single house units it would be more worthwhile to use an aerobic digester, such as the "Clivus" unit, which, though it will not produce fuel gas, is a conveniently prepackaged system which reduces water consumption, disposes of organic wastes, and produces high quality fertilizer.

Anaerobic systems become much more feasible for housing clusters. A proposed waste treatment system is shown for a cluster of approximately thirty houses. Toilet wastes, organic kitchen and garden wastes and a large quantity of cellulose material from the solid waste output of each house are all fed into the digester. The Table opposite gives the estimates of dry weight and volatile solids available per day from such a community, and the probable yield in methane gas. The maximum and minimum estimates are given at each stage of the calculations, since there is little reliable experimental data. Even assuming the minimum output per day, there is more than enough gas to run the necessary mechanical apparatus.

There is very little information available on the cost of methane digesters, and any estimates of their economic practicality are bound to be very approximate. Taking the system shown here however, and assuming an average gas production of 300 cubic feet per day, the accumulated value of the gas collected over twenty years would be around 22,500 dollars (assuming the cost of methane remains at 1.00 dollar per 100 cubic feet — a figure based on the current cost of propane at about 2.4 dollars per cubic foot **

This figure represents an initial investment of about 9,500 dollars, amortized at 10 percent over the twenty year period. Maintenance and operation of the system would be no more than for any other on-site treatment plant, except for the periodic removal and distribution of the sludge, which should pay for itself in fertilizer value. To be economically feasible, therefore, a low-cost anaerobic system must not cost 10,000 dollars more than any other waste treatment system. This should be possible in constructing new housing clusters or large buildings which lack nearby sewer lines, and therefore require on-site sewage treatment.

Daily input and output of an anaerobic digester for a thirty unit housing cluster. From Reference 19.

	max	min
Human waste output per day:		
Feces / person / day lbs	0.5	0.5
From 60-80 people	30.0	40.0
Dry weight of this (27%)	8.1	10.8
Weight of nitrogen (6%)	0.48	0.64
Weight of carbon (48%)	3.84	5.12
Urine / person / day lbs	2.2	2.2
Collectable amount	0.5	1.1
From 60-80 people	30.0	88.0
Dry weight of this (6%)	1.8	5.28
Weight of nitrogen (18%)	0.32	0.90
Weight of carbon (18%)	0.32	0.90
Organic Waste / household / day	1.0	3.0
From 32 units	32.0	96.0
Organic waste from garden	5.0	20.0
Total organic wastes available	37.0	116.0
Dry weight of this(10-20%)	3.7	28.0
Weight of nitrogen (3%)	0.10	0.74
Weight of carbon (50%)	1.85	14.0
Shredded cellulose material, waste paper etc., to make up the required C/N ratio:		
Household output / day	3.5	3.5
Volume req'd by digestor	90.0	250.0
Dry weight of this (50%)	45.0	125.0
Weight of nitrogen (0.1%)	0.05	0.12
Weight of carbon (50%)	22.5	62.5
Total dry weight added	58.6	169.1
Weight of Carbon	28.5	72.5
Weight of Nitrogen	0.95	2.4
C/N Ratio	1:30	1:30
Total volatile solids added / day (60% of dry weight)	35.16	101.46
Volume of gas produced at 5-7 cu.ft. of gas per lb of volatile solids	157.8	710.2
Cu.ft. of methane 60-70%	102.5	497.1
Volume of methane used to drive emulsifier, 2hp. motor for 1 hour	22.0	22.0
Remaining gas	80.5	475.1
B.T.U. value of this	76500.0	390000.0

*Calculated according to L. John Fry's system. Consult References and Further Readings.

**For bottled propane in small quantities.

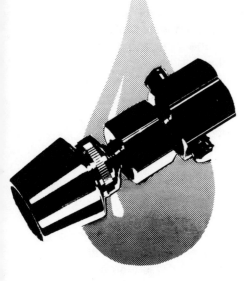

	Purchase and Installation cost.	Yearly Savings—4 person family.
1. Flow control Showers	$ 50	$12
2. Reduced Flush Toilets	$110	$15
3. Dual flush Toilets	$ 30	$20
4. Vacuum Flush Toilets (on basis of 100 homes)	$295	$31
5. Washing Machine (extra cost for level controls)	$ 35	$ 2

*Estimated installation costs and yearly savings of various flow reduction devices (for a family of four). From Reference 4.***

Water Conservation

According to one report published in 1967, the average or typical household in the United States spent between $57 and $87 each year on water and sewage systems depending on the service provided. These figures are probably closer to 100 dollars now, due to general inflation.* In areas without public sewage systems, the average revenue charge for metered water in 1967 was 68 cents per 1000 gallons. At this price there is little to encourage the public to conserve water.

Various "flow reduction" devices are available, however, which will pay for themselves over a number of years by reducing water costs. Also available are flush toilets which use only three to four gallons of water per flush as compared with the usual five gallons. "Dual flush" toilets which only use one gallon of water when urine is to be disposed of, can provide an overall savings of around 2½ gallons. Spray faucets can be as effective as conventional ones and only use half as much water, and pressurized "atomizers" could theoretically provide a whole shower-bath with only one pint of water. The purchase cost and yearly savings for a number of water-saving devices currently available is shown above.

Recycling the household water supply requires the installation and maintenance of some kind of filtration system. It has already been estimated that even the reuse of bath water for toilet flushing would ultimately cost more than the corresponding saving due to reduced water consumption. However, on a larger scale the treatment of water for reuse in the household becomes more feasible. The system outlined in the illustration, recycling (washing water in a cluster of 32 houses), would provide an overall savings of around $4.70 per day (at 70 cents per 1000 gallons), which, over a period of 20 years would amount to over 35,000 dollars. It is difficult to estimate how much of this saving would be offset by maintenance and operation costs, but it seems reasonable to assume that a filtration system would pay for itself. Given a situation where the only alternative is a large septic field, the benefits of an above ground recycling system would be considerable.

*Bailey and Wallman in *Reference 4.* quote the average cost of water supply and sewage treatment per household as $90/year.

For this and other interesting ideas on water conservation and recycling see **The Ecol Operation, *Reference 20*

House Design

Water-Waste Systems and Housing: A Note on Rainwater Collection

If all washing were recycled and a vacuum system or "Clivus" unit were used for toilet wastes, then the overall household water consumption would be reduced to about 50 gallons per day (for drinking and cooking). If well water were not available, then the supply could be provided by collecting, filtering and storing rain water.

The minimum average rainfall per month in New Haven, Connecticut, for example, is 3.2 inches. To provide the requirement of 1500 gallons per month, assuming a loss of 20 percent by evaporation, would require a collection area of 840 square feet. This area is not much larger than the roof area of the average house. Rain water would therefore be used as a decentralized water source. One of the major problems would be the absorption of atmospheric pollutants, particularly lead. In other parts of the world, where water is a more valuable resource, and is not readily available, rain water collection from the roof of the house could become very worthwhile.•••

••• The Brace Research Institute has conducted a comprehensive study of the economics of rainwater collection. *Reference 4.*

The Greenhouse

A self-contained waste treatment facility needs to be located near the house in order to reduce the length of sewage pipes. If a digester or composter is used, it must be near a garden or other area where the sludge fertilizer can easily be put to use.

An anaerobic system would require less heating if it were in a sheltered space. A greenhouse extension to a house provides an ideal situation for above-ground, waste treatment facility. It is heated by solar energy; it is convenient for accepting wastes from toilets, kitchen, and from the greenhouse itself; and provides a visual statement about the connection between man and plant life in which waste recycling is so important.

The "House for People and Plants" (next page) is a fanciful representation of how this and other relationships could be expressed in architectural terms. The same ideas could be used in more conventional house forms. The glass house could function as a semi-conditioned space — as a protection for the living area of the house in winter — and as an extension of the living area at other times of the year. It would absorb, and could be made to retain, solar energy; it could serve as a rain water collector and provide fresh vegetables all year round. As plate glass windows become less common in houses designed to conserve energy, the "greenhouse" could well become more important as an additional living space.

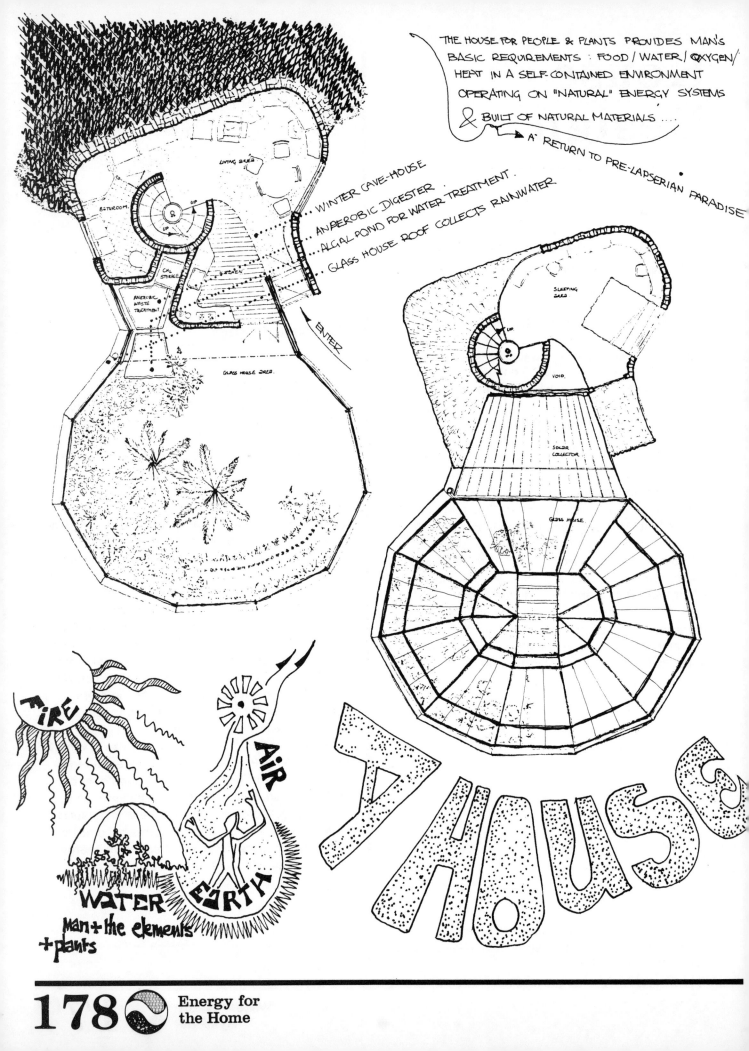

THE HOUSE FOR PEOPLE & PLANTS PROVIDES MAN'S
BASIC REQUIREMENTS : FOOD / WATER / OXYGEN /
HEAT IN A SELF-CONTAINED ENVIRONMENT
OPERATING ON "NATURAL" ENERGY SYSTEMS
& BUILT OF NATURAL MATERIALS ....
A RETURN TO PRE-LAPSERIAN PARADISE

· WINTER CAVE-HOUSE
· ANAEROBIC DIGESTER
· ALGAL POND FOR WATER TREATMENT.
· GLASS HOUSE ROOF COLLECTS RAINWATER

LIVING AREA

BATHROOM

COAL STORAGE

ANAEROBIC WASTE TREATMENT

KITCHEN

GLASS HOUSE AREA.

ENTER

SLEEPING AREA

VOID.

SOLAR COLLECTOR

GLASS HOUSE

FIRE

AIR

WATER

EARTH

Man + the elements
+ plants

A HOUSE

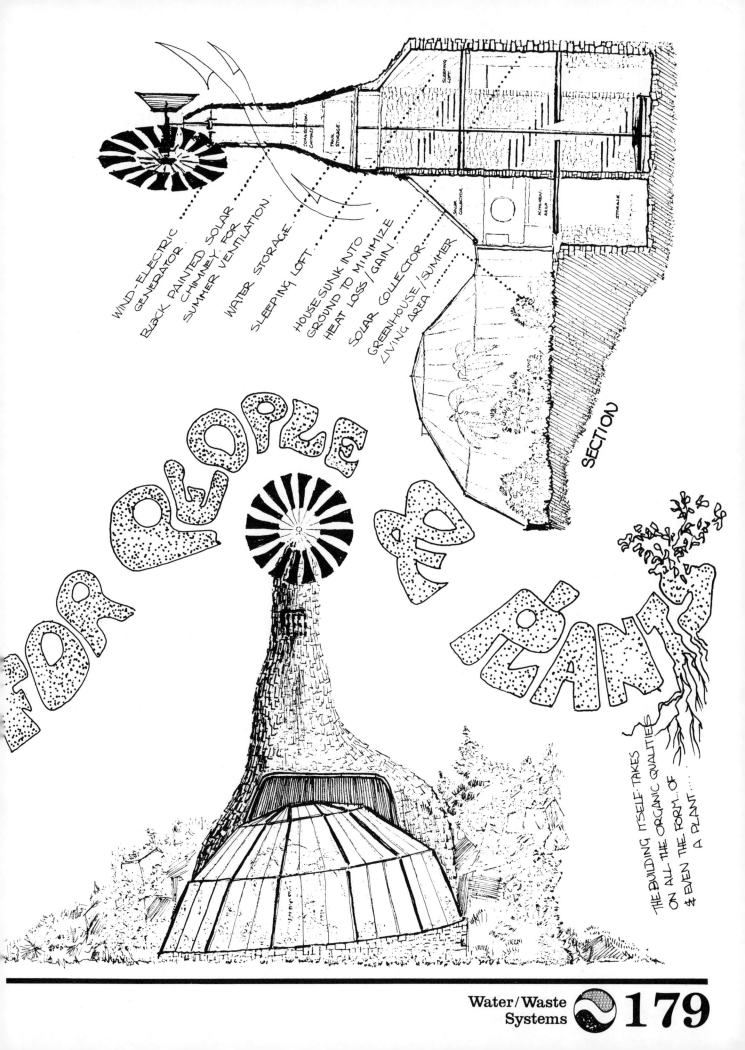

WIND-ELECTRIC GENERATOR

BLACK PAINTED SOLAR CHIMNEY FOR SUMMER VENTILATION

WATER STORAGE

SLEEPING LOFT

HOUSE SUNK INTO GROUND TO MINIMIZE HEAT LOSS/GAIN

SOLAR COLLECTOR

GREENHOUSE/SUMMER LIVING AREA

SECTION

FOR PEOPLE AS PLANTS

THE BUILDING ITSELF TAKES ON ALL THE ORGANIC QUALITIES & EVEN THE FORM... OF A PLANT....

References

1 **Bio-gas Plants: Their Installation, Operation, Maintenance and Use.** M. A. Indiani and C. M. Acharye. Indian Council of Agricultural Research. New Delhi. 1963.

2 **Cleaning Our Environment.** American Chemical Society. New York, 1971.

3 "Directory of the Composting/Organic Waste Recycling Industry". **Compost Science: Journal of Waste Recycling.** January-February 1971.

4 "Flow Reduction and Waste Water from Households". Bailey and Wallman. **Water and Sewage Works.** March 1973.

5 "Literature Review: Water Reclamation and Reuse; Anaerobic Processes." **Journal of the Water Pollution Control Federation.** 45.6. June 1973.

6 **Methane Digesters for Fuel Gas and Fertilizer.** R. Merrill and L. J. Fry. New Alchemy Institute. Woods Hole, Massachusetts, 1973.

7 "Solar Energy: Plant Power." Colin Moorcroft. **Architectural Design.** January 1974 and February 1974.

8 **A Study of Residential Water Use.** F. P. Linaweaver. The Department of Housing and Urban Development. Washington D.C. 1967.

9 "Anaerobic Digestion of Solid Wastes." S. A. Klein. **Compost Science: Journal of Waste Recycling.** January-February 1972.

10 "The Ecological House." Graham Caine. **Architectural Design.** March 1972.

11 "How to Generate Electric Power from Garbage." C. E. Burr. **Mother Earth News.** Number 3, 1967.

12 **Composting.** H. B. Gotass. World Health Organization Monograph Number 31, 1956.

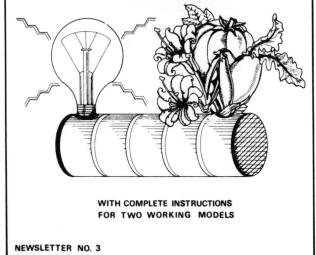

NEW ALCHEMY INSTITUTE

METHANE DIGESTERS
FOR FUEL GAS AND FERTILIZER

WITH COMPLETE INSTRUCTIONS
FOR TWO WORKING MODELS

NEWSLETTER NO. 3

13 "Gobar Gas; Methane Experiments in India." **Mother Earth News.** Number 12, 1969.

14 "Interview sith Ram Bux Singh." **Mother Earth News.** Number 18, 1973.

15 "Microbial Formation of Methane." R. S. Wolfe. **Chemical Abstracts.** 76. 17. 966690t. 1972.

16 "Partial Recycle: A New Sewage System." R. D. Buchanan. **Water and Sewage Works.** January 1972.

17 "Production of Methane by Bacterial Action on a Mixture of Coal and Sewage Sludge." G. E. Johnson. **Chemical Abstracts.** 72. 24. 144650d. 1972.

18 "Use of Solar Energy in Waste Disposal." W. Oswald. **The International Conference on Solar and Aeolian Energy.** Athens. 1961.

19 **Eco-Unity.** Peter Clegg and Ryc Loope. A Project for a cluster of self-sufficient housing. Award-winning Entry for the A.I.A./A.S.C. competition on Energy conservation and Building Design, Yale University 1972.

20 **The Ecol Operation,** A. Ortega et. al. 1972. Available from the Minimum Cost Housing Group, McGill University School of Architecture, Montreal, Canada.

Further Readings

A Homesite Power Unit: Methane Generator. Les Auerbach, William Olkowski, and Ben Katz. Available from Les Auerbach, 242 Copse Road, Madison, Connecticut 06443.

Let it Rot! The Home Gardener's Guide to Composting. Stu Campbell. Garden Way Publishing. Charlotte, Vermont. 1974.

"Biological Conversion of Light Energy to the Chemical Energy of Methane." C. Golueke and W. Oswald. **Applied Microbiology.** 7: 219-227.

"Power from Solar Energy via Algae-Produced Methane." C. Golueke and W. Oswald. **Solar Energy.** 1968. 7(3):86-92.

"Sludge Gas as Fuel for Motor Vehicles." K. Imhoff and C. Keefer. **Water Sewage Works.** 1952. 99:284.

"Methane Gas — An Overlooked Energy Source." S. A. Klein. **Organic Gardening and Farming.** June 1972, pages 98-101.

"Aquaculture: Toward an Ecological Approach." W. McLarney in **Radical Agriculture.** Richard Merrill, ed., Harper and Row, New York; see also "Efficiency in Agriculture: The Economics of Energy." M. Perelman in the same work.

"Methane Production from Farm Wastes as a Source of Tractor Fuel." G. Rosenberg. **J. Min. Agric.** (England) 1952. 58:487-94.

"Anaerobic Digestion of Poultry Wastes." Eliseos P. Taiganides. **World Poultry Science Journal.** October-December 1963, pages 252-62.

Volunteers in Technical Assistance (VITA) has plans for a methane generator. A catalog of "Village Technology Plans" is available by writing to 3706 Rhode Island Avenue, Mount Ranier, Maryland 20822.

EWP

AMERICAN STANDARD

Colt Industries

pollutrol technology inc.

CLIVUS MULTRUM

Cycle-Let

WATER/ WASTE SYSTEMS CATALOG

Dear Reader,

The information appearing on the following pages was forwarded to us from the manufacturer or organization whose name appears in the book. We wrote to each organization requesting information about the work it was doing in the particular field of energy in question, explaining that they were welcome to send to us whatever copy they thought would represent them well.

Our goal was and is to make this helpful information available to you, the reader. Should you become interested in obtaining a product or further information from one of the companies displayed herein, we request that you **not** write to Garden Way Publishing Company but directly to that particular company whose product or research interests you.

clivus multrum

The simplest, cleanest and most efficient piece of equipment for aerobic composting of all kinds of organic wastes. It is now manufactured under license in the States.

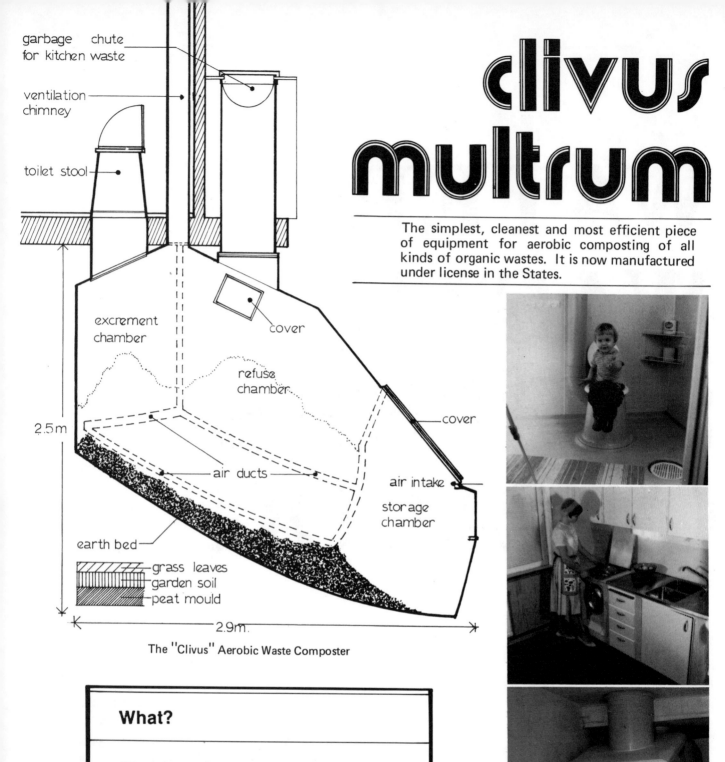

garbage chute for kitchen waste

ventilation chimney

toilet stool

excrement chamber

cover

refuse chamber

cover

air intake

2.5m

air ducts

storage chamber

earth bed

grass leaves
garden soil
peat mould

2.9m.

The "Clivus" Aerobic Waste Composter

What?

Clivus Multrum is a self-contained system for the treatment of organic household wastes. It places toilet and kitchen wastes into an environment where they decompose slowly by composting, producing a humus which can be returned directly to the soil. Multrum uses no water, no energy and no chemicals of any kind. It is not connected to sewers as it has no liquid effluent. It has no moving parts, so requires virtually no maintenance. Capacity ranges from 4-6 people for small unit, to 10-14 for the large unit with mid-sections.
Clivus Multrum means literally "inclining compost room."

Why?

Multrum is designed to meet the need for a convenient, hygenic and natural means of converting organic household wastes into a useful product. Unlike any standard waste treatment system, Multrum solves the major problems in this area without creating new ones (e.g., pollution, waste of energy, loss of nutrients) in the process. It uses no water thus saving 40-50% of that used in an average household, or 10,000 gallons per person per year. It uses no energy except what is supplied by the microorganisms which do the work. The wastes are converted to a usable product on the site so need no transportation to remote treatment plants. In short, the Multrum eliminates the very notion of "waste" and, as such, is truly a device for the post industrial age.

How?

It is simple. The Multrum consists of a large impervious container with tubes connected to toilet and kitchen garbage inlets, and a vent pipe which carries away all odors as well as water vapor and CO_2 produced by the decomposition process. The tank is partitioned into three chambers. The upper one receives toilet wastes, the middle one kitchen garbage. The combined wastes decompose at the same time as they settle and slide slowly down the inclined bottom. By the time the material reaches the storage chamber it is converted to humus. It takes 2-3 years for the first humus to reach the storage chamber. After this time 3-10 gallons of soil may be removed per person per year. The process is from this time on continuous.

Where?

The Multrum is suited for new and existing buildings, vacation homes, campgrounds and small industrial and commercial facilities.

It may be installed indoors (first or second floor), beneath a house in a full or partial basement, or outside as in a comfort station for campgrounds or forest stations.

It may be used seasonally or year round.

It can be placed on or below grade.

Households with a Multrum need to provide for the separate disposal of dish, laundry and bath water.

★ installed in over 2000 Scandinavian homes

CLIVUS MULTRUM:

ORGANIC WASTE TREATMENT SYSTEM.

CLIVUS MULTRUM USA
14 A ELIOT ST.
CAMBRIDGE, MASS. 02138

The price of the Multrum ranges upwards from $975 depending upon size and parts needed. There are two basic sizes: a small model 8 ft. long and a large model almost 10 ft. long. Mid-sections can be added to both models to increase capacity. Cost does not include installation or transportation.

Background information

It is a law of nature that all organic material returns to the soil so that it can provide nutrition for new life.

This cycle has unfortunately been broken for some decades now, the result being depressingly obvious in the form of water pollution.

Sewage outlets are among the worst water pollutants. The availability of clean water is one of the primary conditions for the existence of human life.

Our Humus-Toilet re-establishes natural laws by creating the conditions necessary for the return of nutritive mould to earth. The Humus-Toilet once again closes the natural cycle and thereby improves the structure of our earth.

Function

The sewage is dehumidified through a patented re-circulation system. The air, which is pumped through this system 200—250 times, becomes saturated with moisture before it is carried out through the ventilation pipe. This means that there is no risk of surplus liquid. The re-circulation process also creates a completely natural, **odourless** and optimum breakdown of excrement, urine and kitchen refuse.

Since the humidity in the re-circulating air should be constant the whole time, no matter how many people are using the toilet, a control unit has been fitted on the air outlet. This control is graduated from 0 to 6. There is a hygrometer on the right-hand side of the air outlet to help make the correct setting. The humidity value should be between 65% and 90%.

The temperature of the 15 000 gallons of air re-circulating each hour through the mould formation zone is perfect for the necessary bacteria-growth at 30—35° C/ 85—90° F.

This temperature is attained by means of a thermostat-controlled heating unit above the fan.

When the lid is lowered the stirrer begins to function. This is fully automatic and is intended to ensure even distribution of the pile of sewage, and thereby accelerate the mould formation process.

After having been in daily use for ONE YEAR by 4—5 people, all that remains is about 25 kg (55 lbs.) of garden mould. This mould passes through the lowest screen and continues down into the two connecting boxes which are emptied about once a year. The mould is then completely odourless and is exceptionally suitable as fertilizer. You can easily check the amount of mould at any time by simply looking through the small glass windows located on the cover at the bottom.
Each Humus-Toilet is delivered with a patented diffusor, which functions as a very effective rain protector, decreases resistance in the ventilation pipe and creates a favourable outlet diffusion of 2.5 : 1.

HUMUMAT ltd.

9403-120th STREET
DELTA, B.C.
CANADA V4C 2P3
TELEPHONE (604) 588-5955

humumat

The Humus toilet is similar to the Clivus unit, only it is more compact and uses electrical energy to provide heat and dehumidification and to turn the stirrer in each unit. With these sophisticated controls it is possible to speed up the bacterial processes and thereby minimize the size of the composting chamber. The "mould boxes" collect high quality fertilizer and are emptied about once a year.

Technical data

Material:
Impact-resistant pressed polythene

Ventilation pipe:
PVC standard 2″ (50 mm) or 2,8″ (70 mm)
Pipe to be insulated in attic and over roof

Dimensions:

Width	53 cm (21″)
Height	70 cm (27,5″)
Length	76 cm (30″)
Step	20 cm (8″)
Seat height (from step)	42 cm (16,5″)

Floor area required 55 x 115 cm (21,7 x 45,3″)

Weight:
50 lbs. (22,7 kg)

Electrical connection:
One-Phase, 110 V, 6 A fuse or 220 V

Electrical system:
110/48 V tranformer or
220/48 V transformer
Heater unit (thermostat control): 160 W
Fan and Motor: 20 W

Installation:
Electric plug and ventilation pipe with diffusor

Guarantee:
One year factory guarantee

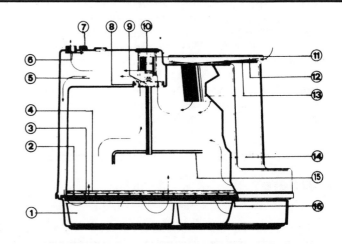

1. Two connected mould boxes
2. Bacteria channel
3. Screen
4. Cellulose tissue mat
5. Pressure chamber
6. Hygrometer
7. Ventilation pipe
8. Air control outlet
9. Fan
10. Thermostat-controlled heater unit
11. Stirrer
12. Cover
13. Seat
14. Funnel
15. Stirrer
16. Mould box cover

Energy for the Home

Operational Flow Diagram

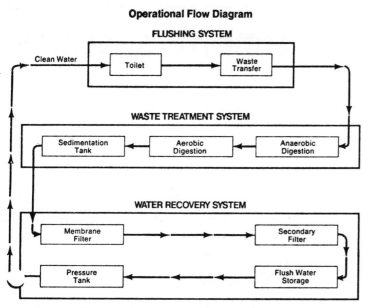

FLUSHING SYSTEM

Clean Water → Toilet → Waste Transfer

WASTE TREATMENT SYSTEM

Sedimentation Tank ← Aerobic Digestion ← Anaerobic Digestion

WATER RECOVERY SYSTEM

Membrane Filter → Secondary Filter

Pressure Tank ← Flush Water Storage

Cycle-Let treatment unit with cover removed.

At last, a toilet waste treatment system with no discharge. That needs no hookup to sewers, septic tanks, disposal fields or holding tanks. That needs no permanent hookup to a fresh water supply, either. Cycle-let® from Thetford Corp. flushes toilets with clear, clean recycled water. This recycling closed-loop toilet waste treatment system is designed to handle all toilet wastes from eight persons on a 24 hour per day basis--or the wastes from 24 persons on an 8 hour per day basis. It can save up to 80,000 gallons of fresh water per year, and eliminate need to process sewage from those 80,000 gallons, The amazingly compact treatment unit is installed indoors. The recycled water for flushing is clear, clean and odorless.

How Cycle-Let® works.

Cycle-Let® is basically a complete and sophisticated sewage treatment plant in an amazingly compact package. The treatment section occupies little more space than a large refrigerator. It digests human waste and recycles flushing water, restoring it to a clear, clean, and odor-free state. One treatment unit can treat waste from one, two or more toilets.

Water recovery system

First, a special membrane filter separates virtually all suspended solids and bacteria from the water. Then water flows through the secondary filter where activated carbon effectively removes odors and colors. Next, water enters into a storage tank, and finally to the pressure tank. Now clean and odor-free, the water awaits reuse for flushing the toilet again.---The entire system holds about 175 gallons when charged for operation.

Maintenance is simple

Four times each year a Cycle-Let® service man inspects the unit and performs preventative maintenance. The service is free the first year of operation. Each year, your service man will replace air filters, fuses, etc. as you have done on your air conditioning unit.

Specifications, Cycle-Let treatment unit

Height	75 in. (190 cm.)
Width	32 in. (81 cm.)
Depth	42 in. (107 cm.)
Weight, dry	325 lbs. (147 kg.)
Operating weight	1,650 lbs. (748 kg.)
Power consumption	450 KW-HR/mo.
Capacity (approximate)	48 flushes per day

The Cycle-Let® is the first commercially available water-flush toilet which actually recycles its own flushing water. It should save about 40% of your household water supply.

For further information, write or phone:

Thetford Corporation
Waste Treatment Equipment Division
P.O. Box 1285
Ann Arbor, Michigan 48106
Telephone (313) 769-6000

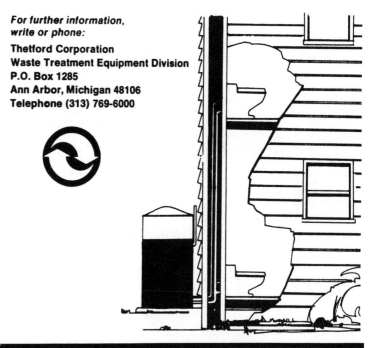

aerobic waste treatment systems

Aerobic waste treatment systems eliminate the sludge build-up of coventional septic tank systems, and reduce the likelihood of flooding. In many cases they can also lead to a reduction in the size of the leechfield. The key element in an aerobic system is a small electrical compressor which aerates the sewage and thus speeds up the digestion process. Provision needs to be made for a power failure, however, and at present very few authorities will permit aerobic systems.

pollutrol

32 Kearney Rd.   Needham Heights, Mass. 02194   Tel. (617) 449-4840

Pollutrol Industries manufactures a wide range of equipment for small-scale waste treatment. Each unit contains two aeration chambers. The first absorbs shock loads and introduces activated sludge for bacterial decomposition; the second is an extended aeration and settling chamber where the clean liquid is filtered off and the sludge returns to the first chamber. The waste liquid can be chlorinated and released into natural waterways.

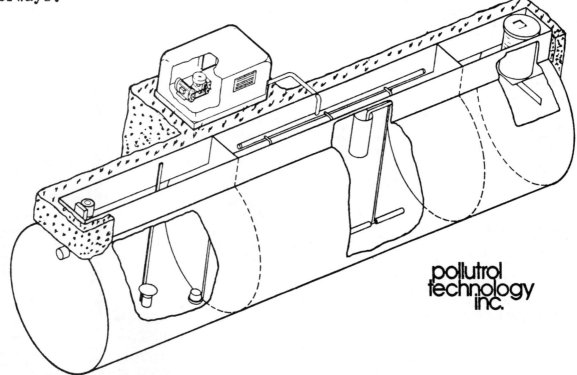

pollutrol
technology
inc.

The Microx is the smallest unit manufactured by Pollutrol Industries, - suitable for single family installations.

CERTIFICATION OF PURITROL PROCESS DATA
BY THE NATIONAL SANITATION FOUNDATION

A Puritrol Sewage Treatment Plant, Model 3M (3000 GPD) has successfully completed the program of testing at the National Sanitation Foundation Testing Laboratory. Complete certified data is available from Pollutrol Technology.

Following is a condensation of two important parameters, BOD and Suspended Solids. Figures are average of values for each of the two test phases.

	Influent	Effluent	Reduction %
SUBDIVISION FLOW PATTERN			
(16-hour runoff pattern)			
Suspended Solids (mg/1)	181	9	95
Biochemical Oxygen Demand (mg/1)	257	15	94
STEADY STATE FLOW PATTERN			
(8-hour runoff-school)			
Suspended Solids (mg/1)	210	8	96
Biochemical Oxygen Demand (mg/1)	303	15	95

Please note that the above treatment efficiencies were achieved by the Puritrol Process of secondary treatment alone. No filtering or tertiary treatment was used. The addition of a filter will give an even higher quality effluent.

MICROX Installation Is Simple...

A SMALL EXCAVATION TO CONTAIN ONE OF THE UNITS DESCRIBED BELOW, HOOKUP OF INLET AND OUTLET LINES, AND PROVISIONS FOR ELECTRICAL POWER (110 VOLT, 20 AMP USING #10 DIRECT BURIAL CABLE) ARE ALL THAT IS REQUIRED. POLLUTROL INSTALLS THE INTERNALS AND STARTS UP THE UNIT.

SECONDARY TREATMENT
Microx provides secondary treatment which gives the same quality effluent as discharged from modern municipal plants.

CHLORINATION
Chlorine treatment can easily be provided to meet the regulations for waterway discharge.

NO SHOCK LOAD PROBLEMS
Operating by an exclusive patented batch process, Microx eliminates shock loading caused by periodic high volume flows.

AUTOMATIC OPERATION
Microx units require minimal attention. Operation is completely automatic.

FEW MAINTENANCE REQUIREMENTS
High quality equipment and components assure the Microx owner of dependable, trouble free operation.

SERVICE CONTRACTS
Under contract, Pollutrol technicians will provide maintenance and service for your Microx unit.

CLEAN, ODOR FREE EFFLUENT
The purity of the Microx effluent eliminates dangerous health hazards.

CLEAN, ODOR FREE PROCESS
Microx extended aeration duplicates Nature's own clean process of biodegredation.

EASY DISPOSAL
The high quality effluent easily meets state and local regulations for a number of disposal methods.

LONGER LASTING ABSORPTION BEDS
The clear effluent and superior efficiency of the batch dosing system assures longer life for your absorption bed. Unlike conventional systems, there is no buildup of slime, sludge or fungus that can plug the field.

WATERWAY DISCHARGE
Microx effluent, after chlorine treatment, may be discharged into any suitable flowing waterway without fear of damage to our environment.

MICROX PROVEN RECORD
The unique Microx process is the result of extensive research and years of testing, both in the laboratory and in the field with operating units.

Steel Tank	Concrete Tank
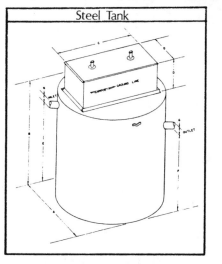	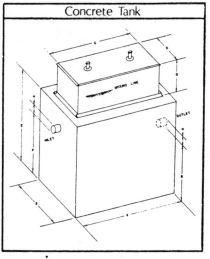

DIMENSION	A	B	C	D	E	F	G
300 GPD II	54	60	41	24	50	46	4
500 GPD III	65	63	50	24	52	47	4
600 GPD II	65	63	50	24	52	47	4
1000 GPD III	84	72	60	24	63	58	6
1250 GPD II	84	72	60	24	63	58	6

DIMENSION	A	B	C	D	E	F	G	H
650 GPD III	96	48	81	24	78	69	65	4
750 GPD II	96	48	81	24	78	69	65	4

FOLLOWING ARE PRICES ON MICROX PACKAGED BATCH SYSTEM SEWAGE TREATMENT PLANTS. THESE ARE COMPLETE SYSTEMS CONSISTING OF A THREE COMPARTMENTED PLANT, POSITIVE DISPLACEMENT BLOWERS, DIFFUSERS, ALL INTERNAL MECHANICAL AND ELECTRICAL COMPONENTS AND START-UP SERVICE.

MICROX II (Inland Discharge)			
Capacity Gallons Per Day	Number of Residents	Price	Shipping Weight
300	4	$1,443.75	650 lbs.
600	8	1,993.75	800 lbs.
750	10	2,118.75	*7500 lbs.
1,250	16	2,693.75	1900 lbs.

*Concrete

envirovac

701 Lawton Avenue
Beloit, Wisconsin 53511
608/364-4411

**Colt Industries
Water and Waste
Management Operation**

The ENVIROVAC vacuum toilet saves water because only about 3 pints is consumed at each flushing, as compared to the 4 to 6 gallons required in conventional systems.

Actually, ENVIROVAC saves water . . . again and again. Gray water can be reused since it is easily and inexpensively purified. This is possible because it is not contaminated by discharges from the toilets.

Lower treatment costs—

Black water reduced by 90%—

Total household waste water reduced by 40%—

A conventional sewage system treatment plant may handle over 60 gallons of waste water per person per day. But with the ENVIROVAC system the volume of black water is reduced to only 2 gallons per person per day. And gray water in either system amounts to 36 gallons per person per day.

Thus the total amount of waste water to be treated in the ENVIROVAC system is only 38 gallons per day—not 60 gallons—which is a 40% reduction.

Savings in treatment costs result even when the black water and gray water are not separated because of the 40% reduction in total volume.

And when the black water, which contains nearly all the contaminants of household sewage, is separated from the gray water, it is possible to process this much smaller volume at a lower cost.

The ENVIROVAC system, expressly designed to save water and overcome the weaknesses of all conventional sewage systems. The basic, patented system and components of ENVIROVAC have been proving themselves in use in large-scale installations, throughout the world, since 1959.

This concept holds great attraction for governmental authorities in areas suffering from a scarcity of water. And in urban developments with inadequate water supply and/or insufficient sewage treatment capacity. Here's why.

ENVIROVAC uses *air*, instead of water, for the transport of sewage.

ENVIROVAC separates black water (toilet waste) from gray water (all other household liquid waste) with resultant lower treatment costs.

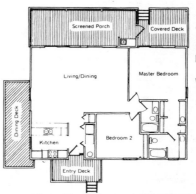

This floor plan and elevation shows a typical private beach residence being developed on Captiva Island, Florida, by South Seas Plantation Land Company. The first phase of the development includes 33 homes which are serviced by Colt Industries' "ENVIROVAC" vacuum sewage system.

cromaglass

Cromaglass manufactures a wide range of aerobic waste treatment systems which have been utilized in water and energy scarce areas such as islands of the Caribbean for recycling effluent used in toilet flushing and gardening.

In addition to the system shown here, they manufacture two additional models suited for treatment of large volume waste from apartment units, mobil home parks and small residential communities.

The large-volume tank and all fittings are made of fiberglass and non-corrosive metals. For full information and specifications, write to:

Cromaglass Corporation
Box 1146
Williamsport, PA 17701

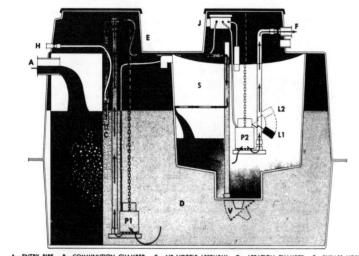

A—ENTRY PIPE B—COMMINUTION CHAMBER C—AIR NOZZLE ASSEMBLY D—AERATION CHAMBER E—BYPASS HOSE
F—DISCHARGE H—AIR SUPPLY J—CONTROL BOX P1-P2—SUBMERSIBLE PUMPS S—SETTLING CHAMBER V—FLAPPER VALVE

MODEL C-5 PROCESS DESCRIPTION

Sewage from source flows through entry pipe (A) to comminution chamber (B). Aeration pump (P1) runs continuously - drawing mixed liquor through bottom and out through air nozzle - venturi assembly (C). Air supply is pulled from within heated area through polyethylene hose (H). Discharge from nozzle is directed toward wire basket and ensuing turbulence causes material in basket to abraid and come apart after which mixed solution passes into main aeration chamber (D).

Small bypass hose (E) directs approximately 25% of (P1) pump flow to settling chamber (S). All power to pumps (P1) and (P2) comes from control or junction box (J). Control box contains a level control switch which activates an alarm circuit within home if water level rises too high in tank (i.e., electrical or pump failure or overloading).

Pump (P2) discharges treated - settled effluent at level L2 and ceases at level L1.

Float assisted flapper valve (V) allows settled solids to void back into main chamber (D) when settling chamber (S) refills after each discharge. Discharge is via PVC fitting (F).

the sewerless toilet

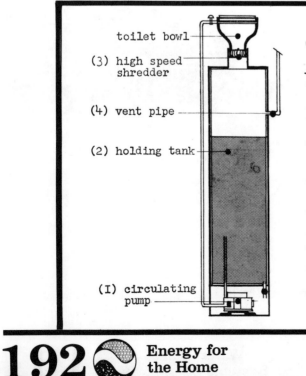

toilet bowl

(3) high speed shredder

(4) vent pipe

(2) holding tank

(I) circulating pump

A device patented by Carl Boester, but not yet manufactured, illustrates the simplicity with which toilet wastes can be treated in small amounts.

The device has a small pump (1) which circulates liquid from a holding tank (2) to the toilet for flushing. At the outlet from the toilet bowl is a high-speed rotary shredder (3) which causes any solid waste to disintegrate as the toilet is flushed, and also introduces enough air into the waste so that it is completely oxidized before it reaches the rest of the liquid in the holding tank. The holding tank is vented (4) and liquid lost by evaporation is made up by the supply of urine. Solids accumulate at the rate of 1/2 to 3/4 lb/user/ year. Apparently the destruction of toilet paper is the main impediment to marketing the system, - if this problem could be solved the unit could revolutionize toilet waste systems.

water conserving appliances

Water-conserving appliances are only just becoming available in the US. They will cost you more money, but will pay for themselves in a fairly short time. Check local plumbing suppliers for fixtures like these.

Water-$aver Cadet toilet

- **Saves one out of three gallons.** And when you consider that the average family of 4 uses 881 gallons* per week. just to flush the toilet, you realize the savings amount to 293 gallons.

- **Saves on the water bill.** Remember that the 293 gallons per week is the savings per toilet. In these days of multiple bathrooms and powder rooms, the 293 figure is likely to be even higher.

- **Saves the environment.** You hear a lot about it these days...here's a practical way to do something about it. The Water-Saver not only uses a third less water. it discharges a third less polluted water.

- **Use it anywhere** a standard fixture would be installed.

- **No mechanical devices.** The system is built right into the elongated bowl trap.

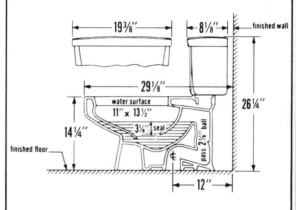

american standard

Compare Aquamizer™ rubber flow control with rigid orifice devices

Low cost and simple installation make Aquamizer™ practical for every showerhead! It will pay for itself in 3 to 4 months average.

Ask your American-Standard distributor for Aquamizer flow controls. Aquamizer is available now. Ordering number 34626-02. You will start saving money right away—instead of pouring it down the drain.

AMERICAN STANDARD

PLUMBING & HEATING DIVISION
40 WEST 40TH STREET / NEW YORK, N.Y. 10018

Simple 3 step installation

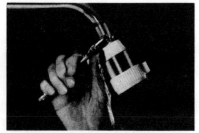

1. Unscrew the shower head.

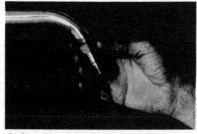

2. Screw on the Aquamizer.™*

3. Screw the shower head back on.*

*Use pipe joint compound for a good seal.

solar distillation

sunwater

Sunwater offers what many a do-it-yourselfer has been looking for equipment and down-to-earth know-how for direct use of solar energy around the house.

The projects are practical and offer the homeowner specific ways to reduce fuel costs through conversion to solar heat.

Heading the Sunwater list of equipment are solar collector panels in three sizes-- 5x6', 4x8' and 3x10'. The firm also manufactures a Suntroller automatic control unit for operation of the panels with a water storage system.

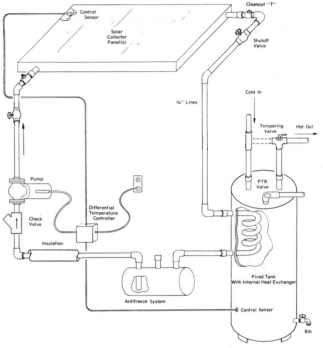

Domestic Heating

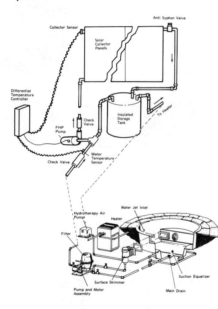

Solar Spa with Storage

Their equipment is in use in swimming pools and spas, in homes for space and hot water heating, in greenhouses, car washes, laundromats, and to meet other low and medium temperature requirements. Sunwater also has published three manuals that will be valuable to the person considering the installations of solar collector panels, since these manuals describe how to figure the panel requirements as well as telling how to install all necessary equipment.

INSTALLATION MANUAL FOR SOLAR WATER PURIFICATION UNITS	$3.00
SOLAR DOMESTIC WATER HEATING	$4.00
SOLAR POOL AND SPA HEATING	$4.00

Sunwater Company

1112 Pioneer Way El Cajon, California 92020 ● Phone (714) 440-3151

  **Energy for the Home**

There are no commercially available methane digesters. Even small scale anaerobic digesters for Primary sewage treatment in small towns would require extensive and complex alterations before they could be controlled to produce methane. There are, however, several sources of do-it-yourself information on building a methane generator for a farm of a homestead,---the most reliable ones are mentioned here.

BIO-GAS PLANTS

Ram Bux Singh is one of the world experts in methane digestion, and India, with over 2000 functioning digesters, is one of the few areas of the world methane is a significant localized source of power. You can buy Ram Bux Singh's "Bio-Gas plant designs and specifications" from:-
The Gobar Gas Research Center,
Ajitmal, ETAWAH, U.P. INDIA.
Price $7.00 Postpaid.

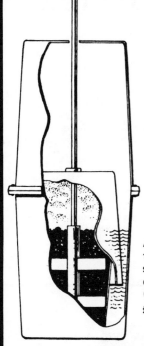

A small fiberglass digester built mainly for experimental purposes. Could be used as a kitchen waste disposal unit. Available from:
Conservation Tools and Technology
4 Lonsdale Rd.
London SW14 England

A small, experimental methane digester which bridges the gap between laboratory test equipment and full-scale digesters. Height 65", diameter 21". Gas capacity approx. 50 litres, slurry capacity 34 litres (7½ gallons).
£28 (inc. VAT & carriage)

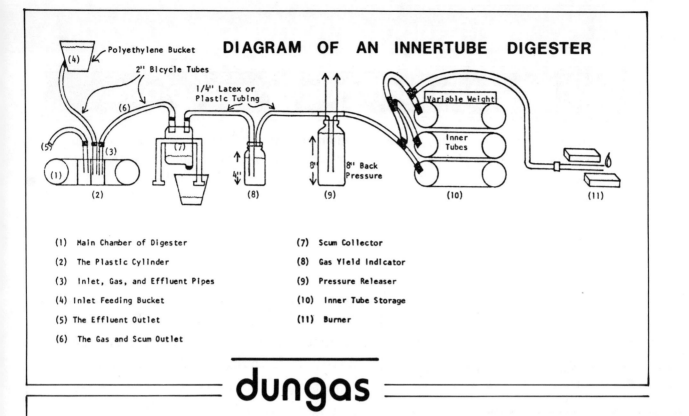

DIAGRAM OF AN INNERTUBE DIGESTER

Polyethylene Bucket
2" Bicycle Tubes
1/4" Latex or Plastic Tubing
Variable Weight
Inner Tubes
8" Back Pressure

(1) Main Chamber of Digester
(2) The Plastic Cylinder
(3) Inlet, Gas, and Effluent Pipes
(4) Inlet Feeding Bucket
(5) The Effluent Outlet
(6) The Gas and Scum Outlet

(7) Scum Collector
(8) Gas Yield Indicator
(9) Pressure Releaser
(10) Inner Tube Storage
(11) Burner

dungas

John L Fry's first book on "Methane Digesters For Fuel Gas and Fertilizer" ($4.00 from New Alchemy Institute, Garden Way Publishing, and other sources) contains information on the planning, design and construction of digesters, and includes plans for two small model digesters. Before actually building a full-scale digester you should consult his "Dungas" book, which offers an even more comprehensive study of the processes and problems involved.

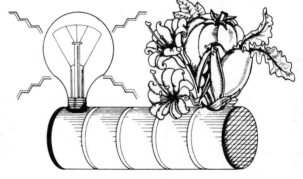

NEW ALCHEMY INSTITUTE

METHANE DIGESTERS
FOR FUEL GAS AND FERTILIZER

WITH COMPLETE INSTRUCTIONS FOR TWO WORKING MODELS

NEWSLETTER NO. 3

do-it-yourself ideas and plans

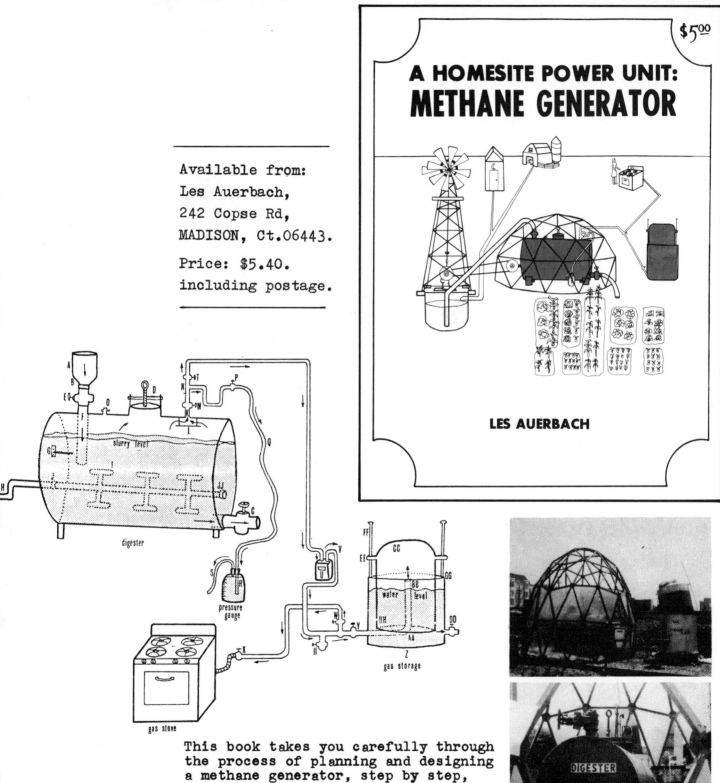

A HOMESITE POWER UNIT:
METHANE GENERATOR

$5⁰⁰

LES AUERBACH

Available from:
Les Auerbach,
242 Copse Rd,
MADISON, Ct.06443.

Price: $5.40.
including postage.

slurry level

digester

pressure
gauge

gas stove

water level

gas storage

DIGESTER

This book takes you carefully through
the process of planning and designing
a methane generator, step by step,
equation by equation. It also provides
a complete description of a small
methane digester one could build for
around $300. A prototype of this
design is now functioning as a
demonstration unit at Berkeley (right).

WOOD HEATING

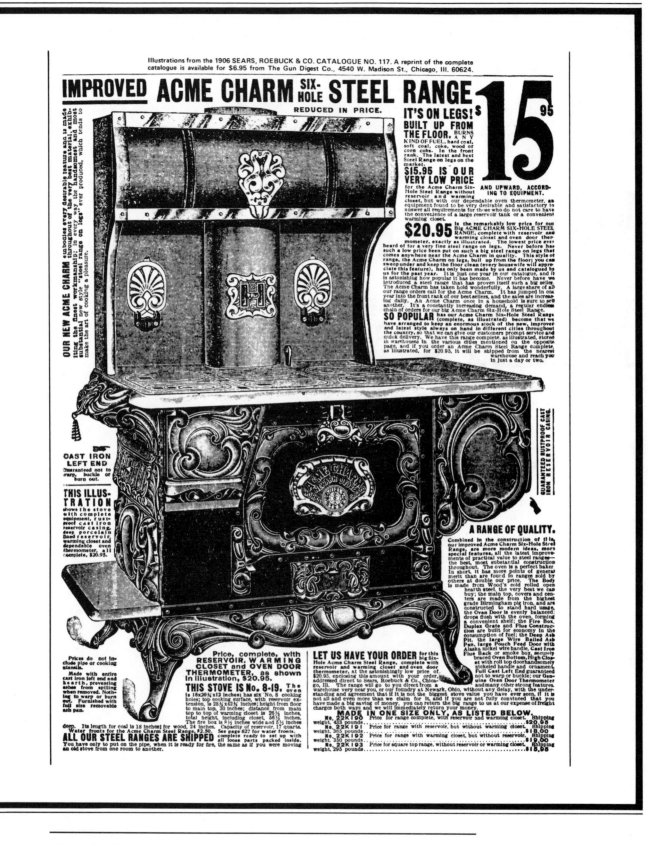

Illustration from the 1906 Sears, Roebuck and Co. Catalog. This kind of stove is still manufactured today, though it costs more than $15 now!

Principles

For centuries the burning of wood was man's only source of heat. Early fireplaces were large, dirty, smoky, and highly inefficient, but during the seventeenth and eighteenth centuries a variety of improvements began to emerge in different countries. America contributed to this advancement (through the work of such early pioneers as Benjamin Franklin) in the design and popularization of more efficient ways of burning wood. In the U.S. during the years 1850-1900, the woodburning cast iron stove was the major source of domestic heating. It was primarily used for cooking and hot water supply until it was supplanted by coal-burners, — and eventually by gas and oil. With the advent of the "energy crisis," the old dies for cast iron stoves have been brought back into use. Stove manufacturers are once again looking for more convenient and efficient ways of heating with wood. The fireplace, which never really died out because it was always either useful, or a luxury the average homeowner wanted, is now available with several modifications to make it a more efficient source of auxiliary heat.

Fireplaces

For those who want to heat entirely with wood, the choice should be between stoves and furnaces. A conventional fireplace is just too inefficient; about 90% of the heat usually goes up the chimney. And it is surprisingly easy to build a fireplace which actually contributes to the heat loss of the house by drawing all the warm air out of the room and up the chimney. When heating was done entirely with fireplaces, a house of moderate size often consumed four times as much wood as does a house using modern wood-burning stoves.

However, for those who must see the flames dancing in an open fireplace, there are a number of ways to improve its efficiency. In 1800 Count Rumford discovered that the heat radiated from a conventional fireplace could be increased by making it shallower (reducing the distance from the front to the back), and by sloping the rear wall forwards. He also discovered that "smoking" could

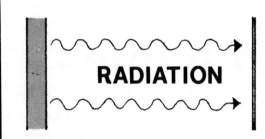

RADIATION

Heat transfer from surface to surface (without affecting the temperature of the air in between) Rate of radiation depends on the surface characteristics and temperatures of each surface. In general, matte black surfaces are good absorbers and emmitters of thermal radiation: white and metallic ("reflective") surfaces are not.

CONDUCTION

Heat transfer through a material, or by direct contact to an adjacent material. Metals are generally very good conductors; air is a poor conductor (though it can transfer heat by convection). The rate of conduction is also dependent on the temperature difference between any two points.

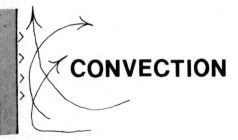

CONVECTION

Heat transfer by the movement of a fluid (such as air or water) Colder (more dense) fluids tend to fall: warmer (less dense) fluids tend to rise. Moving air will pick up or lose heat by conduction to or from anything it comes into contact with, at a rate dependent on the temperature difference, the speed of the air, and the area of contact.

be reduced by inserting a chimney shelf at the bottom (or "throat") of the chimney. This reduces the size of the entrance to the flue, increasing the speed of the air moving upwards and preventing the downdrafts which cause a fireplace to smoke. Rumford recommended a 4" throat. Modern standards recommend 8", but most modern fireplaces have the added sophistication of a damper to regulate the size of the opening.

Other efforts to save more of the heat from a fireplace usually involve changing the heat distribution system. A conventional fireplace *radiates* heat to the walls, furniture, objects (and people) in the room. It does not warm the air in the room, except insofar as the warmed surfaces heat the air next to them. However, with a source of radiant heat it is possible to be comfortable despite low air temperatures (for example, outside on a cold but sunny winter's day).

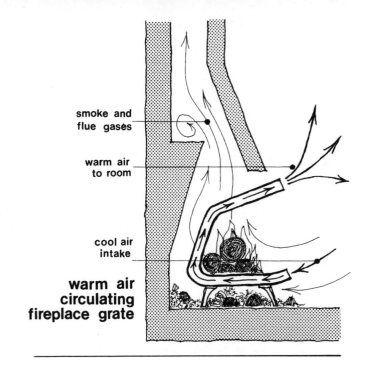

smoke and
flue gases

warm air
to room

cool air
intake

**warm air
circulating
fireplace grate**

*Tubular fireplace grate heats air
in the room by convection.*

Most of the heat *radiated* by a fire is absorbed by the walls of the fireplace and *conducted* through them. If the walls are made of masonry, they will store the heat and gradually release it to the rest of the house (which explains why the early New Englanders soon learned to put the chimney in the middle of the house). Most of the *air* that is directly heated by the embers rises up the chimney, in this way the heat is *convected* out of the room.

A number of methods have been invented which use convection to distribute the heat from the fireplace more efficiently. Specially designed grates made of hollow pipes are heated by both radiation and conduction from the burning embers. Air blown through the pipes and back into the room absorbs a lot of heat which would otherwise be lost. Sometimes these units can be uncomfortably efficient — a blast of hot air is not as pleasant as radiant warmth.

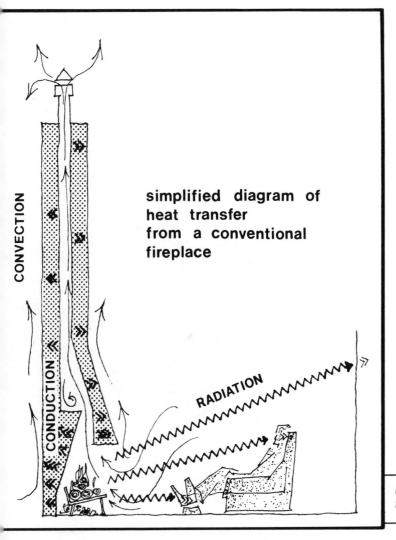

CONVECTION

CONDUCTION

**simplified diagram of
heat transfer
from a conventional
fireplace**

RADIATION

*How heat is transferred from a conventional
fireplace by convection, conduction and radiation.*

The "Franklin"-type fireplace with closing doors is a compromise between the beauty of an open fire and the efficiency of an enclosed stove. Closing the doors considerably reduces the amount of warm air drawn out of the room and up the chimney as well as increasing the efficiency of combustion.

The first "Franklin stove" took in air from a draft beneath the floor. Some of the air was used for combustion, the rest passed around the firebox and flue and back into the room. This ingenious arrangement allowed for the distribution of heat within the room by convection. Modern versions of the Franklin stove do not use this warm air circulating system, and even with their doors closed they do not give nearly as much heat as either airtight stoves or old-fashioned Franklin stoves. However modern warm air circulating fireplaces are available which pass air around the back and sides of the fireplace to pick up extra heat. The air can then be directed out into the room or to the upper floors of the building.

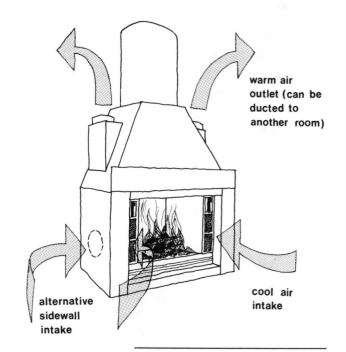

Heatilator-type warm air circulating fireplace (see Wood Catalog).

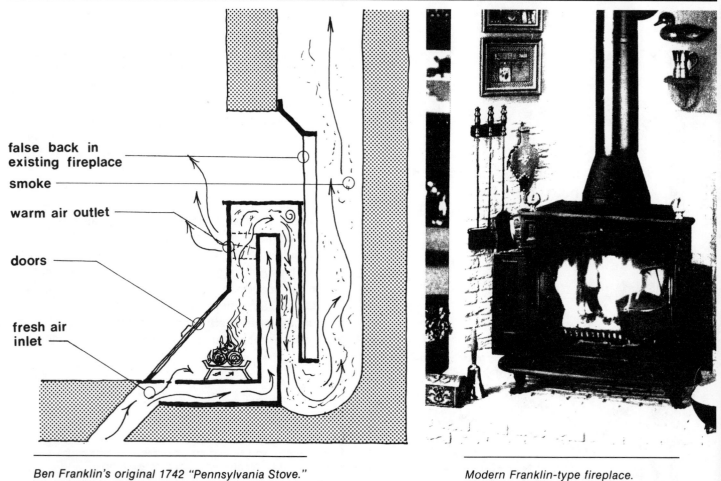

Ben Franklin's original 1742 "Pennsylvania Stove." Modern "Franklin stoves" are much less efficient.

Modern Franklin-type fireplace. Portland Model #2. (see Wood Catalog).

Wood Burning Stoves

The major improvement in wood-burners since the fireplace era has been the gradual reduction in the draft so that no more air goes into the stove and up the chimney than necessary for efficient combustion. Modern "airtight" stoves hold a fire longer and require less attention than others.

The high efficiencies of airtight stoves are achieved by providing air in correct amounts where, and when it is needed, — for example, "primary" air at the base of the fire to burn the coals, and secondary air above the wood to burn the gases that give rise to the long flame characteristic of wood fires.

The modern wood stove routinely holds a fire for 12 or so hours and can be kept going all winter long. This is a great advantage over older stoves, not solely for reasons of comfort, but also because constant kindling of fires is a big nuisance. Long refueling times also mean that those with nine to five jobs can heat their homes with wood. Airtight stoves burn the wood so completely that ashes need be removed only once a week or so. This too is quite an advantage over inefficient wood-burners and coal stoves. All in all, the modern wood stove may be cited as an example of genuine technological progress, at least by comparison with its predecessor, the fireplace.

However, the convenience of modern airtights comes at a price — namely formation of quite flammable creosote in the chimney. Chimney fires were a regular phenomenon in the olden days and are not unique to modern stoves. But the latter are operated in such a way that creosote formation is promoted. At bedtime they are customarily packed full of fuel and the draft turned down. The fire cools to the point where combustion is quite incomplete, and many partially burned gases enter the chimney which

also cools to some extent under these conditions. If cool enough, the unburned gases and water condense to form an acid solution which runs back down the flue until the water re-evaporates leaving solid creosote behind. If your chimney is not in good repair and the creosote in it ignites, there is some chance that the resulting fire could spread to the rest of the house. If it is of an approved safety design and without cracks, you have little to worry about. But before installing a stove, you must be sure you have a sound chimney.*

In the 19th century, cast iron stoves were made in great numbers in this country. Almost every town of any size had a foundry. Technology has changed, so that American stoves today are economically constructed mainly of sheet steel. This modern change is not necessarily for the worse. After all, imperfectly cast plates did crack.

When looking at a steel stove, two important considerations are the thickness of the metal and the quality of the welds. The thicker the steel, the longer it will take to rust out.** If the thickness is less than about one-sixteenth of an inch, the steel will probably bend and bow when heated unless reinforced. But this is not serious unless it interferes with airtightness. In some stoves the sheet metal is protected from the heat of the

---

*A helpful booklet on safety: **Using Coal and Wood Stoves Safely,** National Fire Protection Association, 470 Atlantic Ave., Boston, Massachusetts. (an informative and inexpensive booklet.)

**Thickness of steel is often reported in terms of "gauge" numbers. Fifteen gauge corresponds to about one-sixteenth of an inch and 11 gauge, to one-eighth of an inch.

firebox by cast iron or firebrick linings. (These also promote a higher temperature in the firebox and in theory should help ensure complete combustion.) Good welds show no porosity and are slightly convex, neither very flat nor with lumps higher than either of the parent metals.

Most steel stoves have cast iron doors which cannot be welded to the steel and are bolted on with furnace cement as a sealer. The furnace cement tends to break apart and fall out. When this happens control over the draft and therefore the fire is lost. Once a year, it is wise to inspect the seals and apply more furnace cement where necessary. When the asbestos gasket around the loading door becomes worn, it too will have to be replaced to ensure a tight fit.

American steel stoves with automatically controlled dampers are sometimes said to work on the wood distillation principle, that is, a load of fuel goes through a pattern of drying, burning the combustible gases, and burning the charcoal. The firebox temperature tends to rise through each stage, but the draft is reduced automatically, in order to keep heat production more or less even.

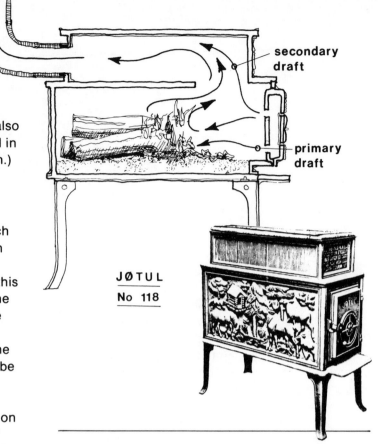

JØTUL
No 118

Draft circulation pattern in a Norwegian stove. Model shown is the Jotul #118 (see Wood Catalog).

Norwegian and Danish cast iron box stoves are based on a wholly different burning principle. Here an even temperature is maintained by inclusion of a baffle in the upper part of the firebox. This forces the draft into an S-shaped pattern, so that the logs burn from front to back like a cigarette. The fire remains qualitatively the same throughout a fuel cycle, and thus heat production is constant and an automatic draft control unnecessary.

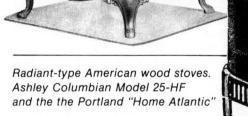

Radiant-type American wood stoves. Ashley Columbian Model 25-HF and the the Portland "Home Atlantic"

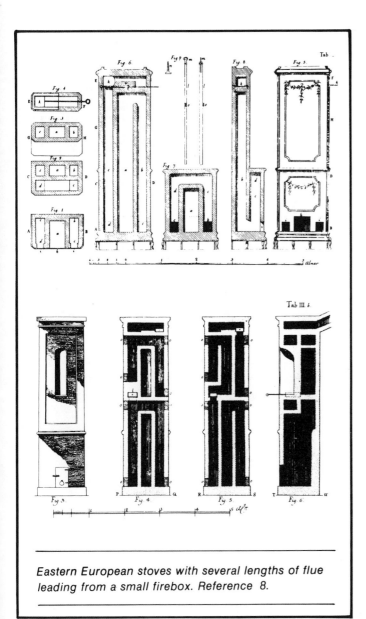

Eastern European stoves with several lengths of flue
leading from a small firebox. Reference 8.

In Austria, Eastern Europe and Scandinavia
there has been a long tradition of building
fireplaces where the flue is extended up and down
inside a large heat retaining box which forms the
exterior of the stove. These models — made of
ceramic tile, soapstone, or firebrick, provided a low
temperature source of background heat. They heat
the air in the room by direct contact — as well
as by radiating heat to surfaces within the room.

Like conventional fireplaces, airtight wood-
burning stoves give off most of their heat by
radiation. To do this effectively, the metal housing
must get very hot. Like warm-air circulating
fireplaces, however, there are also wood burning
stoves which heat the air of the room by
convection. These wood stoves, — generally called
wood "circulators" are equipped with a metal
jacket surrounding the firebox. Air is passed
between the two metal surfaces, heated, and rises
out into the room. Often a small electric fan is
used to pull the warm air down through the cabinet
and out at floor level, for better distribution
throughout the room.

Wood-burning "circulator". Air is warmed
between the firebox and the outer jacket,
then passes out into the room.
Manufactured by Brown Stove Works (see Wood Catalog).

Wood Furnaces

One of the cheapest (but least glamorous) ways of completely heating a large house with wood is to use a wood furnace. Like an oil furnace, it takes up a lot of room and is most conveniently located in the basement of a house along with the wood required to feed it. A wood furnace is similar to a very large circulator-type stove. It has a firebox which operates on the same complete combustion principles as an efficient stove, so that wood and most residue is reduced to a minimum amount of ash. Unlike stoves, modern wood furnaces can easily be converted to burn oil. Some will switch automatically so that you have a choice of fuel, and can leave the furnace to run on oil for lengthy periods. When fueled with wood it will require attention about twice a day.

To distribute the heat from a furnace, air is drawn around the firebox and circulated through ducts in the house just as in a conventional forced air heating system. Some furnaces can be used with hot water distribution systems, in which case the firebox is surrounded by water which is then piped into baseboard radiators or radiant floor systems. Suppliers of wood furnaces also offer automatic humidifiers (with forced air systems) and auxiliary equipment for heating the household water supply. An investment in a wood furnace is equivalent to buying a complete house-heating system, so it is advisable to talk to owners as well as manufacturers before making a purchase.

Choice of Chimney

Stoves and chimney should be thought of together, as a unit. Poor draft and back-puffing are sometimes blamed on the stove when the fault lies with the chimney. The lifting force on chimney gases depends on how hot they are and how high the chimney is. The higher the chimney, the better the draft. A chimney is too high only when it is in danger of being toppled by the wind or when exhaust gases are chilled at the top.

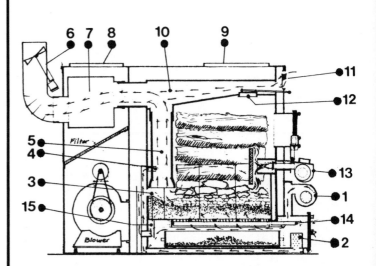

1. Thermostatically controlled blower for primary air intake.
2. Secondary air intake, at base of furnace.
3. Primary air inlet to combustion chamber.
4. Secondary air inlet to combustion flue where gases are burnt.
5. Heavy cast iron combustion flue.
6. Draft inducer in smokepipe automatically operates to ensure complete combustion
7. Heat exchanger at top of fan chamber.
8. Return air intake plenum.
9. Warm air outlet plenum.
10. Air -heating flue along top of furnace.
11. "Barometric "damper mixes room air with flue gases to help stop creosote deposition.
12. Direct draft damper for use when refuelling.
13. Auxilliary oil burner, automatically activated when wood burns out.
14. Heavy cast iron grating.
15. "Fuel selector" damper, regulates air intake according to the type of fuel burned.

Cross-section, front and rear views of the Riteway Fuelmaster Wood-burning Furnace (see Wood Catalog).

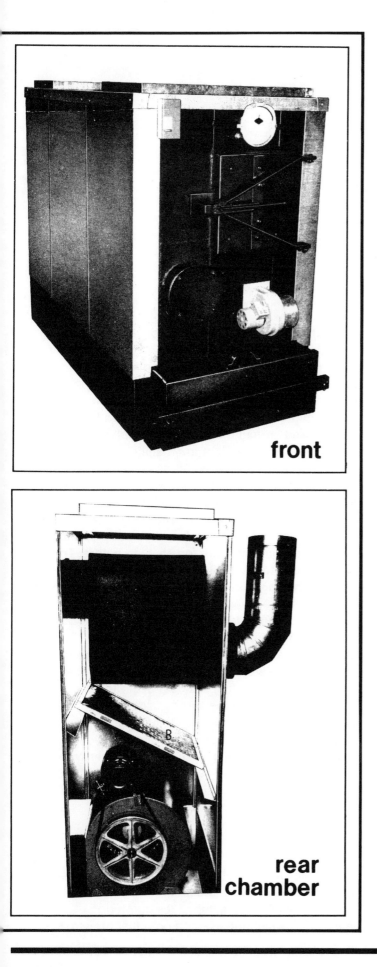

front

rear chamber

The choice in most cases is whether to erect a brick chimney or put up prefabricated stainless steel sections packed with asbestos. The metal chimney has the advantage of being easy to install. If the stove smokes, it is easy to climb on the roof and add another section. On the other hand, a masonry chimney with a flue liner and good thick walls has a lot in its favor while being harder to put up. It acts as a big heat reservoir in the middle of the house, and once warm, provides a good draft even when the fire is low. This helps prevent deposition of creosote and back-puffing. On the other hand, a masonry chimney takes a long time to get warm in the first place, and heavy creosote deposition may occur on the first few days of use in the fall. When a stove is fired only occasionally, a metal chimney is preferable because it heats up fast and draws well almost immediately.

One installation that is unsatisfactory with an airtight stove is a chimney made of prefabricated sections above the roof and plain stovepipe from the roof to the stove. When the fire is low the ordinary stovepipe cools and becomes coated with creosote. Chimney fires are almost impossible to avoid with this setup and especially dangerous here, because the creosote corrodes and seriously weakens ordinary stovepipe in a season or two. Because of the creosote problem, modern slow-combustion stoves should be connected to the chimney with only a short length of pipe. Stovepipes stretching horizontally as far as 50 feet were common in churches in the last century, but with a good hot fire only once a week in an inefficient box stove, there was little chance of depositing tar in the pipe. The long pipe provided a way of getting heat out into the nave after it was swept prematurely out of the firebox by a high draft.

Another point in favor of a brick chimney is that it becomes an air conditioner in the warm season. In winter, with a fire in the stove, gases in the chimney are hotter than the air outside, and an updraft occurs. On hot summer days, the air in the chimney is cooled below the temperature of the outside air, and a downdraft occurs. To take full advantage of this effect, the stove should be disconnected in the summer. This is a good idea in any case to be sure that no rust-inducing moisture enters through the chimney.

Available Energy

Wood as a source of Energy

Fossil fuels, wind, water and wood could all be considered as solar energy sources. Unlike coal and oil, however, wood is a renewable source. Moreover, in countries where there is a plentiful wood supply, generally it is true that the supply has remained constant. The statistics will probably remain so, insofar as human beings take responsibility for caring for their natural resources.

As solar collector the tree is unique. No man-hours nor any fuels are needed to build it. It is also unique as an energy storage device, since the energy can, with some precautions, be retrieved and used centuries after being captured. If one's definition of efficiency is broad enough, therefore, it may be said that the tree is more efficient at capturing and storing solar energy than anything man can make. In addition, the tree is simply a beautiful thing to have around us.

This does not mean that man-made solar energy traps are useless, but it should be clear that they belong where vegetation does not grow — roof tops and deserts for example.

There is presently an abundance of wood, available in the United States, despite many stories in our press to the contrary. It *is* a fact however, that there are serious shortages of certain species, particularly the big trees of high quality. The amount of standing wood in this country, however, is enormous and on the increase, in spite of soaring consumption of paper and plywood.

There are two major reasons for the comeback of wood — (1) the reversion of millions of acres of former cropland in the East to forest, and (2) a reduction in the per capita consumption of wood. When the settlers first arrived they cut timber faster than one would imagine, considering the tools they had to work with. Much of this wood was burned in the field, and potash and perlash from the ashes were sold in England and other countries of Northern Europe for cash used to buy farm tools. As the mid-West of the United States and highly mechanised agriculture took over, small eastern farms were abondoned, a trend still continuing in some places. The deserted farms eventually become forest once again, but without man's intervention the time to reach full production of commercial forest products can be over a century.

Less well known is the fact that *less* wood is demanded from American forests than before. This is largely due to the decline in the use of wood as a fuel. Interestingly, in the early days of the United States there was literally wood to burn, and as late as 1860 the average American family was consuming 17.5 cords annually for heat and cooking. Up until the sixties, steamboats and railroads were wood-powered. Only in the latter part of the 19th century did coal begin to take over. In 1900, 45% of the energy used in the United States still came from wood. Since then it has been almost totally displaced as a domestic source of energy, while the harvest of other wood — "industrial wood" — has stayed fairly constant in spite of rising population. Wood and charcoal have been supplanted by other materials in thousands of applications — such as buildings, vehicles, furniture, iron-making, and the chemical industry.

In the United States about 500 million acres are classified as commercial forest land (not counting some 100 million acres in interior Alaska),on which the average potential growth rate of harvestable wood is near 1 cord per acre per year. Ideally, this means a total growth of 500 million cords in the United States each year, if each of those 500 million acres were well stocked with vigorous trees. They are not, especially in former farmland in the East. Realistically, then, assume an annual growth of 350 million cords on these 500 million acres, of which about 150 million cords are currently used for lumber, veneer, paper, and minor products. That leaves, then, a total of 200 million cords which could be converted to fuel without depleting the forests at all. Five cords will heat the average American house for one year; 200 million cords 40 million houses — or approximately two-thirds the total number of dwelling units in the U.S. There may, in fact, actually be quite a bit more potential fuelwood than this, since trees in backyards, along roadsides, in fence rows, and those on the 250 million acres of so-called "non-productive" forest land are not included in the estimate. Of course much of this wood is in remote areas and simply unavailable for all practical purposes, and much is owned by people who intend to allow it to lie fallow. The calculation does, however, help one begin to visualize the magnitude of this vast renewable resource. It is, however, well to bear in

mind the pessimistic facts of waste, and a growth of population that does not keep pace with the conservation of our natural resources.

These figures do suggest how much woodlot is needed to supply a wood-energized house indefinitely. Five cords of hardwood per winter should be adequate for heating and cooking in a six room house. There are well-built houses in the coldest parts of the country that get by on less. With an annual production of, say, 7/10 cord per acre, 7 acres of woodlot would be the minimum size needed for the average house. But if the total annual growth were taken for fuel each year, this would mean burning some trees suitable for lumber, wasting time cutting up some very small wood, and robbing other wildlife. To be realistic, then, more than 7 acres of woodlot are required to support a hypothetical average house totally heated by burning wood — perhaps as much as twice that many. If the cutting is done with an eye to increasing lumber production, the harvest of fuelwood would then decline in time, and more acreage would be needed to supply 5 cords to the house. Of course these figures must be adjusted for local conditions. They do, at least, provide an initial estimate of the size of woodlot needed.

Annual wood harvest in the U.S. since 1900. From Reference 1.

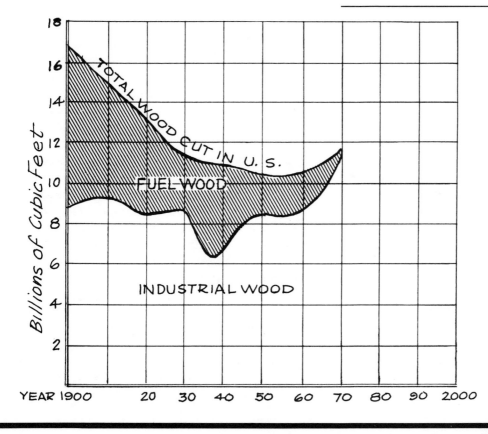

Cutting Fuelwood

Cutting fuelwood in the East, where three out of every four hardwood trees are classed as *cull* or low grade, can substantially increase the growth rate of timber suitable for lumber and veneer. The principle here is simple: If the crooked, twisted, diseased, and economically unimportant trees are removed, then straight, healthy and commercially important trees left standing grow faster. Removing cull trees creates openings in the forest canopy into which the crowns of crop trees expand, intercept more light, and produce more wood each year. Comparison with weeding the garden is apt.

Incidentally, the slash left from the thinning operation provides cover for small game, and the young trees that grow up in the open spaces make good browse for deer.

A *key point* regarding the products of the combustion of wood is that these would be liberated in the forest by decay anyway and culling does not, therefore, lead to a net increase in environmental pollution.*

Decay is slow oxidation under the influence of microorganisms and fungi; combustion is fast oxidation. Complete oxidation of wood is the reverse of photosynthesis, the major products being carbon dioxide , water and energy as heat instead of light. These are the products, whether the oxidation occurs on the forest floor or in the firebox of a stove. Thus burning of wood does not lead to a net increase of atmospheric carbon dioxide, in contrast to coal and oil, since the carbon dioxide would be liberated in the forest by decay anyway.

However, burning of wood is often incomplete. In home and industrial wood-burners a wide variety of other substances, ranging from the common to the exotic, are produced in addition to carbon dioxide and water. But the point here again is the great similarity between these so-called intermediate products of combustion and those liberated in the forest by decay. Many of the intermediate products are volatile, and, when they are formed in decaying wood, escape into the forest air where they undergo chemical reactions with one another under the influence of

See reference 3.

sunlight. The result is the haze characteristic of forests on hot, still summer days — haze so pronounced in the Smoky Mountains that they take their name from it.

Of course, no one should draw the conclusion that it is harmless to breathe smoke from a wood fire.

There are other environmental effects of burning wood which have no direct connection with air pollution. The forest itself is affected. We can cut trees the way it was done all too often in the past, depleting the soil of minerals, causing erosion and destroying wildlife. Or we can do it intelligently.

Choice of Fuelwood

The densest wood makes the best fuel. In the following Table, species are arranged according to density with the densest at the top of each column. All the woods in the left column make excellent fuel; those in the middle are not bad, and those on the right will do. There are people in very cold parts of the world who stay warm and happy with nothing but spruce to burn. But no one with experience chooses spruce over oak if he has a choice. Inspection of the Table shows that the woods used for pulp and construction are by and large in the righthand column. In spite of technical advances in the use of hardwood for pulp, softwood is still preferred, and carpenters like to work with the softer woods. In the lefthand column only the oaks, black birch, black walnut and sugar maple are in much demand for lumber and veneer; thus there is a fortuitous natural division which should go a long way toward preventing cutthroat competition between cutters of fuelwood and of industrial or commercial wood.

The order in the accompanying Table is only approximate, since density varies within each species. There are cases of a beech being more dense than sugar maple, and an elm more dense than cherry, but you will not find a cherry denser than hickory.

Table I

Densities of various North American woods

High	Medium	Low
Live oaks	Holly	Black spruce
Shagbark hickory	Pond pine	Hemlocks
Black locust	Nut pines	Catalpa
Dogwood	Loblolly pine	Red alder
Slash pine	Tamarack	Tulip poplar
Hop Hornbeam	Shortleaf pine	Red fir
Persimmon	Western larch	Sitka spruce
Shadbush	Junipers	White spruce
Apple	Paper birch	Black willow
White Oak	Red maple	Large tooth aspen
Honey locust	Cherry	Butternut
Black birch	American elm	Ponderosa pine
Yew	Black gum	Noble fir
Blue beech	Sycamore	Redwood
Red oak	Gray birch	Quaking Aspen
Rock elm	Douglas fir	Sugar pine
Sugar maple	Pitch pine	White pine
American beech	Sassafras	Balsam fir
Yellow birch	Magnolia	Black willow
Longleaf pine	Red cedar	Cottonwood
White ash	Norway pine	Basswood
Oregon ash	Bald cypress	Western red cedar
Black walnut	Chestnut	Balsam poplar

Costing

Economics of Wood Heating

There are considerations other than price that affect choice of fuel, such as guaranteed availability, ease of handling, and cost of heaters. But it is useful to be able to compare the prices BTU for BTU. See the results in *Tables II* and *III*.

The figures were established as follows: the densities are averages of data found in various technical sources. Any actual density measurement could easily differ from the ones in *Table II* by 15 percent. In fact, close inspection will show minor disagreements between *Tables I* and *II*.

Table II

Fuel values of some common woods

	Average Density	Fuel Value	Price
Shagbark hickory	4400 lb. per cord	31.2 million BTUs	$60 per cord*
White oak	4400	31.2	60
Sugar maple	4100	29.1	56
American beech	4000	28.4	55
Red oak	3900	27.6	53
Yellow birch	3800	27.0	52
White ash	3700	26.3	51
American elm	3400	24.1	46
Red maple	3400	24.1	46
Paper birch	3400	24.1	46
Black cherry	3300	23.4	45
Douglas fir	2900	21.5	41
Eastern white pine	2200	15.8	30

Assumed efficiencies: wood stove, 50%; oil furnace, 65%

*Based on equivalent amount of oil at 35¢ per gallon.

Energy for the Home

Table III

Comparison of heating costs

	Unit Price	Cost of 1 Million BTUs	Heater Efficiency	Cost of 1 Million Useful BTUs
Electricity	2.5¢ per kilowatt-hour	$7.33	100%	$7.33
Oil	35¢ per gallon	$2.50	65%	$3.85
White Oak	$50 per cord	$1.60	50%	$3.20
White Ash	$40 per cord	$1.52	50%	$3.04

The energy released on burning a pound of bone-dry wood completely is called its fuel value — about 8600 BTUs. Air-dried wood is nearly 20 percent water by weight (relative to dry wood), and the heat liberated on burning a pound of air-dried wood is therefore less — about 7100 BTUs. (The heats of combustion of bituminous coal and No. 2 heating oil are 13,500 and 19,000 BTUs per pound respectively). The third column is obtained from the second by multiplying by 7100 for the hardwoods and 7400 for Douglas fir and 7200 for white pine to take into account the resins in the latter two. Thus, the figures in the third column represent maximum heating effect from a cord of wood and must be modified by an efficiency factor to estimate the amount of heat actually transferred to the house. The best wood stoves are about 50 percent efficient under household conditions, hence, *all the figures in the third column should, realistically, be halved to find actual heating effect.* [**]

Oil furnaces are about *65 percent* efficient under household conditions.[***]Since the fuel value of one gallon of heating oil is 140,000 BTUs, the heating effect from one gallon is *91,000* BTUs. At 35¢ per gallon, that amounts to 0.384¢ per thousand useful BTUs. At the same price, the 14.2 million useful BTUs from a cord of American beech would cost about $55. Thus beech at anything less than $55 a cord is cheaper than oil at *35¢* a gallon. All the figures in the fourth column have been calculated similarly. Should the price of oil change, new figures for that column can be calculated by simple proportions. For example, if oil were 45¢ a gallon, then you could pay up to $71 (55 x 45/35) for a cord of beech and still save money.

For comparison, electric heat at 2.5¢ per kilowatt-hour is equal to 0.733¢ per 1000 BTUs of heat (1 kw-hr = 3413 BTUs). That's almost twice as expensive as beech at $55 per cord.

[**]Data on wood stove efficiencies is meagre. The **Char-Wood Heater,** a stove designed by Prof. Lauren E. Seeley of Yale, achieved efficiencies near 65% under carefully controlled conditions in experiments during World War II.]

[***] Standard tables used by engineers to estimate oil furnace efficiencies from stack temperature and Carbon Dioxide measurements have an efficiency range of from 40 to 90 percent. See Reference 4, p. 151.

House Design

Wood Heat and House Design

Before installing a wood-burning stove in an existing house it is necessary to decide whether the house is best suited to a warm air "circulator" or a radiant-type stove. Radiant stoves will heat the fabric of the building, — so are well adapted to houses where walls and partitions are made of materials which will absorb and retain heat (such as brick or stone). They are not well-suited to buildings with poor insulation, large unprotected window areas, etc., where the heat absorbed by

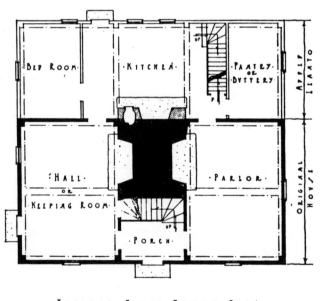

·TYPICAL FIRST FLOOR PLAN·

♪CENTRAL CHIMNEY TYPE♪

Floor plan of a typical early New England house. The masonry fireplace in the center of the house was the only source of heat.
From **Early Domestic Architecture of Connecticut** by Frederick Kelly, Yale University Press, 1924.

the walls is easily lost to the outside. On the other hand, circulator stoves are best suited to houses where the walls provide good insulation but not necessarily thermal storage (such as conventional timber frame houses). Since they heat the air inside the house they are least suitable for drafty buildings where the hot air can easily escape through the fabric of the building. Whichever stove is used however, it is of course worth retaining as much of the heat it produces for as long as possible, — and that means taking all the usual precautions such as insulating walls, covering windows at night, and preventing the escape of warm air.

Whether you have a furnace in the basement or stoves on the ground floor, the chimney should be placed in the middle of the house and not on an outside wall. It is also important to check building codes regarding the placement of fireplaces and flues. The standard clearance required between stovepipes and combustible surfaces is generally 18", — but this can be reduced by adding various layers of fireproof and insulating materials. This helps keep the chimney drawing well and also means that heat lost from the chimney helps warm the house. To put the chimney in the middle takes up valuable space, but where the winter is severe there is no doubt that the central part of the house is the most efficient place for the chimney. Colonial houses in the South may have had chimneys at either end, but settlers in New England soon learned to put them in the middle of the home.

If there are several flues they should be close together in one chimney to help keep one another warm. In this way the flue connected to the parlor stove will draw well right away, and you will not have to put up with smoke every time you wish to use it.

A masonry chimney in the middle of the home will take the chill off upstairs bedrooms, so that they can be used for sleeping without any other heat. Stainless steel-asbestos chimneys are not nearly as effective at warming the upstairs because they are too well insulated.

Stoves installed on the second floor are apt to be smoky because of short flue length. It is generally preferable to heat the upstairs by the chimney and by warm air from downstairs coming through registers or openings in the floor.

A stairwell in the center of the house, or openings in the ceiling near the fireplace or stove will allow the hot air to rise. Slits in the floor near

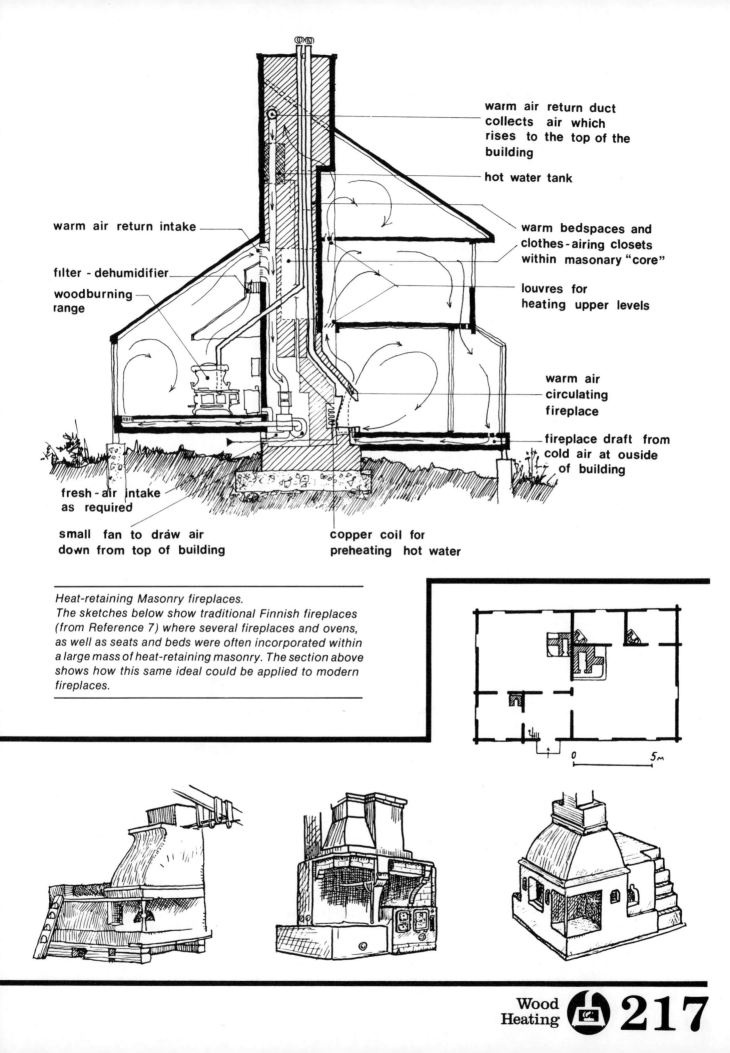

warm air return duct collects air which rises to the top of the building

hot water tank

warm air return intake

filter - dehumidifier

woodburning range

warm bedspaces and clothes-airing closets within masonary "core"

louvres for heating upper levels

warm air circulating fireplace

fireplace draft from cold air at ouside of building

fresh-air intake as required

small fan to draw air down from top of building

copper coil for preheating hot water

Heat-retaining Masonry fireplaces.
The sketches below show traditional Finnish fireplaces (from Reference 7) where several fireplaces and ovens, as well as seats and beds were often incorporated within a large mass of heat-retaining masonry. The section above shows how this same ideal could be applied to modern fireplaces.

0   5ᴍ

the outer wall of the house will allow the colder air to fall down and it can then be directed towards the source of heat. This simple principle was developed by Wendell Thomas and has the great advantage of eliminating drafts from windows and doors to the outside. It could be adapted to many different house designs and result in more comfortable conditions being achieved using less heat. Any house is a constantly changing thermal environment, the air is always moving, and the temperature of the building fabric is continually changing. Understanding how heat moves around your house and how it eventually escapes can provide you with valuable insights into energy conservation.

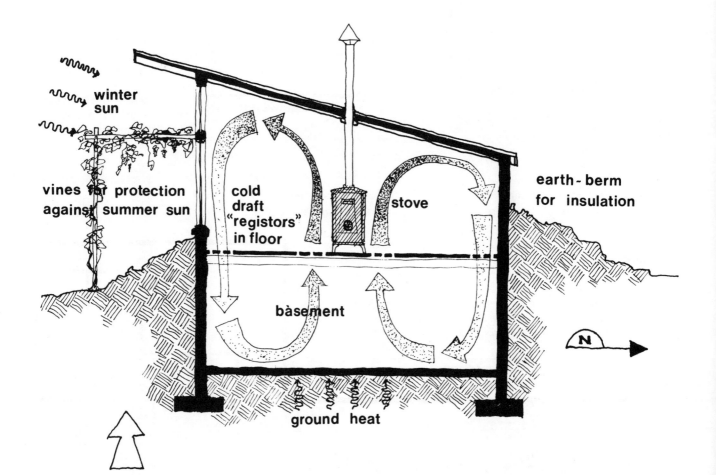

Wendell Thomas's house in western North Carolina. Registers in the floor encourage air movement around the stove, thus creating warm air convection currents within the room. Cold air from windows, door and outside walls falls down into the basement thus creating a draft-free living area.

The use of radiant heaters in a building constructed of heat retaining materials. Wall construction is of exposed block or brickwork **inside,** *(high "thermal capacity")* covered on the **outside** *(never **inside** the house) with sprayed foam insulation (high "thermal resistance"). The foam is protected by siding or intumescent paint. The masonry walls store the heat and re-radiate it back into the room. Note: Most Plastic foam products are very flammable. Check local building codes and use them wisely.*

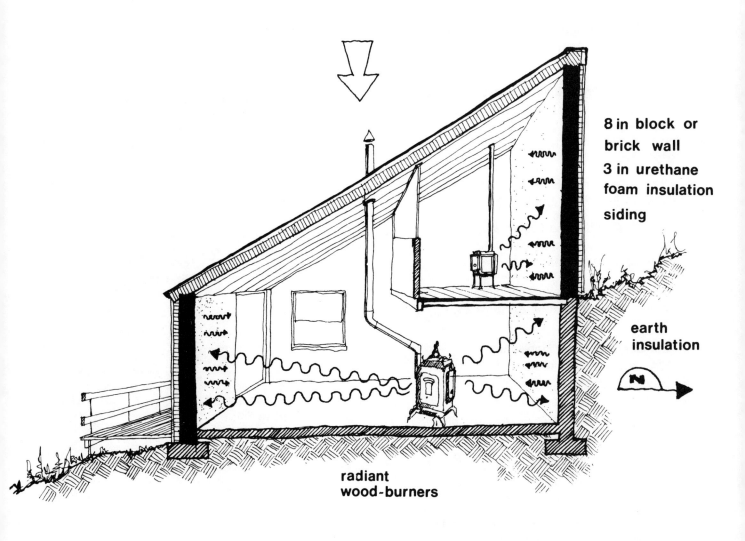

8 in block or brick wall

3 in urethane foam insulation

siding

earth insulation

N

radiant wood-burners

References

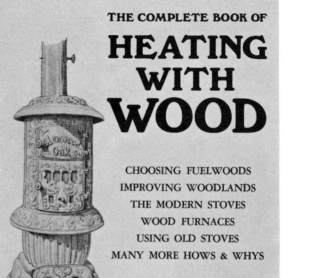

THE COMPLETE BOOK OF

HEATING WITH WOOD

CHOOSING FUELWOODS
IMPROVING WOODLANDS
THE MODERN STOVES
WOOD FURNACES
USING OLD STOVES
MANY MORE HOWS & WHYS

LARRY GAY

1 **The Outlook for Timber in the United States,** Forest Service, United States Department of Agriculture, Forest Resource Report No. 20, 1973.

2 **Energy in the American Economy, 1850-1975,** S. H. Schurr and B. C. Netschert, Johns Hopkins Press, Baltimore, 1960.

3 **Forest Fuels, Prescribed Fire and Air Quality,** J. A. Hall, Pacific Northwest Forest and Experiment Station, United States Department of Agriculture, Portland, Oregon, 1972.

4 "The Conversion of Energy," C. M. Summers, **Scientific American,** Sept., 1971.

5 **Using Coal and Wood Stoves Safely,** National Fire Protection Association, 470 Atlantic Ave., Boston, Massachusetts.

6 "The Self-heating, Self-cooling house," Wendell Thomas, **Mother Earth News,** Reprint #39.

7 **Zur Geschichte der Finnischen Wohnstuben.** N. Valonen. Helsinki, 1963.

8 **Kakelugnar.** B. Tunander. I.C.A. Forlager AB. Vaseras, Sweden, 1973.

9 **Rumford Fireplaces.** G. Curtis Gillespie, Comstock, New York, 1906.

10 **Heating With Wood.** Larry Gay 128 pp $3.95 paperback from Garden Way Publishing Charlotte, VT 05445

11 **Wood Stove Know-How.** Peter Coleman 24 pp $1.50 paperback from Garden Way Publishing, Charlotte, VT 05445

Wood Stove Know -how

by PETER COLEMAN
Director of
Garden Way Research

GARDEN WAY PUBLISHING
CHARLOTTE, VERMONT 05445

Further Readings

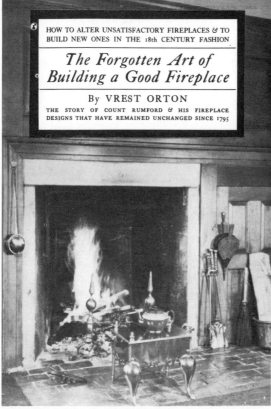

Firewood for Heat. Peter H. Allen. Society for the Protection of New Hampshire Forests, 5 South State St., Concord, New Hampshire 03301.

Wood Stove Know How. Peter Coleman. Garden Way Publishing, Charlotte, Vermont, 1974.

Antique Wood Stoves. Will and Jane Curtis. Cobblesmith, Ashvill, Maine, 1974.

The Complete Book of Heating with Wood. Larry Gay. Garden Way Publishing, Charlotte, Vermont, 1974.

The Woodburners Handbook. David Havens. Media House, Box 1770, Portland, Maine, 1973.

Fire on the Hearth. J. H. Peirce. Pond-Ekberg, Springfield, Massachusetts, 1951.

Home Fires Burning: The History of Domestic Heating and Cooking. Lawrence Wright. Hillary, London, 1964.

The Forgotten Art of Building a Good Fireplace. Vrest Orton. Yankee Inc., Dublin, New Hampshire, 1969.

Mother Earth News, Michael Wassil. "Stovepipe Power," No. 24.

"A Rudimentary Treatise on Warming and Ventilation," Charles Tomlinson, London, 1870. (A very good "exposition of the general principles.")

One Man's Forest, R. P. Stephens, Garden Way Publishing, Charlotte, Vermont, 1974.

Curing Smoky Fireplaces, Douglas Merrilees, Garden Way Publishing Company, 1973.

STYRIA

Portland Stove
Foundry Co.

RADIANT GRATE INC.

The Majestic Company

ASHLEY®

Jotul

BROWN STOVE WORKS, Inc.

HEATILATOR

GARDEN WAY RESEARCH
CHARLOTTE, VERMONT 05445

LOCKE STOVE COMPANY

FUEL-MASTER M

WOODLAND SUPPLY CORP.

MARTIN INDUSTRIES

LEDA 18 73

RITEWAY

WOOD HEATING CATALOG

Dear Reader,

    The information appearing on the following pages was forwarded to us from the manufacturer or organization whose name appears in the book. We wrote to each organization requesting information about the work it was doing in the particular field of energy in question, explaining that they were welcome to send to us whatever copy they thought would represent them well.

    Our goal was and is to make this helpful information available to you, the reader. Should you become interested in obtaining a product or further information from one of the companies displayed herein, we request that you **not** write to Garden Way Publishing Company but directly to that particular company whose product or research interests you.

The Home Atlantic Wood Parlor

---WITH ITS---

NEW AND ORIGINAL RETURN FLUE →
for #122 and #125 models only

We consider this FLUE so valuable an addition that we strongly recommend the purchase of the RETURN FLUE STOVE.

Hitherto stoves of this class have had an outer shell bolted across the main back of the stove to make a return flue. This carries all the heat from the back, which is the hottest part of the stove, into the smoke flue and loses it up the chimney. In our construction WE SAVE THAT LOST HEAT. We make a gracefully designed radiating flue box, a part of the body of the stove, and separated entirely from the main back by an air space 1 1-8 inch thick. The heat from the back of the stove and the inside wall of the hot return flue is radiated into this space causing a rapid circulation of heated air from beneath the bottom of the stove upward across the whole back of the stove.

This forced circulation will heat a room with extraordinary rapidity.

A damper permits the smoke when building a fire to pass directly into the chimney and controls the passage of the smoke around the return flue when desired.

We thus secure two large and efficient heating surfaces more than can be found on any other stove.

The Queen Atlantic

Attractive Nickel Finishings

Available Options
Hot Water Reservoir, Single High Shelf, Warming Oven, Box High Shelf or Canopy Shelf

Other Models Available:
Empress & Empire Atlantics. Send for brochures.

Shown — #408 Queen with single high shelf and hot water reservoir.

Basic Dimensions
Width: 52"
Depth: 30¾"
Height: 32½"

ALL CAST IRON CONSTRUCTION

Atlantic Wood Cook Stove
A PLAIN, HEAVY, DURABLE STOVE

This time-tested COOK STOVE, made especially for wood burning, assures you many years of dependable, rugged service.

Where wood is the only available fuel, the ATLANTIC WOOD COOK STOVE gives you maximum cooking comfort — and ECONOMY.

Castings are exceptionally strong and well-adapted to hard usage. OVEN is 20" x 22" with doors on each side. FIREBOX is 24" long. FLUE construction permits easy cleaning. BAKING qualities cannot be excelled.

HOT WATER RESERVOIR . . . of ample proportion, with removable copper tank, can be supplied at back end of stove. In stove blacking finish only.

We pledge that our stoves are made today, as they were 97 years ago, by skilled Yankee Craftsmen. Each casting painstakingly fitted.

Our Franklin stoves **are not** made with steel sides and backs as are some competitive models.

Our Franklin stove fronts are one piece, solid cast iron, not made in several pieces and screwed together.

Our Franklin stove hearths (bottoms) are one solid piece, not two pieces screwed together.

Check for these quality features when you consider purchasing your stove.

Portland Stove Foundry Co.
Division of Fitchburg Foundry, Inc.
PORTLAND, MAINE

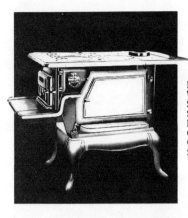

**Model 8316 Winner Cast Iron
Wood Burning Cookstove**

Size of oven	13½" x 13" x 10"
Size of top	30¼" x 21½"
Ht. to cooking top	28¾"
Covers	Four 8"
Collar oval	6"
Shipping weight	155 lbs.

Atlanta manufactures a wide range of cast iron coal and/or wood-burning cookstoves as well as Franklin fireplaces, radiant and circulator-type wood heaters.

**Model 51-15SB Cast Iron Coal
and Wood Range**

Style 5 shown. Comes semi-enameled with polished top.

Size of oven	15" x 14" x 11"
Size of top	33" x 21½"
Ht to cooking top	31"
Covers	Six 8"
Collar oval	7"
Shipping weight	335 lbs.
Available in Styles 1 and 5	

STYLE 1
RANGE ONLY

**Model 16-36 Cast Iron Coal and
Wood Range**

Style 3 shown. Cast iron and plain black finish. Oven thermometer.

Size of oven	16" x 16" x 12"
Size of top	37" x 23"
Ht. to cooking top	30¾"
Covers	Six 8"
Collar, oval	7"
Shipping weight	335 lbs.
Available in Styles 1 and 3	

STYLE 1
RANGE ONLY

THE ATLANTA STOVE WORKS, INC
PO Box 5254, Atlanta GA 30307

— *and* —

BIRMINGHAM STOVE & RANGE CO
Birmingham Alabama 35203

--Over 80 Years of Knowing How--

Combines the good cheer of a fireplace with the warm comfort of a stove.
You can put this authentic Ben Franklin fireplace almost anywhere. Install it easily, either free standing or built-in. You can use it as a fireplace, or for warmth as a stove.

Fill it with charcoal, and you can have year 'round charcoal broiling! It's made from strong, durable cast iron and styled to add a touch of Early American elegance to any atmosphere! A variety of useful and decorative accessories are available!

Thermostatically Controlled Super Automatic

There is nothing quite like this original, patented wood-burning heater with the adjustable thermostatic controls that make day or night warmth so completely automatic ...with outstanding efficiency and economy. The top, bottom, and doors are heavy cast iron, and you can load fuel at the front or from the top. The heavy gauge blue steel jacket radiates heat throughout the room. The ash door is removable to make ash handling easier. There's a 6" round, reversible collar for flue connections.

Easy-to-read patented thermostat controls adjustable for completely automatic heating. Also has manual control for fast starting.

For extra convenience, the smooth cast iron top can be used as a cooking surface.

Two popular sizes
Model 2501
Inside
diameter 22" x 17" x 23¼"
Height overall   35½"
Actual weight   140 lbs.

Model 3001 (Shown)
Inside
diameter 25" x 18" x 23½"
Height overall   35½"
Actual weight   151 lbs.

Patent Nos. 2376409
and 122151.

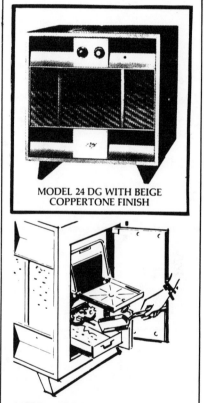

MODEL 24 DG WITH BEIGE
COPPERTONE FINISH

Several U.S. companies make thermostatically controlled wood circulators (like the model on the left) and radiant heaters (above). They all have similar features and prices,—the radiant heaters being less efficient and cheaper, the circulators are more efficient and expensive. The styling is generally from the 1940s and 50s, and —compared to some foreign models the efficiency is fairly low. If these stoves suit your requirements, check out each individual manufacturer (see the next few pages) before making your choice.

MODEL 24 DG For coal or wood burning
Available in a beautiful Beige Coppertone baked enamel finish, this heater burns either coal or wood with amazing economy. A large cast iron pouch fire door makes fueling easy. Heavy cast iron lining holds the heat for hours of extra warmth, air-tight ash door keeps ashes out of the room, but makes ash removal clean and simple.

Wood lgth., 21" • Firebox lgth., 21½" •
Firebox width, 11½" • Firebox ht., 21" •
Fuel door, 8½" x 9½" • Flue size 6" • Ht. to
cntr. of flue, 27" • Cabinet lgth., 35" •
Cabinet ht., 36½" • Cabinet width, 21" •
Shipping wt., 328 lbs.

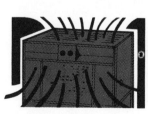

Directional louvers on top increase warm air circulation. Extra heat radiates from front grill and both sides.

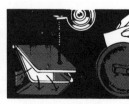

Automatic Draft Control works day and night. Paper-tight Manual Draft Control for extra draft . . . and fast warm-ups.

No. 24 and 24T Blower Kits. No. 24 is manually operated, No. 24T is controlled by a thermostat. Easily installed on all 24 Series Heaters. 1250 rpm, delivering 150 cfm of warm air to the floor.

locke

Wood-Burning Deluxe Circulator

products of
LOCKE STOVE COMPANY
114 West 11th Street - Kansas City, Mo. 64105

MODEL 701
With
Porcelain Enamel Cabinet Finish
Automatic Draft Regulator
Firebrick Lining
Cast Iron Grates
Ash Drawer

Porcelain Enamel Finish! Beautifully styled cabinet has attractive dark brown finish of porcelain enamel for lasting beauty. Won't rub off or discolor!

Hinged Smoke Curtain! Keeps smoke from coming into room when loading door is open.

Primary Air Vents! Round openings in firebrick liner sections bring in primary air from automatic draft regulator and distribute it evenly in burning zone.

Cast-Iron Grates! Three sections of heavy, slotted grates are ventilated for extended life. Slotted design permits ashes to sift by gravity into container below. No stirring of ashes required!

Hinged Ash Chute! Cast-iron chute drops down when door is opened, keeping ash from spilling out.

Large Slide-Out Ash Drawer! For convenient, muss-free ash removal!

Built-in Automatic Thermostat! Automatically adjusts primary draft to maintain desired burning rate and to keep temperatures steady. Control knob conveniently located at top rear of cabinet.

Cast-Iron Liner Plates! Upper sides and end of combustion chamber are fitted with cast-iron liner plates for longer operating life.

Firebrick Lining! Two-inch thick firebrick protects both sides of firebox.

Large Side Door. Loading door and ash door are constructed of cast iron with asbestos seals for tight fit. Loading door opening measures 10" X 14" to permit insertion of large sections of firewood.

Secondary Draft Slide! Provides supplementary air needed for quick starting of fires.

Two more wood "circulators" well worth consideration ▶

▼

U.S. Stove

UNITED STATES STOVE COMPANY
South Pittsburg,
Tennessee.

The "All Night" Heater— Extra capacity firebox provides "all night" heating with one loading—and up to 24 hours!

The "Comfort Controlled" Heater—An amazingly sensitive heat control device operates draft control door. Choose your comfort setting, then forget it. No electricity is needed, unless optional blower is used.

And low prices—Check the following "plus" features against much higher priced units. You'll find many features at less cost!

• Replaceable grate sections assure complete combustion. Ashes are almost 100% powder!

• Optional 2 speed blower operates only when heat is radiated. You choose gentle breeze or powerful surge of warm air. Discharges at floor level.

• Full size ash pan. Easy disposal of ashes, necessary for longer grate life.

• Airtight construction includes asbestos sealed doors. Entire heater sealed to give the most efficient (money-saving) temperature control.

• Choice of rigidized steel firebox linings for rapid heat transfer, or firebrick linings for heavy service requirements.

ashley

HOW PATENTED ASHLEY DOWNDRAFT SYSTEM WORKS:

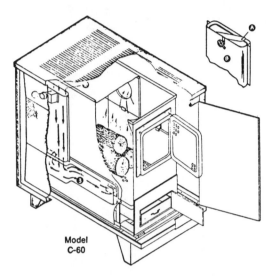

Model C-60

Firebox and ash doors are airtight. The only air admitted to primary combustion area of firebox enters at top (2) of down-draft stack, is preheated as it is drawn down stack, then is distributed evenly through air intake manifold (3) to bottom of firebox along its entire length, assuring even, more complete combustion, and eliminating hot spots (which also assures longer life of all firebox components). Thermostatic control (1) consists of damper (A) in top of downdraft stack activated by a bi-metal helix coil (B) which is temperature sensitive, opening and closing damper just enough to admit precisely the amount of combustion air necessary to maintain the level of comfort you have selected.

Please note that the Ashley introduces combustion air at FRONT of firebox (not at one end) so flow to flue is ACROSS the fire — not across one end or corner of it, as in other heaters. This promotes even, efficient burning along entire length of firebox.

Patented Secondary Air Intake — To increase further the efficiency of combustion, a patented automatic secondary air intake has been added. Responding automatically to temperature and atmospheric conditions, it admits to the firebox ABOVE the primary fire zone the proper amount of oxygen to burn wood gases that in other heaters would go unburned.

Ashley has been making wood-burning stoves for over a century. Currently they produce two wood circulators (the larger one can heat up to 4-6 rooms), and one radiant heater (shown at right). The circulator can be fitted with an electric fan for better heat dispersion. The radiant model is listed as part of their 'economy line' and sells for much less than the circulators.

By providing forced circulation of air, the blower (1) eliminates hot and cold spots for more even heating, (2) increases heater efficiency, and (3) decreases fuel consumption. You get more comfortable heating from less fuel.

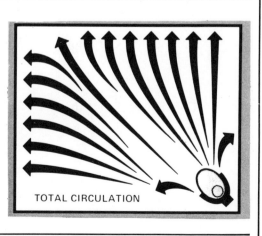

TOTAL CIRCULATION

Ashley COMPACT CONSOLE
Model C-62
Mahogany

Heats 3 or 4 average rooms. 20¾-inch firebox takes logs up to 18 inches long. Firebox capacity 3.2 cu. ft. Lift-off top. Mahogany baked enamel finish on steel cabinet, with contrasting decorator panel. Access door to concealed fire-box door, and separate ash removal door and pan. Holds 50 lbs. of wood at one filling.

ASHLEY®

Products Division
MARTIN INDUSTRIES
PO Box 730
Sheffield Alabama 35660

shenandoah

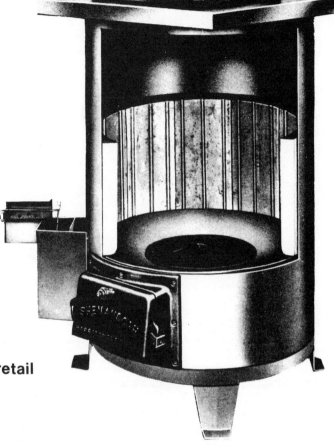

EMERGENCY HEATER
When your present heating system leaves you in the cold, warm up to a Shenandoah Heater. In an emergency, this inexpensive heater installed in your basement will keep you warm and insure against damage from freezing (burst water pipes, etc.).

HEAT YOUR HOME ECONOMICALLY
Supplement your present heating system by burning wood. One cord of air-dried wood is equal to 100 to 200 gallons of no. 2 fuel oil (depending on whether you burn a hard or soft species). By comparing the cost of obtaining wood with the cost of oil, you can determine whether it is feasible to use wood for supplementary heat.

IT'S A VERSATILE ALL-PURPOSE HEATER
Ideal for garages, utility rooms, work shops, cabins, small homes, cottages (one to two rooms). Thermostatically controlled, this heater is designed to burn with either a very hot flame or with a "simmer" flame. With a simmer flame, the fire will burn a full 24 hours.

$150 - $275 retail

SHENANDOAH MANUFACTURING CO
PO Box 839
Harrisonburg, Va 22801

---

other manufacturers

Autocrat Corporation . . . . Cookstoves and Space Heaters
Illinois & Benton Sts
New Athens IL 62264

Birmingham Stove & Range Co . . . . Cookstoves and Space Heaters
Box 2593
Birmingham AL 35203

King Stove & Range . . . . Cookstoves, Space Heaters, Laundry Stoves
Martin Industries
Box 730
Sheffield AL 35660

Malleable Iron Range Co . . . . Cookstoves and Wood/Gas, Wood/
Beaver Dam   Electric Combination Stoves
WI 53916

Automatic Wood Circulator

SPECIFICATIONS

Height	32"
Length	35"
Depth	22"
Fire Box	25 1/4" L x 13 1/2" D
Wood Length	24"
Height to top of lining	9 1/2"
Feed door opening	11 3/4" H x 11" W
Collar	6"
Shipping Weight	225 lbs.

A modern cabinet circulator especially designed for wood fuel. Combines unusual smartness and beauty with efficiency, dependability and long life. Standard features include: Fire brick lining, cast iron grate, large ash pan, cast iron feed and ash doors and automatic draft control.

BROWN STOVE WORKS, Inc.
P.O. Box 490
CLEVELAND, TENNESSEE 37311
615/476-6544

other manufacturers

U.S. Stove Co. . . . . **Thermostatically-Controlled Space Heaters**
S Pittsburg TN 38376

Vermont Soapstone Co . . . . **Soapstone/Steel Box Stoves**
Perkinsville VT 05151

Washington Stove Works . . . . **Cast Iron Box Stoves, Parlor Stoves**
Box 687   **Franklins and Modern Fireplaces**
Everett WA 98206

Whitten Enterprises . . . . **Franklin Fireplaces, Kitchen Ranges**
Arlington VT 05250

riteway ~ marco

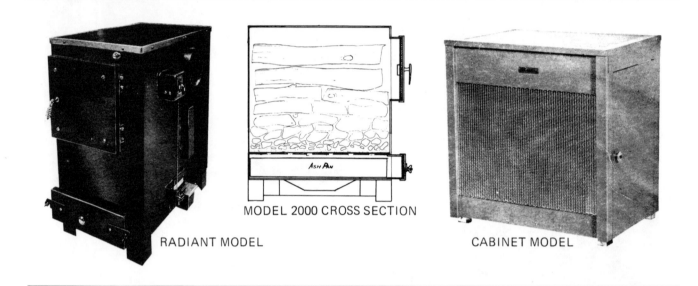

RADIANT MODEL   MODEL 2000 CROSS SECTION   CABINET MODEL

● *IMPROVED TEMPERATURE CONTROL*—Automatic magnetic draft damper, either fully open or fully closed, largely eliminates creosote.

● *MAXIMUM TEMPERATURE IN GAS COMBUSTION FLUE*—Further minimizes creosote formation and facilitates burning of fuel gases.

● *STURDY CONSTRUCTION*—Heavy steel plate electrically welded forms a permanently air-tight unit.

● *LARGE FUEL CAPACITY*—Load the fuel magazine morning and evening and let the model 2000 do the job with trouble-free heating.

● *50,000 BTU OUTPUT*—One heater should supply ample heat for four well-constructed rooms of average size.

● *ALUMINIZED STEEL LINER*—Weight-saving and long-lasting for high temperature service.

• *CABINETS AVAILABLE IN MAHOGANY AND GOLD BLEND*

——RITEWAY STOVES——

manufactures a furnace that will burn any combination of wood, coal, oil or gas. When heating with this combination unit, an independent control system automatically starts the oil or gas burner when the wood or coal supply fails to maintain the temperature selected at the thermostat. Complete combustion of gases is achieved with a downdraft flue that forces them back into the fire before exiting through the chimney. Temperature is maintained by a magnetic damper. Fuel savings of up to 80% have been reported by owners of these furnaces.

—————— SPECIFICATIONS ——————

RADIANT MODEL—28" long, 17" wide, 33" high
CABINET MODEL—36" long, 24" wide, 37" high
HEATER WEIGHT—225 lbs.
CABINET WEIGHT—75 lbs.
WOOD LENGTH—24" long
PIPE COLLAR—6" diameter
FUEL DOOR—12" x 12"
WOOD CAPACITY—4 cu. ft.

LIST PRICE
RADIANT—$295.00
CABINET—$140.00
HEATER WITH CABINET—$430.00
PRICES SUBJECT TO CHANGE WITHOUT NOTICE

MANUFACTURED & DISTRIBUTED BY
RITEWAY MANUFACTURING CO.
DIV. OF SARCO CORP.
P.O. BOX 6, HARRISONBURG, VA 22801
703-434-7090

BOILERS & FURNACES

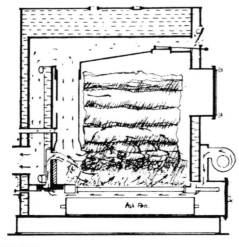

ECONOMY

● FUEL SAVINGS REPORTED AS HIGH AS 80% FOR FURNACES AND BOILERS — THANKS TO REVOLUTIONARY COMPLETE COMBUSTION PRINCIPLE.

● WITH THE CONSTANT THREAT OF THE ENERGY SHORTAGE, IT'S TO YOUR ADVANTAGE TO OBTAIN AN "ALTERNATE FUEL" SYSTEM. DON'T BE DEPENDENT ON ONE FUEL — FUELMASTER PRODUCTS OFFER YOU THE VERSATILITY OF HEATING WITH COAL, WOOD, OIL OR GAS.

COMFORT

● COLD MORNINGS CAN BE PART OF THE PAST — EACH FUEL LOADING LASTS 12 HOURS AND MORE!

● AUTOMATIC THERMOSTAT CONTROLS ON ALL MODELS MEANS CAREFREE, EVEN HEAT FOR YOU, THE HOME OWNER.

BEAT THE ENERGY CRUNCH

● THE COMPLETE COMBUSTION DESIGN BUILT INTO ALL FUELMASTER PRODUCTS IS THE RESULT OF MORE THAN 35 YEARS' ENGINEERING EXPERIENCE IN WOOD BURNING EQUIPMENT.
● MARCO ENGINEERS WERE THE FIRST TO PERFECT PRACTICAL COMPLETE COMBUSTION WOOD BURNING EQUIPMENT FOR THE AMERICAN MARKET.
● FIRST MARKETED UNDER THE "RITEWAY" NAME, THESE UNITS SOON EARNED AN ENVIABLE REPUTATION FOR RELIABILITY AND SUPERIOR PERFORMANCE, THE FUEL-MASTER LINE IS AN EVEN FURTHER REFINEMENT BASED ON THE COMPLETE COMBUSTION PRINCIPLE.
● FUELMASTER PRODUCTS OFFER UNUSUAL ECONOMY AND REMARKABLE EFFICIENCY, SAVING HALF THE FUEL NEEDED BY OLD-FASHIONED "UP DRAFT" HEATING EQUIPMENT.

HOW IT WORKS

● WOOD IS PLACED IN A LARGE MAGAZINE (CLOSED AT THE TOP) WHERE IT IS GRADUALLY REDUCED TO CHARCOAL. TWO PRIMARY AIR JETS, LOCATED IN BACK OF THE COMBUSTION CHAMBER AND ON EACH SIDE OF A LARGE GAS COMBUSTION FLUE, DELIVER A STRONG FLOW OF AIR OVER THE CHARCOAL BED WHEN THE THERMOSTAT CALLS FOR HEAT.
● A VERY HIGH TEMPERATURE RESULTS NEAR THE GAS COMBUSTION FLUE INLET, MAKING IT POSSIBLE TO ESTABLISH AND MAINTAIN THE REQUIRED TEMPERATURE (1200 DEGREES) TO IGNITE THE WOOD GAS.
● AFTER ENTERING THE GAS COMBUSTION FLUE, PRE-HEATED SECONDARY AIR IS ADDED TO PROVIDE NECESSARY OXYGEN FOR THE COMBUSTION OF THE ALWAYS PRESENT WOOD "CREOSOTE" AND TARS.
● FULLY ONE-HALF THE HEATING VALUE OF WOOD IS REPRESENTED BY COMBUSTIBLE GASES — GASES NORMALLY LOST IN TRADITIONAL WOOD BURNING EQUIPMENT.

RITEWAY FURNACES & BOILERS —— SPECIFICATIONS

	FURNACES				BOILERS		
	LF20	LF30	LF50	LF70	LB30	LB50	LB70
BTU Output	Up to 125,000	Up to 160,000	Up to 215,000	Up to 350,000	Up to 160,000	Up to 200,000	Up to 350,000
Length	68"	73"	85"	103"	56"	68"	84"
Width	34"	36"	36"	40"	36"	36"	40"
Height	53"	65"	65"	65"	66"	66"	66"
Smoke Pipe Diameter	7"	8"	8"	10"	8"	8"	10"
Wood Length	24"	24"	36"	48"	24"	36"	48"
Fuel Capacity (cu. ft.)	13.5	20	30	45	17.5	26.2	43.4
Fuel Door Size (inches)	13 x 14	14 x 16	14 x 16	16 x 16	14 x 16	14 x 16	16 x 16
Warm Air Plenum Opening	16 x 30	18 x 32	24 x 32	28 x 36			
Flow & Return Tappings					2"	2½"	3"
Approx. Shipping Wt.	1000 lbs	1800 lbs.	2400 lbs.	3050 lbs.	2000 lbs.	2600 lbs.	3200 lbs.
Prices	$1442.00	$1950.00	$2110.00	$2760.00	$3088.00	$3221.00	$3840.00

FUELMASTER FURNACES INCLUDE A COMPLETE SET OF ELECTRIC THERMOSTATIC CONTROLS, BAROMETRIC DAMPER, DRAFT INDUCER, FORCED DRAFT AND WARM AIR CIRCULATION, FILTERS, GALVANIZED CASING, HEAT EXCHANGER, AND MOUNTING TUBE FOR FUTURE INSTALLATION OF OIL OR GAS BURNER.

FUELMASTER HOT WATER BOILERS ARE EQUIPPED WITH COMBINATION TEMPERATURE, PRESSURE AND ALTITUDE GUAGE, DUAL CONTROLS INCLUDING PRESSURE AND RELIEF VALVE, DRAFT INDUCER, BAROMETRIC DAMPER, AND A COMPLETE SET OF ELECTRIC THERMOSTATIC CONTROLS. STEAM BOILERS ARE EQUIPPED WITH WATER GLASS, TEST COCKS, PRESSURE GUAGE, RELIEF VALVE, AND A COMPLETE SET OF ELECTRIC CONTROLS.

THE KEY IS VERSATILITY

● OIL OR GAS BURNERS MAY BE INSTALLED ON THE FURNACE OR BOILER YOU CHOOSE, PRACTICALLY INSURING YOU OF HEAT, DESPITE THE SCARCITY OF ONE PARTICULAR FUEL. KNOWING YOU CAN BURN WOOD, COAL, GAS OR OIL SETS YOUR MIND AT EASE IN A TIME WHEN SOME FUELS ARE IN SHORT SUPPLY.
● IN OUR COMBINATION EQUIPMENT WE INCLUDE TWO INDEPENDENT CONTROL SYSTEMS AND TWO ROOM THERMOSTATS. WHEN WOOD IS TO BE BURNED, SIMPLY SET THE OIL OR GAS THERMOSTAT 2-3 DEGREES LOWER THAN THE WOOD AND COAL TEMPERATURE CONTROL. WHEN THE WOOD OR COALS BURNS OUT, THE OIL OR GAS BURNER AUTOMATICALLY KICKS IN AND MAINTAINS THE CORRECT TEMPERATURE.

OPTIONAL EXTRAS

OIL, NATURAL GAS OR BOTTLED GAS BURNER COMPLETE WITH FULL SET OF ELECTRIC CONTROLS, SPECIAL COMPONENTS NECESSARY FOR EFFICIENT AUTOMATIC OPERATION OF BURNER IN CONNECTION WITH WOOD OR COAL BURNING UNIT

OIL BURNER—$570.00
WATER HEATER (FURNACE)—$147.00
WATER HEATER (BOILER) 3½ GPM—$94.00 4½ GPM—$112.00

GAS BURNER—$640.00
HUMIDIFIER—$36.00

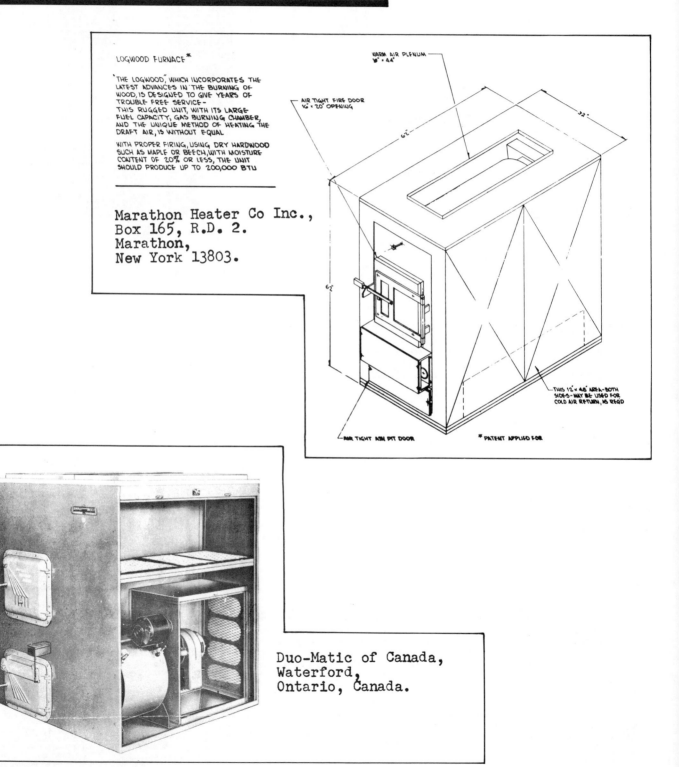

LOGWOOD FURNACE *

"THE LOGWOOD", WHICH INCORPORATES THE LATEST ADVANCES IN THE BURNING OF WOOD, IS DESIGNED TO GIVE YEARS OF TROUBLE FREE SERVICE —
THIS RUGGED UNIT, WITH ITS LARGE FUEL CAPACITY, GAS BURNING CHAMBER, AND THE UNIQUE METHOD OF HEATING THE DRAFT AIR, IS WITHOUT EQUAL

WITH PROPER FIRING, USING DRY HARDWOOD SUCH AS MAPLE OR BEECH, WITH MOISTURE CONTENT OF 20% OR LESS, THE UNIT SHOULD PRODUCE UP TO 200,000 BTU

Marathon Heater Co Inc.,
Box 165, R.D. 2.
Marathon,
New York 13803.

Duo-Matic of Canada,
Waterford,
Ontario, Canada.

The New BELLWAY Hi-Temp Heaters, Furnaces and Boilers operate on the principle that the fuel is stored in the top section of the heat exchanger, where it doesn't burn, and is completely dried out before feeding down by gravity when needed, to the high temperature burner in the lower section.

All BELLWAY units burn green or dry wood, garbage and old paper and will produce up to 40% more heat by burning the wood gas or blue smoke instead of wasting this energy up the chimney. The thermostat control combined with the Bellway designed crossflow burning unit with afterburner and feedback system maintains even heat for over ten hours in zero weather without attention.

Manufactured from heavy steel, these furnaces have full-length shaker grates, large feed door, and heavy weight casings for gravity heat or forced hot air. Their boilers have insulated casings and will supply hot water as well as hot air. The water system is rust-proof and can be operated dry without damage.

Bellway furnaces can also burn oil as a supplement to wood and will kick in when the wood supply runs out or temperatures cannot be maintained at the desired level with wood. All units come complete and ready to install.

* Clean Burning
* Proven In 17 Vermont Winters
* Ten Hour Wood Storage-- Feeds Down As Needed
* Burns Green Wood, Garbage & Catalogs
* Thermostatically Controlled Draft

**BELLWAY MFG
GRAFTON VT 05146
802 843 2432**

jøtul

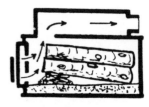

**Aksjeselkapet,
Jøtul,
Postbox 6206, ET
Oslo 6, NORWAY.**

JØTUL, one of the oldest and largest woodstove manufacturers in Europe, was founded in 1853. Jøtul cast iron wood heaters, fireplaces, coal and peat heaters, cook stoves and combi-fires are generally acknowledged by authorities as the most efficient on the market today.

Kristia Associates, Portland, Maine is the exclusive importer of Jøtul stoves in the U.S.

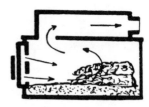

The Jøtul 602

- This popular little wood stove is only eighteen inches long yet will heat a medium sized room.
- Traditional Norwegian design. Available with a decorative top.
- A more even heat is radiated because of the heavy enamelled cast iron construction and interior cast iron baffle plates.
- Like the other Jøtul wood stoves, No. 602 has an extremely efficient front end combustion system which allows wood to burn slowly for long periods, without reloading.

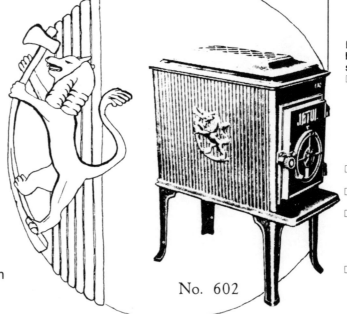

No. 602

Facts about JØTUL wood-burning and coke-burning stoves.

- ☐ Excellent for keeping a fire burning day and night. Jøtul wood-burning stoves burn from the front, giving an exceptionally long burning time for each replenishing. (See figs. 1 and 2).
- ☐ Rapid heat emission and high fuel economy.
- ☐ Specially designed air valve for wood-burning.
- ☐ Patented air pre-heating chamber on inside of door, distributing the primary and secondary air currents in the correct manner.
- ☐ Specially designed heat plates give higher temperatures in the fire chamber, distribute the heat and protect the sides of the stove.
- ☐ Asbestos packing in door – no false draught reaches the fire and no individual fitting required if doors are renewed.
- ☐ Efficient, robust door closers with heat-insulated handles.
- ☐ Sweeping is easy – and clean. Simple, attractive design.
- ☐ Available in heat-proof, deep green Jøtul enamel – no stove-blacking needed.

JØTUL WOOD STOVES FROM NORWAY

All Jøtuls are 100% heavy duty cast iron. Unusual front end combustion system allows wood to burn slowly over long periods of time without reloading. Truly efficient, durable, handsome wood heaters. Prices range from $200-$800.

(Here are four JØTUL favorites)

Jøtul No. 118
Classic box stove has been a Jøtul front-runner for over 30 years. Traditional Norwegian bas-relief design. Available in dark green enamel or matte black. Accommodates logs up to 2 feet long. Max. heating capacity: 7,060 cu. ft.

Jøtul No. 4
Known for quick-change artistry. One minute it's a roaring fireplace ... the next it's an airtight wood stove. Takes up so little space and yet it's the champ among Jøtul's in total heating capacity. Available in dark green enamel or matte black. Max. heating capacity: 8,825 cu. ft.

Jøtul No. 404
Only 18 inches wide by 25 inches long, this Norwegian cook stove readily finds niche in your kitchen. Adjustable damper for cooking and baking. Efficient oven with enameled baking sheet and solid steel roasting tin. Black fireproof enameling throughout. Max. heating capacity: 2,649 cu. ft.

Jøtul No. 602
Little brother of Jøtul 118. Only foot and a half long little box stove still heats average size room. Traditional bas-relief lion design. Available in dark green enamel or matte black. Max. heating capacity: 4,766 cu. ft.

Jøtul No. 606
An all-time favorite back in production due to great demand for small, efficient wood burners. The heated air rising from the firebox rests in the heating chamber rather than rising up the chimney. Arch design is very traditional and provides larger surface of heat radiation.

Send $1 for new Resource Guide to Woodburning, featuring full line of Jøtul cast iron heaters, fireplaces, coal heaters and combi-fires, to:

No. 118

No. 4

No. 404

No. 602

No. 606

IMPORTERS:

KRISTIA ASSOCIATES

343 Forest Avenue • P.O. Box 1118
Portland, Maine 04104

Distributors:
The Burning Log/Lebanon, New Hampshire/(603) 448-4364
Glowing Embers/Bloomingburg, New York/(914) 773-4331
The In Grates/Braintree, Massachusetts/(617) 848-5550
Kristia Associates/Portland, Maine/(207) 772-2821
Mother's General Store/Flat Rock, North Carolina/(704) 693-4109

National Glass Works/Worcester, Massachusetts/(617) 753-7200
Northern Lights Ltd./E. Wilton, Maine/(207) 645-4292
Stove Pipe Associates/Bloomington, Indiana/(812) 332-2940
Stove Pipe Associates/West Lafayette, Indiana/(317) 567-2513

Model K 6.14

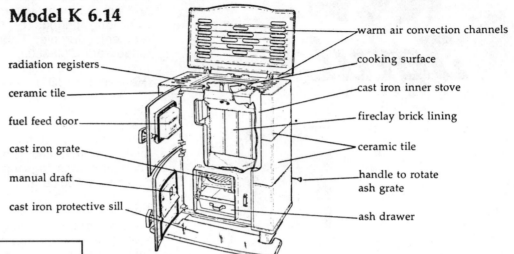

radiation registers

ceramic tile

fuel feed door

cast iron grate

manual draft

cast iron protective sill

warm air convection channels

cooking surface

cast iron inner stove

fireclay brick lining

ceramic tile

handle to rotate ash grate

ash drawer

The Berliner: *Quality plus Efficiency*

The Danish Woodburning Stove has a newly designed interior Draft Plate which makes the logs burn slowly from front to back (like a cigar) not consuming the entire log at once as in most conventional box stoves. The addition of the Draft Plate allows the wood to burn slowly for long periods of time without reloading (conserving fuel) and to maintain an overnight fire without loss of heat efficiency.

The *Berliner* stove has a large cast iron firebox which is lined with firebrick for maximum durability and efficiency. The slow-combustion firebox produces intensive heat from a minimum amount of solid fuel: wood, charcoal, or coal.

The *Berliner* Model 6.14 R has an automatic, non-electric draft regulator to control the amount of air supplied to the fire. The Model 6.14 has a manual draft and is therefore best suited for burning only wood. Both models disperse heat through means of the warm air convection channels as well as a gentle radiation through the old-fashioned ceramic tiles. The two large service doors (lined with brass trim), the top and protective sill, are all enameled deep brown to contrast with the burnt amber glaze of the ceramic tiles to produce a tasteful design.

Model 6203

Heat capacity approx. .....18,000 BTU
Total height with decorative
    outlet ....41 in.

HDI IMPORTERS
Schoolhouse Farm
Etna, N.H. 03750

The Austrian KACHELOFEN

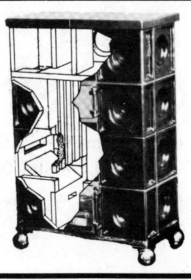

These beautiful and durable ceramic tile stoves operate on the "heat accumulation" principle. Heat energy from a small amount of fuel is stored in the four-inch thick walls and is gently released over a period of time...for up to 15 hours. Kacheloefen are thus one of the most efficient stoves ever built...up to 85%. Austrians have been using them for heating castles, inns, and homes for over 425 years.

These transportable Kacheloefen are designed and built by Austrian craftsmen to our exact specifications. One may select tile shapes from any architectural period: Gothic, Renaissance, Baroque, Rococo, or modern. A variety of colors and glazes are available.

A customed designed Kachelofen can be built into your home for the ultimate in heating comfort, efficiency, and beauty... and at a cost only slightly higher than that of building a fireplace.

The L. Lange Company of Svendborg, Denmark is 125 years old, and follows a stove-making tradition even older. They are manufacturers of a large selection of cast iron air-tight stoves, from a small coal-burning ship's stove to the model 6302A with horizontal baffles which heats up to 9,000 cu. ft. to their combination fireplace/stove with removable front and firebrick lining. As with other Scandinavian 'air-tights' now available in the U.S., they are excellent and efficient heaters.

Distributed in the U.S. by:

SCANDINAVIAN STOVES INC
Box 72
Alstead NH 03602

Lange Model 6302A

This is a powerful heater of very sturdy design. Curved plates for extra strength. Unique baffle system for extra heat output. Baffle can be by-passed for quick starting fire. Can be used for cooking.

Lange Model 6302K

The base is the same as the 6302A, but a second heating chamber has been added. The chamber contains an oven (with vent for temperature regulation) and cooking plates. The "K" will heat a very large area, and handle cooking and baking at the same time.

Lange Model 6303A

This is an especially strong heater with a long firebox and big wood capacity for a small stove. Curved side plates add strength. All stove plates near fire, so no baffle is needed. Can be used for cooking.

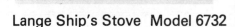

Lange Ship's Stove Model 6732

A small ship's stove for use with coal, coke or charcoal. Removable rings in cookplate permit pot to sit securely as ship rolls. Stove bolts to ship. Black enamel finish avoids rust. Firebrick lined. Uses pea coal.

wood burning heaters & ranges

STYRIA Wood-Burning Heaters and Styria Wood/Coal Cooking Ranges are made in Austria. They are ruggedly built, using enameled steel panels, nickel-plated trim and cast iron doors, plus **FULL FIREBRICK LINING.** All Styria products are built along the lines of European Ceramic (Tile) Stoves ... the heat is 'Built up' or accumulated, and the Styria Heaters, for example, do not cool off rapidly! The heat is even and the wood consumption is very economical. Styria Ranges can hold the fire overnight too; they burn wood, coal, fuel briquets, charcoal & burnable trash.

Prices range from $870 to $2000, which includes duty & shipping from Austria to Maine. Send $ .80 for your Styria Catalogue ... or write for a free brochure. Most models are in stock, ready for shipment via motor freight.

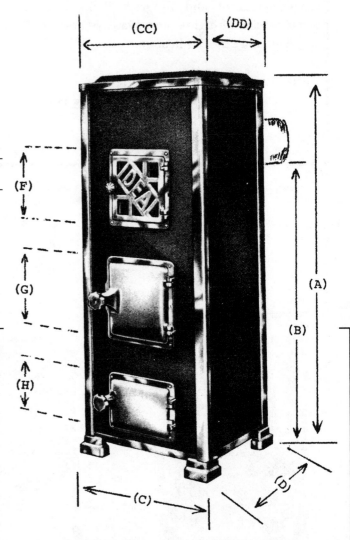

Illustrated above: Model THREE
STYRIA Ideal Heater

Shown above: Model "130" STYRIA Cooking Range

Description		Model (2)	Model (3)	Model (4)
(A)	Total HEIGHT:	39"	42½"	48½"
(B)	Pipe-to-Floor:	31½"	35¼"	40"
(C)	Total WIDTH:	18"	18"	21¾"
(CC)	Upper Width:	17"	17"	21"
(D)	Total DEPTH:	15"	15"	18½"
(DD)	Upper Width:	14½"	14½"	17¾"
(F)	Humidification Chamber: All Models, 7¼" square			
(G)	Fuel Door with Keylock Knob: All Models, 7½" square			
(H)	Ash-Emptying Door with Keylock Knob: Models (3) and (4), 7½" by 4½"			
	[Note: Door "G" serves both purposes for Model (2)]			
WEIGHT, uncrated:		130 kg	157 kg	240 kg
		289 lbs	349 lbs	533 lbs
[Add approximately 100 lbs. for a shipping crate]				

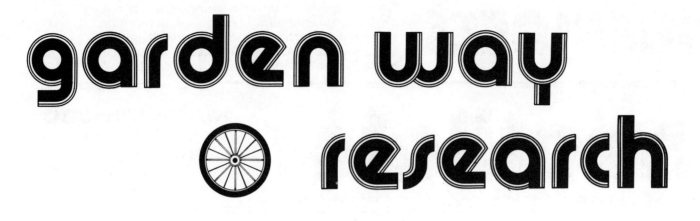

garden way · research

Fireplace Grates

Garden Way's fireplace grate provides an inexpensive means for solving the problems of a smoky fireplace. Fully adjustable, the grate will hold logs in the position they are placed, allowing for complete control of the draft. It comes in two sizes and the prices range from $32.30 (Model B) to $35.70 (Model A). In addition to the box stove shown below, the company also offers log carriers, racks, puff-pokers (which you can blow through to rekindle flames) and a full line of carts for hauling wood, removing ashes, etc.

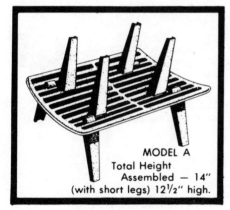

MODEL A
Total Height
Assembled — 14"
(with short legs) 12½" high.

Height--14" Base Size--15" x 21"

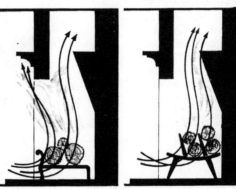

Adjustable legs and topside log supports keep the fire up and back, keep smoke from escaping.

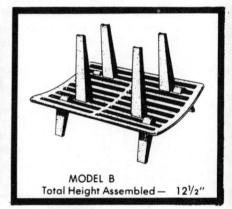

MODEL B
Total Height Assembled — 12½"

Height--12½" Base Size--13" x 19"

$159.95

& Box Stoves

AN EXTREMELY EFFICIENT BOX-STYLE STOVE WHICH WILL HEAT YOUR LIVING ROOM, DEN OR BEDROOM.

The Garden Way Box Stove is a simple and economical way to cut the costs of space heating. It's attractive enough to use in your living room and the Shaker design is an extremely efficient use of materials as well as a high-efficiency space heater. The stove is constructed of 1/8" steel and will last for many years of burning.

The nearly air-tight construction assures good control of the fire; with the door and draft vents closed, the fire will go out in a short time.

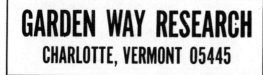

GARDEN WAY RESEARCH
CHARLOTTE, VERMONT 05445

FIREPLACES

Local fireplace shops and hardware stores can provide you with most of your needs in terms of stovepipe and fittings, sheet metal hoods, grates, etc. Sears also has a wide range of accessories and sells conventional fireplace units as well.

heatilator

HEATILATOR FIREPLACE • *A Division of Vega Industries, Inc., Mt. Pleasant, Iowa 52641*

MARK 123-38C
HEAT CIRCULATING
FIREPLACE
MODEL 3138
PATENTS PENDING

Amongst a wide range of less efficient designs, Heatilator manufactures a simple, well-designed warm-air circulating fireplace. Their complete installation manual makes it possible for the homeowner to install a fireplace on his own.

MARK 123C

A COMPLETELY NEW FIREPLACING SIMPLIFIED CONCEPT

A real fireplace and heating system in one unit. This lightweight, built-in, fully controllable woodburning heat-cirulating fireplace has easy to handle components that quickly install for a complete, operating fireplace. Position anywhere, (see diagram A), along any wall; 45° across corner; in chase, closet or garage area or to act as an attractive room divider. Install flush with wall, partially or fully projecting with a flush or raised hearth. Leave Flat Black as finished, paint any color to harmonize or contrast with brick, stone, marble, glass, slate, etc. Finish trim options are unlimited.

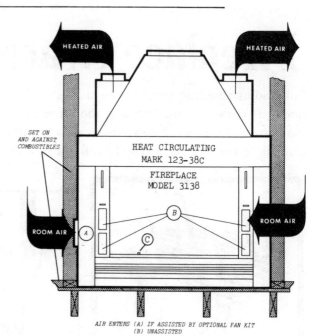

HEATED AIR   HEATED AIR

SET ON AND AGAINST COMBUSTIBLES

HEAT CIRCULATING
MARK 123-38C

FIREPLACE
MODEL 3138

ROOM AIR   ROOM AIR

AIR ENTERS (A) IF ASSISTED BY OPTIONAL FAN KIT
(B) UNASSISTED

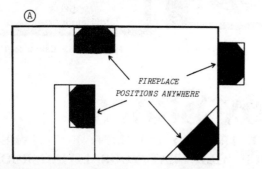

FIREPLACE POSITIONS ANYWHERE

CONTROLLABLE HEAT CIRCULATION WHEN AND WHERE DESIRED

Individually controllable left and right ducts from fireplace to wall outlets carry clean, warm air which is heated in special chambers inside the fireplace. One outlet only may be used from each side. The outlets are not, however, required to be in the same room (see diagram B). Outlets may be installed in the fireplace room, or in any other room, or one outlet per room. The warm air rises naturally, or may be assisted by the optional fan-equipped inlets. Heat circulation through outlets may be stopped by use of pull-chain controls. Internal air circulation within the fireplace does not stop, however, but continues in order to maintain safe temperatures of all metal parts and of combustible construction of the building. ALL AIR FLOW CEASES when fire is completely out and damper has been closed.

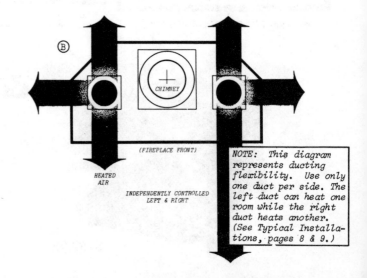

CHIMNEY

(FIREPLACE FRONT)

HEATED AIR

INDEPENDENTLY CONTROLLED LEFT & RIGHT

NOTE: *This diagram represents ducting flexibility. Use only one duct per side. The left duct can heat one room while the right duct heats another. (See Typical Installations, pages 8 & 9.)*

MARK 123-

CIRCULATING FIREPLACE OPERATING INSTRUCTIONS:

DAMPER (CENTER CONTROL): ALWAYS FULL-OPEN WHEN FIREPLACE IN USE, HANDLE UP. PULL DOWN TO CLOSE, WITH LARGE BEAD OF CHAIN LOCKED UNDER BRACKET.

HEAT (LEFT & RIGHT CONTROLS): TO CIRCULATE HEAT, RELEASE HANDLES. TO TURN OFF HEAT, PULL HANDLES FULL-DOWN, LOCK CHAIN IN BRACKET. USE FANS, IF SO EQUIPPED, ONLY WHEN HEATING.

NOTE: LEFT AND RIGHT HEAT OUTLETS INDEPENDENTLY CONTROLLED.

CAUTION: KEEP GRILLES CLEAR. NEVER INSTALL GLASS DOORS.

Easy Do-It-Yourself Installation

1. Platform to hold fireplace and provide raised hearth in place.
2. Fireplace unit in position on wooden platform and against wall. (U.L. listed for zero clearance to combustible surfaces.)
3. Conceal fireplace and heat circulating duct with 2x4 framing and wall material. Complete installation directions provided.
4. Final finish as you want it. The choice of non-combustible surround and room finishing treatment is endless. Catalog color photos illustrate some of the possibilities.

1

2

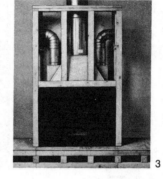
3

4

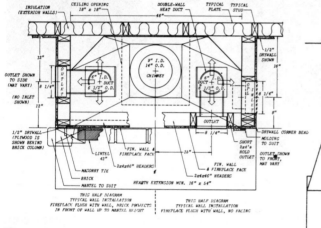

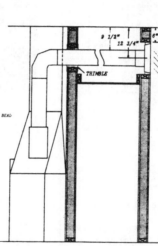

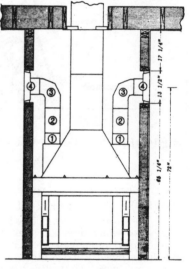

HEATILATOR

TYPICAL INSTALLATION "G" — SIDE VIEW

Showing: Method of locating Outlet in remote room;
Duct penetrates partition wall;
Partition Thimble use to maintain clearance.

TYPICAL INSTALLATION "A" — FRONT VIEW

Showing: Fireplace against a wall;
Fireplace on floor;
8'0" ceiling room (96 inches);
Supplied duct parts used;
Outlets in left and right walls.

Wood Heating Catalog 243
Wood Heating Catalog **243**

ƒtovalator

American Stovalator Corporation
MANCHESTER, VERMONT 05254

IMPROVED EFFICIENCY WITH STOVALATOR IN PLACE

STOVALATOR BLOCKS MY FIREPLACE? HOW DOES THE AIR FEED THE FIRE?

The air intake is limited to a damper at the base of the unit which directs cold air from your floor under the fire at an increased velocity. This creates a furnace-like efficiency and directs the air where you want it. You now have a controlled fire. In fact, it is so efficient we recommend that you burn wood or coal.

HOW DOES STOVALATOR HEAT MY HOUSE?

By recycling the heat in your fireplace, instead of going straight up the chimney, the heat is forced to stay in your fireplace, minimizing the loss up the chimney. STOVALATOR'S scientifically designed heat chamber extends into your fireplace blocking the direct escape of heat. It forces the heat to work for you and ultimately returns it to your home. This recycling process super heats the chamber and starts the convective process that supplies you with valuable heated air.

HOW DOES STOVALATOR'S HEAT CHAMBER SUPPLY HEAT?

The chamber operates on the same principle as a hot air furnace. It requires two vents: an intake and an exhaust. The lower intake vent pulls cooler air into the chamber. A tongue in the chamber directs the air over the fire, heats it, and forces it out the exhaust vent. The hotter the fire, the greater the volume of heated air coming into your home.

No matter which kind of 'heat return' fireplace you install, you will certainly get better efficiency than with an open fire. Stove enthusiasts may point out that the increased efficiency will be nothing like that of an "airtight", and open fire addicts will complain that a fire behind glass doesn't look, or feel, the same. But one of these many various approaches to the heat loss problem with fireplaces must surely suit someone.

American Stovalator Corporation
BOX 435 • TEN SEMINARY PLACE
MANCHESTER, VERMONT 05254
Manufacturers of Fireplace Furnaces and Accessories

el fuego

Here is a new way to beat the high cost of heating. El Fuego units are scientifically designed to capture and heat the air in your room. Cool air is drawn into the bottom of the unit, heated and expelled through vents in the top.

These units are so uniquely designed that El Fuego has applied for a U.S. patent.

FUEGO III — The basic convector Firebox module for improving the efficiency of an existing masonry fireplace. Three sizes adapt to most fireplaces.

FUEGO IV — A pre-built unit for the home. Installs on existing floor with zero clearance to any wall surface, framing or paneling. No expensive masonry is required.

FUEGO V — A free-standing stove with the aesthetic appeal of a real fireplace. Outer steel surfaces are comfortable to the touch. Uses hardwood as a fuel.

The diagram at the right shows how the cool air from the room is drawn into the area beneath the firebox, is heated as it circulates up and around the heated firebox and returns to the room through the top front grill. In a conventional fireplace, heated air escapes up the chimney. Glass doors on the Fuego units minimize this heat loss. The doors also help to prevent sparks, soot and smoke from entering the room.

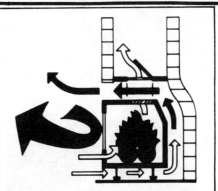

EL FUEGO
INDUSTRIES, LTD.

puts heat in your room
...not up the chimney!

PO BOX 33 OAKVILLE CT 06779

radiant grate

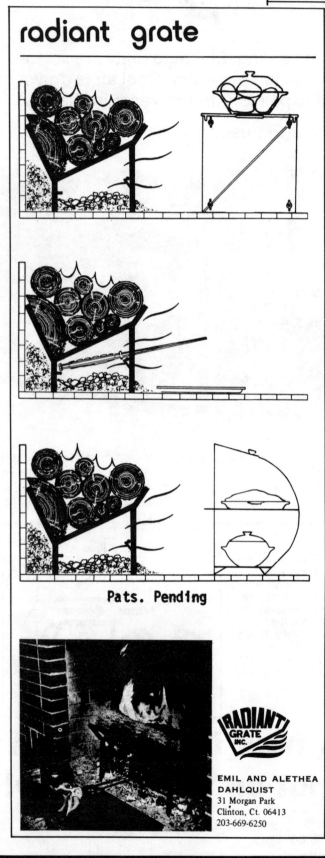

Pats. Pending

A simple, well-designed grate can improve the efficiency of your fireplace enormously. Emil Dahlquist developed the "Radiant Grate", which exposes the ashes so that they can radiate heat into the room. This makes the fireplace ideal for cooking, — and you can buy all the equipment you need from the Dahlquists at reasonable prices. There are several versions of the convecting grate available. The simplest versions can be made easily enough from mild steel exhaust pipe,— get your local muffler shop to cut and bend it to suit your grate. For heating large rooms the blower pays off.

thermograte

Fireplace furnace

Your blazing hearth looks cozy —but most of the heat goes up the chimney. It won't, if you cradle your fire on this grate: C-shaped tubular steel, welded into a sturdy basket, draws cool room air in at the base, pours hot air out at the top. Thermograte, 51 Iona Lane, St. Paul, Minn. 55117.

löeffler grate

LOEFFLER HEATING UNITS MFG. CO.
R. D. 1 - BOX 503
BRANCHVILLE, NEW JERSEY 07826

CONVECT-O-HEATER DESIGN FEATURES

DETACHABLE BLOWER ASSEMBLY — Connects to either side of unit

PORTABLE — Just lift it out

CONCENTRATED BURNING AREA — Conserves fireplace fuels — up to 40 percent

SILENT BLOWER OPERATION

Model A62 and B11

Model C43

GENERAL PRODUCTS CORPORATION INC.

655 PLAINS ROAD • MILFORD, CONNECTICUT 06460

UNIT SPECIFICATIONS	MODELS		
	A62	B11	C43
Height	20 in.	20 in.	26 in.
Width	25 in.	25 in.	32 in.
Depth	* 17 in.	* 17 in.	22 in.
Number of Chambers	6	6	8
Diameter of Chambers	1⅛ in.	1⅛ in.	1⅛ in.
Material (steel)	16 ga.	16 ga.	16 ga.
Flex-Steel Duct Length .	24 in.	24 in.	24 in.
Blower Fan Output	60 cfm	100 cfm	100 cfm
Blower Fan Input	36 watts	61 watts	61 watts
Shipping Weight	33 lbs.	35 lbs.	45 lbs.

*Recommended for fireplaces up to 28 inches deep; convection tube extensions available for deeper fireplaces.

convect~o~heater

HOW EFFECTIVE IS CONVECT-O-HEATER?

This performance test compares the heat output of the same fireplace. both with and without a CONVECT-O-HEATER. Equal amounts of firewood were used for both parts of the test. Two temperature recorders were used; one at 6 feet and the other at 26 feet from the fireplace. AT NO TIME DURING THIS COMPARISON TEST WAS ANY OTHER HEAT SOURCE USED.

COMPARISON TEST RESULTS	°F at 6 feet	
	without Convect-O-Heater	with Convect-O-Heater
Starting Room Temperature	52°F	52°F
Room Temperature After ½ Hour	61°F	68°F
Room Temperature After 1 Hour	65°F	73°F
Room Temperature After 2 Hours	67°F	75°F

CONVECT-O-HEATER model used A62   Room size 26 x 15 feet

COMPARISON TEST RESULTS	°F at 26 feet	
	without Convect-O-Heater	with Convect-O-Heater
Starting Room Temperature	52°F	52°F
Room Temperature After ½ Hour	53°F	63°F
Room Temperature After 1 Hour	55°F	70°F
Room Temperature After 2 Hours	56°F	73°F

Observe the even room temperatures achieved with CON-VECT-O-HEATER. Also the dramatic increase in heat output of the fireplace — at 26 feet — when equipped with CON-VECT-O-HEATER.

Better 'n Ben's
the Fireplace Stove

Convert your fireplace to an efficient home heater...with Better 'n Ben's

SAVE UP TO 60% IN HOME HEATING COSTS THIS WINTER

This unique combination wood stove and fire-place cover panel installs in minutes without masonry alterations. It burns seasoned wood throughout the night, will heat your home and cook your meals. Homeowners report up to 60% fuel savings. Also great for camps, cabins, ski-lodges and as an emergency unit in case of power failures. Firebox: 18" high; 18" wide; 24" deep. Door Opening: 9" x 13". Weight: 145 lbs. Back Panel: Std. 34½" high x 42" wide. Other sizes available.

Heat Deflector

Damper (must be in open position)

Fiberglass Insulation

Stove Damper Control Handle

Lintel

Adjustable Lintel Clamp

Stove Damper

Baffle

Adjustable Screw Leveler

13"

BETTER 'N BEN'S has a one year limited warranty from date of purchase covering defects and workmanship.

For descriptive brochure, send 25 cents to:

C&D
DISTRIBUTORS, INC.
P.O. Box 715, Dept. CJ
Old Saybrook, CT.
06475   (203)388-5665

SouthEastern Vermont — Community Action, Inc.

The S.E.V.C.A. stove was designed to provide low-income families with an efficient wood-burning stove, at a price suited to their means. The stove is fabricated from discarded propane tanks. The 3/16" walls assure a very strong and lasting fire-box. All additional structural parts of the stove are made from 3/16" hot rolled steel plate.

The upper chamber acts as a secondary wood-gas burning chamber and offers a larger heat transfer surface, suitable for cooking.
Preliminary tests on this new design put the S.E.V.C.A. stove in competition with any of the airtight stoves currently on the market.

Retail price for this stove is a little over $200. For qualifying low-income people, there is a reduced price.

South Eastern Vt Community Action Inc
7-9 Westminster St
Bellows Falls VT 05101

HEAT-RECOVERY UNITS

Residential-Type Fuel Miser
4 sizes . . . . $106.00 each

Edmund Scientific Corp.
555 Edscorp Bldg.
Barrington, NJ 08007

A conventional heat reclaiming device that breaks down the flue into several smaller pipes and blows wasted chimney heat over them. Thermostatically controlled to turn itself on when flue temperatures reach 125°F.

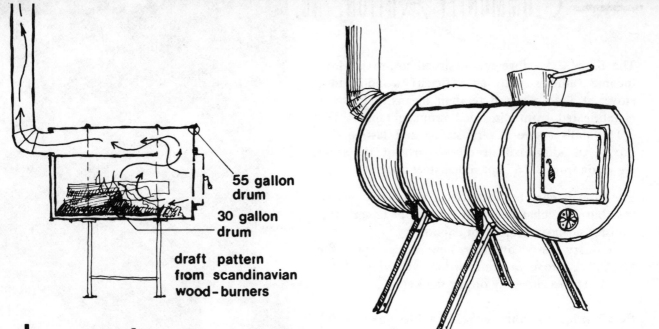

55 gallon drum

30 gallon drum

draft pattern from scandinavian wood-burners

drum stoves

Secondhand oil drums are cheap, well-made, and ideally suited to do-it-yourself stove construction. Horizontal "Yukon"-type stoves can be fairly easily constructed out of a 55 gallon oil drum, with the use of tin-snips and welding equipment. For loading doors and drafts it is best to use cast iron fittings from old stoves. For greater efficiency you might try to incorporate ideas from commercially available stoves (such as the Scandinavian draft-pattern or the "Riteway" secondary combustion flue), and if you feel really confident you might try to build Ken Kern's sophisticated design (see "Producing Your Own Power", Rodale Press, 1974). Stove plans and/or kits are available from:

Washington Stove Works, Box 687, Everett, Washington 98206.

Markade Sureheat, Box 11382, Knoxville, Tennessee 37919.

Stoves Limited, Box 178, Lee Center, New York 13363.

Oil Drum Stove Kit

(Oil drum not included) $66.00

The Drum Stove comes to you in four easy to assemble parts: flue collar, hearth and door assembly, and two pair of legs. Drum Stove measurements, when complete, approx. 2' x 3'. Flue size 6". Shipping weight 45 lbs.

THE STOVE STORE NO. 1
Route 314
Grand Isle, Vermont. 05458

sawdust stoves

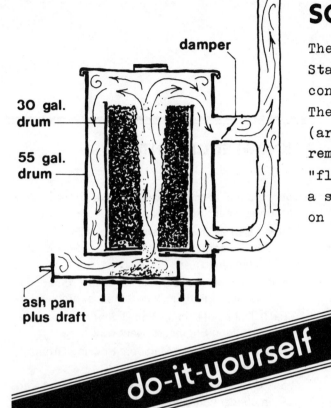

damper

30 gal. drum

55 gal. drum

ash pan plus draft

The Northeastern Forest Experimentation Station provides information on how to construct a simple sawdust burner (left). The inner drum is packed with sawdust (around a wooden pole which is then removed to provide the central combustion "flue"). One barrel of sawdust will heat a small room for 6 to 10 hours, depending on the moisture content of the sawdust.

do-it-yourself ideas and plans

fireplace water heaters

There are many different ways to heat hot water from a fireplace. The most common method is to install copper piping within the flue or in the the back of the fireplace. This system uses iron piping (corrosion?) to pass water through the grate itself.

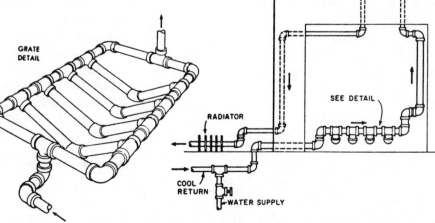

GRATE DETAIL

EXPANSION PIPE

VENTURI AND RELIEF VALVE

SEE DETAIL

RADIATOR

COOL RETURN

WATER SUPPLY

Fireplace
Fireplace heater plans for the hot water system and grate can be obtained from Frank Fusco, 56 Upland Drive, East Northport, N.Y.

Plumbing
Venturi valves, piping, shut-off valves and new radiators available from most plumbing supply stores. Used radiators can usually be found from second hand outlets.

A word about the author

Peter Clegg was born in the Yorkshire village of Saxton, in the north of England. His father was an educational administrator who spent all of his free time in the garden, producing food for his family. Peter was educated in the local schools and later attended Cambridge University where he studied architecture for three years.

He first came to the United States on a Mellon fellowship and entered Yale University in the Master's of Environmental design program. There most of the research for this book was done.

Peter presently teaches a course on energy conservation and environmental design. He has worked for architects in Great Britain and the United States and is a design consultant in the field of solar energy.

In 1974, Peter Clegg shared with a colleague an **American Institute of Architects (AIA) Award** for his excellent work in energy conservation and building design. The award was open to all students of architecture in this country. His design for a self-sufficient community was published in the **American Institute of Architects' Journal.**

New, Low-Cost Sources of Energy for the Home is his first full-length book.

ACKNOWLEDGEMENTS

I am very grateful to the following people for the support and encouragement I received:

Everett Barber Jr., Assistant Professor in Environmental Technologies, Yale School of Architecture.

Donald Watson, Advisor, Master of Environmental Design Programme, Yale School of Architecture.

Fred S. Dubin, of Dubin, Mindell, Bloome Associates, Consulting Engineers, New York.

The William N. Feater Memorial Housing Group, Center Church, New Haven.

Larry Gay, in Vermont for his advice and good work in connection with the chapter on wood.

Robert Vogel and Doug Merrilees, in Vermont, for a number of fine illustrations which appear here.

Laura Kautz and the Yale School of Architecture for putting people in touch with one another and helping us start out right.

Herman Spiegel, Dean, Yale School of Architecture.

Loretta Trezzo and Ken Braren.

Edward Miller, Editor.

and many others including Ryc and Gene Loope, Derry Watkins and Alex Pike of the Technical Research Division, Cambridge School of Architecture, who first aroused my interest in the subject.

Research for this book was done in the Environmental Design Program, at Yale School of Architecture in New Haven, Connecticut.

This book was typeset and printed during March-April, 1975 in Vermont by The Essex Publishing Company, Inc. at Essex Junction.